DAILY LIFE OF

WOMEN IN POSTWAR AMERICA

DAILY LIFE OF

WOMEN IN POSTWAR AMERICA

NANCY HENDRICKS

The Greenwood Press Daily Life Through History Series

 GREENWOOD

An Imprint of ABC-CLIO, LLC

Santa Barbara, California • Denver, Colorado

Library of Congress Cataloging-in-Publication Data

Names: Hendricks, Nancy, author.
Title: Daily life of women in postwar America / Nancy Hendricks.
Description: Santa Barbara : Greenwood, 2021. | Series: The Greenwood Press daily life through history series | Includes bibliographical references and index.
Identifiers: LCCN 2020027521 (print) | LCCN 2020027522 (ebook) | ISBN 9781440871283 (hardcover) | ISBN 9781440871290 (ebook)
Subjects: LCSH: Women—United States—History—20th century. | Women—United States—Social conditions—20th century. | United States—Social life and customs—20th century. | Television and women—United States. | Feminism—United States.
Classification: LCC HQ1420 .H425 2021 (print) | LCC HQ1420 (ebook) | DDC 305.4097309/04—dc23
LC record available at https://lccn.loc.gov/2020027521
LC ebook record available at https://lccn.loc.gov/2020027522

ISBN: 978-1-4408-7128-3 (print)
       978-1-4408-7129-0 (ebook)

25 24 23 22 21   1 2 3 4 5

This book is also available as an eBook.

Greenwood
An Imprint of ABC-CLIO, LLC

ABC-CLIO, LLC
147 Castilian Drive
Santa Barbara, California 93117
www.abc-clio.com

This book is printed on acid-free paper (∞)

Manufactured in the United States of America

CONTENTS

PREFACE

After World War II ended in 1945, things began to change in the daily lives of American women. The shifts started so slowly that few were aware of the enormous transitions occurring all around them. Much of it came down to one small pill that revolutionized the destiny of females for the first time in the history of the human race.

Daily Life of Women in Postwar America follows the trajectory of the 1950s, a decade that many consider to be sleepy, uneventful years. However, it was in the 1950s that the seeds took root for the social turmoil of the 1960s as well as the massive advances for women that followed in the 1970s and beyond.

This book will illuminate the effect of those events on the daily lives of average women in postwar America. It will not lose sight of the fact that the daily lives of African American women, Hispanic women, Native American women, and women of other groups were quite different from the daily lives of the white middle-class suburbanites who often symbolize the postwar era.

ABOUT THIS BOOK

Daily Life of Women in Postwar America can be studied for academic purposes, as a historical reference, or for the pleasure of reading the story itself, as one might enjoy a historical novel. As will be seen in this book, many women of the postwar era were influenced by growing up amid the deprivation of the Great Depression in the 1930s and living through the austerity of the war years in the 1940s. They found the postwar years to be a world apart on many levels.

The book can be read by individual sections for specific interests, or perhaps from beginning to end as a narrative. It will show how values were shaped and how they often collided.

Daily Life of Women in Postwar America will examine how the juggernaut of advertising, consumerism, technology, and television affected the women of the nation. It will underscore the impact made by the politics of the era, which was always just beneath the surface of postwar life. Moreover, while it concentrates on the decade of the 1950s, it will illustrate how the seeds planted at that time directly affected the lives of postwar women and their daughters well into the 1960s and 1970s. During that time, today's world took form.

A READER'S GUIDE THROUGH *DAILY LIFE OF WOMEN IN POSTWAR AMERICA*

The "Introduction" provides an overview of postwar America, placing the era in its historical context.

The "Timeline" follows the chronological progression of the postwar era, illustrating the flow of significant events and introducing people who became well-known figures during that time.

The "Glossary" defines terms from the postwar era that the reader will find in the text.

"Domestic Life" centers on women's role within the home and family, including subtopics such as children, teenagers, marriage, relationships with men, sexuality, and rites of passage.

"Economic Life" takes a look at issues that pertained to financial and commercial matters in the postwar era, including advertising, consumerism, race, rural life, suburban life, and urban life.

"Intellectual Life" examines topics such as communication, education, health, literature, medical advances, news media, popular culture, and science.

"Material Life"—which came to the forefront for American women in the postwar era—includes subtopics such as automobiles, clothing, food and drink, housing, and possessions.

"Political Life" looks at government and politics as they pertained to women in postwar America and how postwar political life would affect those women who came after.

"Recreational Life" observes how the average women in postwar America experienced greater leisure time through subtopics such as athletics, dance, movies, music, television, theater, and the visual arts.

"Religious Life" examines spiritual matters that were part of the daily lives of women in postwar America in such areas as the female presence in religion and the role religion played in secular life.

The "Bibliography" offers suggestions for further information on specific topics.

Above all, this book aims to illuminate how the postwar years impacted the daily lives of average American women, not only at that time but for generations to follow. Under what appeared to be a tranquil surface in the 1950s, there were undercurrents propelling women into the unknown. This book will look beneath the surface to discover how it happened and where those forces would ultimately lead.

ACKNOWLEDGMENTS

The author wishes to thank Michael Millman, former senior editor, ABC-CLIO; Kaitlin Ciarmiello, senior acquisitions editor, ABC-CLIO; Dr. Peg Lamphier, California State Polytechnic University, Pomona; and Dr. Guy Lancaster, editor, *Encyclopedia of Arkansas History and Culture*.

INTRODUCTION

In the year 2000, Gloria Steinem, a leader in the field of women's rights, got married for the first time at age 66. She was criticized by some people for appearing to change her stance on the issue of whether a female needed to be married to feel fulfilled. Author Karen Karbo (2018) claims that Steinem's response to critics was that *she* hadn't changed, *marriage* had changed: "We spent 30 years changing the marriage laws" (49), Steinem stated, adding that if she had wed in her younger years, she would have lost her name, her legal residence, her credit rating, and many of her civil rights.

The 30 years of change cited by Steinem had their roots in women's roles during the postwar era. From the end of World War II in 1945 to the early 1960s, the daily lives of average American women reflected societal expectations of a female's "proper place" solely as wives and mothers. Many of those expectations were established around the dawn of civilization. The names of women who attempted to make a place for themselves outside the limits placed upon them have usually been lost.

MRS. SHAKESPEARE

Throughout most of recorded history, virtually all of what was being recorded pertained to *"his* story," not "hers." Women quietly stayed at home while males went out and did things that attracted attention. That narrative is exemplified in the oldest existing works of Western literature, the *Iliad* and the *Odyssey*, two epic poems written by the poet Homer hundreds of years before the birth of Christ.

In the *Iliad*, one of the few female characters, Helen of Troy, basically acted only as what 20th-century moviemaker Alfred Hitchcock would have called the "MacGuffin," defined by the *Merriam-Webster* dictionary as an object, event, or a character that sets off the action. The action in this case was the Trojan War, which lasted for 10 years. As recounted in the *Iliad*, that conflict immortalized male warriors such as Achilles and Agamemnon.

The *Odyssey* follows Greek hero Odysseus as the champion of 10 more years of adventures as he made his way back to Greece after the Trojan War. His wife loyally waited at home with their son for two decades, fending off suitors who tried to convince her that Odysseus was dead. She never lost faith in her husband, who eventually arrived home.

There is no shortage of males through history with names that are instantly recognizable, including Aristotle, Caesar, Columbus, Confucius, Edison, Einstein, Galileo, Gandhi, Geronimo, King, Lincoln, Michelangelo, Mozart, Napoleon, and Shakespeare to name but a few. However, most people cannot recall noteworthy females apart from Cleopatra and Queen Elizabeth I.

It is not known precisely what Shakespeare's wife was doing all those years after her husband left her in Stratford when he went off to write plays in London. However, we have a fairly good idea. Exactly like the wife of Odysseus, Mrs. Shakespeare stayed home with the children and did her best to provide for them. The pattern was the same for women over thousands of years.

SEEDS OF CHANGE

During the postwar years that followed America's involvement in World War II, there was one radical change that took place for average American women in one generation. When she was 10 years old, a hypothetical postwar-era girl born in 1950 would see the approval of something that completely altered what had been the destiny of females from the beginning of human history.

The advent of the birth control pill in 1960 was so revolutionary that it was often simply known as the "Pill." Everyone knew exactly what that meant. Safely and effectively, it allowed females to avoid becoming pregnant, something unavailable to any previous generation of women since the dawn of time.

That same hypothetical girl born in 1950 would have had to wait until she was in her mid-20s to see significant changes in some things, but eventually, change did come. Unmarried women in America had access to the Pill for the first time in 1972. Title IX of the Education Amendments of 1972 barred discrimination on the basis of gender in educational programs receiving federal financial assistance. In 1973, the U.S. Supreme Court banned gender-segregated "Help Wanted-Male" and "Help Wanted-Female" ads for employment, allowing both men and women to apply for their job of choice. In 1974, the average American woman was able to receive a credit card in her own name.

The seeds of those changes were sown in the postwar years, which some consider merely to be a time of conformity and complacency when nothing much happened. In fact, monumental changes were beginning to take root in the daily lives of women in postwar America, reflecting the kind of events that took place in the nation itself during the 1950s.

Far from being bland years, it was a time of contrasts. The postwar era was a time of Beatniks and Sputnik, the baby boom and the Bomb, and Princess Grace and *Peyton Place*.

LEAVING THEIR "PLACE"

As the decade of the 1950s began, there was opposition to the proposed construction of an interstate highway system to carry automobiles across the country, a proposal that was considered futuristic by some and socialistic by others. However, as the decade came to a close in 1959, the nation's first astronauts were announced as America set her sights on the Moon. In the short postwar period of nine years, the future had arrived, and it was not limited to carrying cars from coast to coast.

As the postwar years progressed, some women began to feel that there was more to life than spending their daily lives confined to the home for the rest of their existence, with only children and kitchen appliances for company. Women in minority groups such as African Americans and Hispanics started to feel that there was more to life than laboring all day as maids in white people's houses before coming home to work in their own.

During the postwar era, some minority women departed from their traditional "place" in American society. In 1955, Hispanic American activist Dolores Huerta helped organize a community group in California that fought for economic improvements aimed at people of Latin descent, especially the migrant agricultural workers whom few white Americans ever thought about. In 1956, Asian American Patsy Mink, after fighting discrimination in her own education, began a political rise in Hawaii that would ultimately lead her to becoming the first woman of an ethnic minority to serve in the U.S. Congress.

Civil rights for African American citizens increasingly came to the forefront in the postwar era, with a number of average women in the spotlight. Linda Brown, an African American third-grader, who was forced to travel long distances to attend a racially segregated school in Topeka, Kansas, although she lived close to a public school that was for whites only was at the center of 1954's landmark *Brown v. Board of Education* Supreme Court decision declaring the mandate of "separate but equal" to be unconstitutional.

In 1955, Rosa Parks of Montgomery, Alabama, an African American seamstress, defied a local law requiring that she give up her seat on a city bus to a white man, triggering widespread civil rights protests. The six girls among the nine young black students in Little Rock, Arkansas, who became known worldwide as the Little Rock Nine faced daily torment in 1957 as they sought to lawfully desegregate that city's Central High School amid televised pictures of angry white mobs.

Although all these women would have considered themselves "average," they departed from the expectations of their daily lives in the postwar era, only to find themselves in the spotlight.

DISTORTED REALITY

People in the United States who had lived through World War II in the 1940s found that during the postwar years, the world began to seem distorted, rather like a fun house mirror. Germany, Italy, and Japan—America's wartime enemies—became U.S. allies in the 1950s. Similarly, allies during World War II became adversaries in the 1950s as Russia and China turned into the enemy.

At home too, there was a strange contrast. On the whole, American women enjoyed an unparalleled feeling of confidence in the course of their daily lives. However, there was also an underlying sense of anxiety due to the threat of Communism, the "witch hunts" under McCarthyism, and the ever-present specter of nuclear war.

Fabulous new goods were easily available to average postwar Americans, including labor-saving devices aimed at women, but some observers protested against the nation's materialism. Even though postwar America was the richest nation in the history of the world, there were huge pockets of poverty—women living in Appalachia, the rural South, and the urban "inner cities" that were a short drive from affluent new suburbs.

Minority groups who had fought for freedom in Europe and the Pacific during World War II came home to find their own freedoms denied by law in parts of the United States and curtailed by practice in others.

STIRRINGS OF DISCONTENT

In the course of their daily lives, most American women of the postwar era tended to trust what they were being told by their government. They had faith in what they saw on television. They tended to believe politicians. However, events in the 1950s, such as unsubstantiated accusations under McCarthyism, would erode that trust. Even something as seemingly inconsequential as the discovery of fraud on television quiz shows left American women feeling they had been cruelly deceived.

In the postwar era, many American women had money to spend for the first time in their lives, having lived through the deprivation of the Great Depression in the 1930s and wartime austerity in the 1940s. The nation's advertising industry urged them to spend it. Average women trusted that the nation's economy would always provide more. But sometimes they found that material possessions as well as the reality of their "perfect" daily lives did not bring happiness.

Just as females started to feel the stirrings of discontent, their male partners sometimes found themselves locked into unsatisfying situations that had ramifications for women. Young men who had led troops into battle during wartime sometimes found themselves in bleak, menial jobs during the postwar era. In the corporate world, office politics could be vicious. Some men became frustrated and angry due to the ongoing demands of providing for a growing family. Males sometimes took out their frustration on the women in their lives. Domestic abuse was not a topic that was generally discussed in the 1950s, with the result that many women thought they were alone in facing it.

On the other hand, at least men could find work. After helping America win the war by working in factories and other jobs in the 1940s, females were discouraged from seeking jobs at all in the 1950s. Some women who had ferried aircraft thousands of miles in wartime found themselves relegated to walking children to the school bus.

BOOMERS AND THE BOMB

Children of the postwar baby boom were in many ways the glue that held the 1950s together. Disillusioned men stayed on the job to provide for their families. Discontented women believed what they were told in magazines: that their purpose in life was to be a wife and mother.

Americans of the 1950s wanted to make their children's lives better than their own had been. As mothers, many women did their utmost to give their offspring an ideal childhood. When the 1960s ushered in the countercultural revolution, many American parents felt the cruel irony. Their children rebelled against the very things men and woman had fought for and cherished.

The concept of warfare changed radically in postwar America with the hydrogen bomb, or what came to be known simply as "the Bomb." It packed far more destructive power than the atomic weapons that had annihilated the Japanese cities of Hiroshima and Nagasaki in World War II. At first, the United States was the only nation to have nuclear weapons, but in 1955, the Russians successfully tested their own hydrogen bomb. The postwar years saw nuclear tests by both nations spewing radiation into the Earth's atmosphere.

Many American women lived with a sense of anxiety about the Bomb destroying their families. Some oversaw the construction of underground fallout shelters if the worst happened.

IMAGES

The Bomb was not the only device in the postwar years that captured the attention of American women. One took center stage right in their living rooms. It was called television.

It is impossible to overstate the effect of television, or "TV," in the postwar years. Many American women found their daily lives to be at odds with the female images on televised situation comedies as well as in commercials.

There were some subtle signs of dissent. Betty Furness was an extremely popular TV spokesperson for Westinghouse appliances throughout the 1950s. She refused to wear an apron in her ads as directed, opting instead for a more fashionable and sophisticated professional look rather than that of a "housewife."

In 1957, writer Betty Friedan began conducting research that would lead to the publication of her groundbreaking bestseller, *The Feminine Mystique*. It revealed the widespread unhappiness of many women in the postwar years. Despite living in material comfort, many felt trapped as housewives regardless of the way women's idealized daily lives were presented on TV.

DREAMS DEFERRED

Today, there are many who think of the postwar years as the decade that most personified the "American Dream," the concept that all citizens of the United States had an equal opportunity for success through hard work and determination. For the middle class, especially white males, the postwar years have been seen in many ways as an idyllic time. Others found their postwar-era dreams deferred.

Women who had found fulfillment by working outside the home during World War II lost their jobs afterward, being expected to get married and stay at home with toddlers. Women were advised to live through their husband and children, having no fulfillment outside the home, in a state of what Elaine Tyler May (2008) calls "domestic containment" (17).

Many postwar women became frustrated by that lack of fulfill-ment. Friedan (2013) identified this malaise as "the problem with no name" in her landmark book *The Feminine Mystique* (18). Even if women had a college education and were permitted by their husbands to work outside the home, the career paths open to females of the postwar era were generally limited to being either a nurse, a teacher, or a secretary.

Future Supreme Court justice Ruth Bader Ginsburg tried a dif-ferent path, being one of the few women accepted at Harvard Law School in 1956. Karbo (2018) relates that as one of only nine females in a class of more than 500 males, the dean asked the nine women to a dinner where, in front of their professors, they were compelled to justify "taking a man's spot" (60). Even after Ginsburg graduated from law school first in her class, no law firm would hire her, being quite open about their policy not to hire women.

GIVING BIRTH TO CONFLICT

For the first time in history, the advent of the birth control pill brought greater freedom for women to determine when or if to have children. However, it also created conflict between postwar women and their daughters who developed much different ideas than their mothers about their lifestyle choices.

Far from being a sleepy decade, the era in which women in postwar America lived their daily lives was a tipping point. Those years ultimately spurred the fight for many of the rights for females that are often taken for granted. Some of those battles had to be fought all the way to the Supreme Court, shaping the world as we know it today.

FURTHER READING

Friedan, Betty. *The Feminine Mystique*. New York: Norton, 50th anniversary edition, 2013.

Karbo, Karen. *In Praise of Difficult Women: Life Lessons from 29 Heroines Who Dared to Break the Rules*. Washington, DC: National Geographic Books, 2018.

May, Elaine Tyler. *Homeward Bound: American Families in the Cold War Era*. New York: Basic Books, 2008.

TIMELINE OF EVENTS

Women in postwar America did not exist in a vacuum. This time-line features cultural highlights that were significant to women in the United States during that era. It indicates the rise of prominent individuals, including those who set feminine standards such as Marilyn Monroe and Doris Day. It also includes world and national events that were on the minds of women in postwar America, such as McCarthyism, Sputnik, and nuclear weapons. Cultural mile-stones, including television shows that reflected the entertainment industry's concept of women, are also noted, as well as landmark scientific discoveries such as the contraceptive pill. Finally, it lists significant legal decisions pertaining to the status of women that did not arrive until after the immediate postwar years. Many had to be fought all the way to the U.S. Supreme Court in order to secure rights that American women enjoy today.

1950   Doris Day (1922–2019) rises to become symbol of whole-some postwar American womanhood with three movies released this year: *Young Man with a Horn*, *Tea for Two*, and *The West Point Story*.

U.S. senator Joseph McCarthy (1908–1957) first gains national attention for his anti-Communism campaign with "Enemies from Within" speech to Republican women in West Virginia on February 9.

Margaret Chase Smith (1897–1995), first woman elected to both the U.S. House of Representatives and the U.S. Senate (serving cumulatively from 1940 to 1973) is first member of Congress to oppose McCarthyism, delivering "Declaration of Conscience" speech on June 1.

Korean War begins on June 25 as North Korea, aided by Communist China, invades South Korea, which is supported by the United Nations with the United States as principal combatant.

Ethel Waters (1896–1977) becomes the first African American actress to star in her own television situation comedy program, *The Beulah Show*, which premiers on October 3 and runs through 1952.

Hattie Caraway (1878–1950), first woman elected to the U.S. Senate and first woman reelected to the Senate (serving 1932–1945) dies on December 21.

1951 American citizens Ethel and Julius Rosenberg are convicted of espionage on March 29 for allegedly passing atomic secrets to the Soviets; they are executed in 1953.

Hydrogen bomb, more powerful than the atomic bombs that destroyed Hiroshima and Nagasaki in Japan during World War II, is tested by the United States on May 9 at the Pacific islands of the Eniwetok Atoll, releasing radiation into the atmosphere.

In Cleveland, Ohio, radio disc jockey Alan Freed (1921–1965) begins hosting a program on July 11 featuring rhythm and blues records that he calls "rock and roll" music.

I Love Lucy starring Lucille Ball (1911–1989) makes its television debut on October 15; it remains a consistently popular hit comedy until the end of its run in 1957.

1952 England's new queen, Elizabeth II (1926–), ascends to the throne on February 6 upon the death of her father King George VI. Her official coronation on June 2, 1953, spurs tremendous increase in television sets purchased by Americans in order to watch the historic event.

Dwight Eisenhower (1890–1969), Republican candidate for president, wins the first of two terms, defeating

Democratic candidate Adlai Stevenson (1900–1965) on November 4.

1953   Korean Armistice Agreement is signed on July 27 creating the Demilitarized Zone (DMZ) to separate North and South Korea; no formal peace treaty was signed.

Groundbreaking book *Sexual Behavior in the Human Female* by Dr. Alfred Kinsey (1894–1956) is published, joining first half of what was called the "Kinsey Report," *Sexual Behavior in the Human Male*, which was published in 1948.

Marilyn Monroe (1926–1962) begins reign as America's leading postwar female "sex symbol" with release of the movie *Gentlemen Prefer Blondes*.

Jonas Salk (1914–1995) announces successful test on November 13 of vaccine to combat the crippling disease of polio.

1954   *Annie Oakley* starring Gail Davis (1925–1997) in title role debuts on January 9 as America's first TV western to star a woman, making Davis a role model; show runs through 1957.

Marilyn Monroe weds star baseball player Joe DiMaggio on January 14 amid media frenzy.

In landmark *Brown v. Board of Education* decision on May 17, the U.S. Supreme Court declares the concept of "separate but equal" in public schools along racial lines to be unconstitutional.

"Rock Around the Clock" is recorded by Bill Haley & His Comets on April 12, with its release igniting national craze for rock and roll music.

"Davy Crockett," a serial on the *Disneyland* television series debuts on December 15, inspiring nationwide craze among American children for coonskin caps and Crockett-related items.

1955   Coya Knutson (1912–1996) begins the first of her two terms in the U.S. House of Representatives (1955–1959) on January 3; she is defeated for reelection in 1958 after infamous "Coya, Come Home" smear campaign in which the opposition enlists her estranged husband.

Disneyland, Walt Disney's amusement park in Anaheim, California, opens to the public on July 17, becoming an immediate hit.

Vietnam War officially begins on November 1, as recognized by the Vietnam Veterans Memorial.

Elvis Presley (1936–1977) begins recording contract with RCA Records on November 21, skyrocketing to fame as rock and roll icon.

Soviet Union detonates its first thermonuclear bomb on November 22.

African American Rosa Parks (1913–2005) is jailed in Montgomery, Alabama, on December 1 for not giving up her seat on a city bus to a white man, triggering civil rights protests.

1956 Elvis Presley makes his first appearance on television's *Ed Sullivan Show* on September 9.

American actress Grace Kelly (1929–1982) marries Prince Rainier of Monaco on April 18 amid media frenzy, becoming "Princess Grace."

Interstate Highway Act becomes law on June 29 to create coast-to-coast roadways across America.

Peyton Place, best-selling novel by Grace Metalious (1924–1964), is published on September 24, shocking many Americans with its steamy realism and portrayal of female sexuality.

Dwight Eisenhower wins the second of two terms as U.S. president on November 6, once again defeating Democratic candidate Adlai Stevenson.

1957 *American Bandstand*, a teen-centered television show spotlighting rock and roll music, debuts on national television August 5.

Little Rock, Arkansas, makes international headlines beginning on September 4 as the African American "Little Rock Nine" (six girls and three boys) face angry white mobs in lawful attempt to desegregate the city's Central High School.

Civil Rights Act of 1957, the first federal civil rights legislation passed by Congress since 1875, is signed into law on September 9.

Sputnik, the first artificial space satellite to orbit the Earth, is launched by the Soviet Union on October 4, marking the start of the "Space Race."

1958   President Eisenhower signs National Aeronautics and Space Act on July 29, creating the National Aeronautics and Space Administration, popularly known as NASA.

1959   Fidel Castro (1926–2016) is named prime minister of Cuba on January 1 after waging a guerilla war against Cuban dictator Fulgencio Batista.

Alaska becomes America's 49th state on January 3.

Barbie doll is introduced on March 9 and becomes female ideal for many, selling over 1 billion dolls.

Hawaii becomes America's 50th state on August 21.

1960   First oral contraceptive, Enovid, is marketed as a birth control pill after being approved by the U.S. Food and Drug Administration.

1963   Equal Pay Act is passed by Congress, promising equal wages for equal work regardless of race, color, religion, national origin, or gender of the worker.

1964   Title VII of the Civil Rights Act is passed by Congress, prohibiting gender discrimination in employment; Equal Employment Opportunity Commission is created.

1965   U.S. Supreme Court establishes the right of married couples to use contraception, although millions of unmarried women in 26 states are still denied birth control.

Weeks v. Southern Bell decision in Appeals Court marks victory against restrictive labor laws regarding women, opening many arbitrary male-only jobs to females.

1968   President Lyndon Johnson (1908–1973) signs executive order prohibiting gender discrimination by government contractors and also requires affirmative action plans for hiring women.

1969   California adopts the nation's first "no fault" divorce law, allowing divorce by mutual consent without alleging wrongdoing by either of the parties.

1970   In *Schultz v. Wheaton Glass Co.* lawsuit, U.S. Court of Appeals sets a legal precedent regarding equal pay for both men and women.

1971   *Reed v. Reed* case sets gender equality precedent in the U.S. Supreme Court, ruling that women are "persons" and that it is unconstitutional to give automatic preference to males as administrators of wills.

The U.S. Supreme Court outlaws the practice of private employers refusing to hire women with young children.

1972   Title IX of the Education Amendments Act prohibits gender discrimination in all aspects of educational programs that receive federal funding.

In *Baird v. Eisenstadt,* the U.S. Supreme Court legalizes the right to use birth control by all citizens of the United States, regardless of marital status.

1973   *Frontiero v. Richardson* is heard by the U.S. Supreme Court, setting legal precedent against gender discrimination.

Supreme Court bans gender-segregated "Help Wanted-Male" and "Help Wanted-Female" classified advertising.

1974   Congress outlaws housing discrimination on the basis of gender as well as prohibiting credit discrimination against women.

1975   Supreme Court decision in *Weinberger v. Wiesenfeld,* regarding widows and widowers who are caring for minor children, sets precedent for gender equality.

GLOSSARY

These are common terms that were familiar to average women in postwar America as they went about their daily lives. Many, such as the Bomb and the Cold War, were on everybody's mind, but for women, they were less of an ideological or political issue than anxiety about the fate of their children. During the postwar years, the new mass medium of television quickly spread the same information from coast to coast at the same time, so that concepts such as McCarthyism and the civil rights movement resulted in women in postwar America speaking the same language whether they lived in Portland, Maine, or Portland, Oregon.

"American Dream": The concept that any U.S. citizen, regardless of social class, has an equal opportunity to attain success through hard work and determination.

Baby boom: The rising birthrate among women in postwar America that started in 1946, following the end of World War II, and ran roughly through 1964. Children of that generation, called "baby boomers," are often closely identified with postwar America.

Beatnik: Deprecating term to describe a group of men and women in the postwar years, often avant-garde writers and artists who tended to explore alternative lifestyles and who usually referred to themselves as Beats.

Bomb, the: General term for nuclear weapons, especially the hydrogen bomb, or H-bomb, that was being developed and tested in the postwar years. The H-bomb was thousands of times more powerful than the atomic weapons that destroyed the Japanese cities of Hiroshima and Nagasaki at the end of World War II.

Brown v. Board of Education: Landmark decision by the U.S. Supreme Court in 1954 declaring that the racial concept of "separate but equal" was unconstitutional and ordering public schools to desegregate "with all deliberate speed."

Civil rights movement: Postwar-era protests against widespread racial segregation and discrimination.

Cold War: The ideological hostility that existed between the United States and Communist countries from 1945 to 1990, characterized by measures short of open combat. Women were told it was their patriotic duty to stay at home and raise children who would keep America strong.

Communism: Official political and economic ideology of the Union of Soviet Socialist Republics (USSR), also known as Russia, during the Cold War. In the Communist system, as opposed to capitalism, property and production are publicly owned, with most private property being eliminated.

Conformity: A sense of uniformity that pervaded American society during the postwar years due to the belief that it would give the United States an advantage over Communism and was also motivated by fear of appearing different during the McCarthyism of the postwar years.

"Domestic Containment": Phrase coined by writer Elaine Tyler May in 2008 to signify postwar women's role to be living through their husband and children, having no fulfillment in their daily lives outside the home.

Fallout: Deadly radioactive debris from nuclear explosions that spread in the atmosphere across the United States and around the world during the nuclear bomb tests in the 1950s.

Fallout shelter: A small reinforced bunker, often buried underground in suburban backyards, designed to protect occupants from nuclear war; women were tasked with keeping it stocked with food and other supplies for their family's survival.

Feminine Mystique, The: Groundbreaking 1963 bestseller by Betty Friedan addressing women in postwar America who were frustrated by a lack of fulfillment in their daily lives.

GI Bill: Popular name for the Servicemen's Readjustment Act of 1944, which provided benefits for returning World War II veterans such as low-cost mortgages, low-interest loans to start a business, and educational opportunities that few could have afforded otherwise. The GI Bill made a tremendous contribution to America's postwar prosperity.

Great Depression: Severe economic crisis in the 1930s during which many women in postwar America had grown up amid poverty; some experts said it contributed to the widespread materialism of the postwar era.

Great Migration: Movement of millions of African Americans out of the South to cities in the North and to western regions of the United States as a way of escaping the widespread discrimination and violence against blacks that was pervasive in the Southern states during the Jim Crow era.

Inner city: Euphemism for urban residential districts that are primarily populated by low-income minorities in areas that are usually older, deteriorating, and more densely populated.

Jim Crow: State and local statutes in the postwar era, generally in the South, that legalized racial segregation and discrimination. Jim Crow laws often resulted in jail, violence, or death if they were defied.

Juvenile delinquents: A postwar term referring to rebellious young people whose antisocial acts ran from street crime to a bad attitude.

"Kinsey Report": Common terminology for two groundbreaking postwar books on American erotic activities, *Sexual Behavior in the Human Male* (1948) and *Sexual Behavior in the Human Female* (1953), written from a scientific standpoint by Dr. Alfred Kinsey.

McCarthyism: Based on congressional hearings in the postwar years attempting to expose alleged Communists. Named for Joseph McCarthy (1908–1957), U.S. senator (R-Wisconsin), who led the investigations.

Migrant workers: Low-paid laborers, often Hispanic, who picked the nation's fruits and vegetables. They were usually unnoticed by most Americans until postwar activists such as Dolores Huerta (1930–) drew attention to their plight.

Peyton Place: A 1956 novel by Grace Metalious (1924–1964) that focuses on small-town women seeking fulfillment, shocking America for its portrayal of female sexuality. It becomes one of the best-selling books not only of the postwar years but in all publishing history.

Pill, the: Popular shorthand for oral contraceptive tablet that women could take to avoid unwanted pregnancies. Approved in 1960 but not available to all women in the United States regardless of marital status until 1972.

Planned obsolescence: A concept in consumer culture in which products have a short life due to changing fashion and / or poor quality, so businesses will profit from the sale of new ones.

Polyester: General term for man-made synthetic fibers that are strong, wrinkle resistant, and quick drying, often advertised to housewives in the postwar years as labor-saving "wash-and-wear."

Postwar: Any period that occurs after a war, but most commonly used in the United States as the era after World War II from 1945 through the latter part of the 1960s.

Red Scare: The perceived threat of Communism within the United States—an internal danger that was called the "Red Menace," referring to people who had allegiance to the red Soviet flag. The anti-Communist fervor reached a fever pitch between 1950 and 1954, when Senator Joseph McCarthy staged congressional hearings that made allegations but provided little proof.

Rock and roll: Term first used in 1951 by radio personality Alan Freed (1921–1965) to describe the rhythm and blues type of music he played on his program.

Sex symbol: Celebrity who is noted for sex appeal. The term was openly promoted in the postwar years, with top female sex symbols of the era including actresses Brigitte Bardot (1934–), Jayne Mansfield (1933–1967), and especially Marilyn Monroe (1926–1962).

Sitcom: Abbreviation for "situation comedy," with the first known usage in 1951. Postwar television sitcoms usually centered on idealized families with a consistent set of characters who are often involved in wacky situations that are lovingly resolved by the end of the program.

Space Race: Competition between the United States and the Soviet Union to claim superiority and gain strategic advantage in the skies.

Sputnik: From Russian phrase "traveling companion," an artificial satellite launched by the Soviets in 1957, sparking the Space Race and causing great anxiety among postwar Americans.

Suburbia: Housing developments near cities, usually white and middle class, often exemplified in the postwar years by developments such as Levittown, New York.

"Togetherness": Word coined by *McCall's*, a women's magazine, in 1954, to promote the concept of the ideal American family unit in which a husband and wife, within their strictly defined roles, centered their lives on home and children, all of whom enjoyed doing things together.

Tranquilizers: Popular anti-anxiety drugs of the postwar era that were prescribed to manage anxiousness over the problems of daily life, sometimes called "Mother's little helpers."

War brides: Women, usually from war-torn countries, who married American servicemen and came to the United States in the postwar years as sanctioned by the War Brides Act of 1945.

Women's rights movement: Postwar effort to attain equal rights and opportunities for women as well as greater personal freedom for females.

World War II: Global conflict than ran from 1939 to 1945. America's entry in 1941 caused societal upheavals on the "home front" in the United States including more freedom for women as they were recruited for traditionally male types of jobs; women were generally forced out after the war ended.

1

DOMESTIC LIFE

World War II and its aftermath changed the trajectory of America. The aftereffects of the war, which was fought by the United States from 1941 to 1945, led to both comforts and conflicts in the daily lives of American women in the postwar era.

Since the earliest days of the nation, women's roles were strictly defined. There may have been some variations in their workload according to their socioeconomic status, such as women in the families of wealthy Southern planters who had numerous servants. But primarily, a woman's place was working in the home. There, women raised children, often while pregnant with another. They cleaned house, did the washing by hand, made soap, prepared food, spun cloth, sewed the family's clothes, and literally kept the home fires burning.

Since early Americans generally lived on family farms, according to Claudia Johnson (2017), most women also "plowed, planted, tended livestock, slaughtered animals, and knew basic carpentry" (48).

With the advent of the Industrial Revolution in the late 19th and early 20th centuries, some women outside rural areas found work outside the home in mills and factories. Still, they also had chores at home. This was especially true after they married.

Being unmarried was considered abnormal. It was vital for women to find husbands. In the past, with transportation limited, many couples lived near each other and knew each other since childhood, attending the same schools and houses of worship. Often, domestic life began with newlyweds moving in with parents, in-laws, or other family members.

However, with America's entry into World War II, women were exposed to new surroundings in which they met men they would not have otherwise known. Women were recruited to work in defense plants that were often far from home. Men were trained for military service at bases around the country, often coming into contact with local girls. Some women served in new types of roles—such as nurses in the armed forces or as clerks called "government girls" in Washington, DC. Because of the war, couples married each other in circumstances that were far removed from the years before the war when they almost certainly would not have met.

The postwar years brought low-interest home loans and booming new suburban housing developments in which to raise a family. Newlyweds could often move into their own house, far away from their childhood home.

There were books to provide them with the kind of information that was traditionally received from parents or other relatives (or not at all). Alfred Kinsey's *Sexual Behavior in the Human Male* (1948) and *Sexual Behavior in the Human Female* (1953) were books of the postwar era that were considered scandalous. However, many women found them to be valuable educational tools.

Inevitably, postwar domestic life meant having children. There was even a book to help with that. *The Common Sense Book of Baby and Child Care*, published in 1946 by Dr. Benjamin Spock, became a "how-to" guide for many anxious young mothers who lived far from parental advisers.

The domestic life of women in postwar America was played out amid strictly defined roles. Conformity was the norm. The "nuclear family" was defined as father, mother, and dependent children living in one household. Women became housewives, defining themselves as someone's wife and someone's mother rather than as individuals. For some women during the postwar years, performing that role began to take its toll.

CHILDREN

The daily lives of women in postwar America revolved around their homes, husbands, and especially children. What was called the "postwar baby boom" impacted American life not only for those who lived during that era but for generations to come. As prompted by both the nation's government and the popular culture, children became an all-consuming focus in the daily lives of postwar women.

According to O'Rourke (2014), "The Baby Boom has an exact definition, a precise demography. [It is] the children who were born during a period after World War II when the long-term trend in fertility among American women was exceeded" (3).

Trends in marriage and childbearing during the 20th century reflected the general status of the nation at that point in time. During the Great Depression of the 1930s, America's fertility rate mirrored a general sociological tendency for birthrates to drop during periods of economic decline. With the widespread poverty of the Great Depression wreaking havoc, young couples worried about their finances and therefore put off having children. According to the National Center for Health Statistics, the U.S. fertility rate, or the number of children born to women ages 15–44, declined by almost 20 percent during the Depression years.

With America's entry into World War II in 1941, the nation's financial picture greatly improved, as war industries hired large numbers of people to produce everything from bullets to tanks. However, the reality of wartime created its own set of impediments to fertility. Millions of young men were stationed overseas in the military, delaying their prospects for marriage and family.

After 1945, when the war ended, Americans made up for years of deferred parenthood by reproducing at record rates, creating the baby boom. According to the National Center for Health Statistics, in 1928, America's fertility rate was 93.8 per 100,000. During the Depression year of 1936, it dropped to 75.8. By the end of World War II in 1945, it crept up to 85.9. However, during the postwar years between 1946 and 1964, the average fertility rate in the United States soared to 113.4 per 100,000.

Not only that, but, as Friedan (2013) states, "the number of American women with three or more children doubled in twenty years" (214). More women were having babies, and more mothers had a larger number of children than in the past. Combined with the societal expectations of the era, the daily lives of women were necessarily centered on their children.

An additional element in the postwar baby boom was the fact that Congress provided a number of benefits to American soldiers after World War II. By doing so, they hoped to avoid the kind of unrest among veterans that had taken place after World War I, which America had fought in 1917 and 1918.

After World War II ended, many young couples were able to afford their own home with the help of low-interest government loans. They did not have to feel cramped by living in crowded conditions with parents or other family members as in the past. They could move to the new suburbs, where women could raise their children in safe, pleasant surroundings.

Developers understood the realities of the postwar baby boom, constructing houses with mothers in mind. Suburban homes began to be built with a large expanse of glass, called a picture window, so that women, spending most of their daily life in the house, could keep an eye on their children playing in the yard.

During the Cold War years, many postwar women considered it their patriotic duty to have children. It was a way to show the world that compared to conditions under Communism in countries such as the Soviet Union, the American way of life was the best environment in which to raise a family.

In addition to the government, America's popular culture celebrated pregnancy, parenthood, and large families. At the height of the baby boom, it was said that a child was born in the United States every seven seconds.

Once the baby boom began, the trend was for the average American woman to get married around the age of 20 instead of 22, as had been the norm in the past. Young women who moved to one of the new suburban developments found other young women like themselves, all of whom seemed to be having children. With encouragement all around them, more women started having babies earlier in their lives, ultimately living their own lives through their children.

Women of the postwar era were encouraged to take on their "proper roles." In their daily lives, they received constant reinforcement that their highest duty and greatest fulfillment, along with keeping a husband happy, was being a good mother to their children.

Motherhood was celebrated all around them. Messages everywhere emphasized the need for women to have children and devote their lives to their families.

It was as much an economic imperative as it was a patriotic duty. American industry had quickly retooled after the war, rolling peacetime consumer goods off the assembly lines where jeeps and fighter planes had been. Along with items including cribs, playpens, and baby carriages, new businesses such as diaper services mushroomed to meet the needs of women in postwar America and their children.

One growth field that targeted the children of women in postwar America was the manufacturing of baby food. Bentley (2014) claims that during the baby boom years, "breastfeeding rates were at their lowest levels in U.S. history" (1). Mass-produced baby food was readily purchased, surpassing previous infant-feeding practices. Postwar women and their children were labeled as consumers, with various factors feeding into each other. Bentley states, "Manufacturers supplied grocers with statistics showing that [female] customers who purchased baby food spent the most dollars per visit and bought more expensive items as well" (56). Another element impacting women in postwar America in raising their children was one of the most revolutionary developments of the century: television. Also called TV, the new medium joined newspapers, magazines, and radio as advertisers sought to stimulate demand by celebrating pregnancy, childcare, and motherhood. Children grew up to be consumers.

All the messages made it clear what women in postwar America were expected to do. There were more children born in the United States during the seven years after World War II than in the previous 30. By the end of the 1950s, about 40 percent of the population had been born since 1946.

Children of the postwar era enjoyed nutritious food, superior healthcare, and universal education. Young mothers even found an instructional manual for raising their children in the form of the best-selling book *Baby and Child Care*, by Dr. Benjamin Spock.

Many previously fatal childhood diseases, such as diphtheria, smallpox, and whooping cough, were eliminated through the use of vaccines. For many, the greatest breakthrough for postwar children came in 1954, when scientist Jonas Salk developed a vaccine against polio. Often called infantile paralysis, polio generally attacked children, becoming a mother's worst nightmare. After being administered to millions of schoolchildren in the postwar era, the vaccine was so effective that by 1979, polio was declared to be eradicated in the United States.

With their sheer numbers and a new sociological dynamic in the nation, postwar American children were a generation apart from any previous one. From birth, they enjoyed a new kind of lifestyle. Most young parents of the postwar era had grown up amid the poverty and deprivation of the Great Depression in the 1930s. They often had to find work from an early age to help support the family, with girls often hiring out as maids. During the Depression, they had often seen their own parents suffer from unemployment, struggling to put food on the table.

When World War II erupted, there was greater opportunity for employment, but at a cost. There were austerity programs and rationing on the home front along with even greater sacrifices on the battlefield. According to the National World War II Museum, there were well over a million young American men who were killed or wounded in the war, leaving wives, mothers, and sweethearts to mourn or to help them adjust to lives with disabilities.

After decades of sadness and struggle in the 1930s and 1940s, mothers in the postwar years were determined that their children would enjoy the kind of childhood that they themselves rarely had.

Although there was certainly poverty in the postwar era among Native Americans, Hispanics, rural blacks, and poor whites, huge numbers of middle-class white children grew up amid prosperity and affluence. They enjoyed the sort of privilege once reserved for the upper class, rarely seeing the kind of hardships their mothers' generation had faced.

Children of the postwar era actually provided vital links for their mothers, especially women in the suburbs. With young mothers often isolated without transportation in new suburban developments, children connected women with other young mothers in their neighborhoods and schools.

Even before children went to school, women in postwar America were providing an education for their children, especially daughters, whether it was a conscious effort or not. Little girls were brought up to emulate their mothers, often through the influence of television and women's magazines. Girls of the postwar era usually wore neatly pressed dresses or skirts. While some were allowed to play in slacks or shorts, wearing blue jeans among most middle-class white children was shunned as being lower class.

Many of the tastes that postwar mothers passed down to their daughters were shaped by television. Most sources estimate that by 1950, around 10 million American homes had a TV. That number grew every year. By 1960, there were more than 50 million, or a television in about 9 out of 10 American households.

Television advertisers and producers found a fertile new market for their products, specifically targeting children. Television was soon labeled the "electronic babysitter." TV producers recognized the times when women were not likely to be in the room with their children, such as when housewives were preparing meals. Children of the postwar era were the first to be studied regarding the influence of television on their mental health, even spurring Congressional hearings.

Instant gratification became the norm. Children were directed by advertisers to "tell Mom and Dad to buy" such and such a product. Often, both the children and the parents did so.

However, when their daily chores permitted, many young mothers read stories to their children or encouraged them to look through books instead of watching television. There was a rise in children's literature during the postwar era as publishers began to produce lighthearted books with colorful illustrations that were geared to a child's imagination. Little Golden Books, selling for $0.25, were displayed at children's eye level in places such as supermarkets so they could be easily spotted when children went shopping with their mothers. Golden Books usually dealt with childhood fears and insecurities such as shyness, along with helping children to find their place in the wider world.

Even amid the general affluence of daily life in America after World War II, there were some women and children of the postwar era who knew their place in the world quite clearly without the help of books. Many children of minority groups lived quite different childhoods from their white middle-class counterparts.

The women and children who were migrant farmworkers, usually Hispanic, were not a group whom most Americans thought about during the postwar years. After the Industrial Revolution, when millions of Americans left family farms for urban and suburban areas, most did not consider who made it possible for food to appear in shops and supermarkets. With mothers working in the fields, children of migrant workers traveled with their parents, performing child labor and often suffering health problems from insecticides and repetitive stress. Because of their transitory life, they were usually unable to go to school, thus repeating the cycle of poverty in their own children, who were equipped for little else.

Among Native Americans, the Indian Adoption Project was started in 1958. Ostensibly to help Native American children assimilate into mainstream postwar culture, it was a federal program that removed hundreds of Indian children from their mothers to place them with whites.

By the postwar years, little had changed in decades for African American children in the rural South as well as urban black children in areas such as New York's Harlem. Often, poor blacks as well as poor whites from the rural South migrated northward toward what they hoped would be new lives. In those places, postwar women did their best for the children, often sacrificing so that their children might at least have the hope of a better future.

TEENAGERS

The union of mass media and the consumer culture of America's postwar years might be said to have given birth to an entirely new species of people. It was as if anthropologists discovered a remarkable civilization that was then studied in microscopic detail. In the postwar era, those people were called "teenagers." Among marketers, they were also called "consumers"—very affluent, impressionable consumers.

In previous decades, human beings basically passed from childhood to adulthood without a specific label for the adolescent years between 12 and 20. Legally, young people were considered children until they came of legal age at 18. For much of the past, the labor of young people was usually needed to help support the family. At the point when they took on an adult's workload in factories, farms, or as domestic servants, their childhood was essentially over.

When America entered World War II in 1941, it brought full employment. For the first time, young women had money to spend on nonessential goods for themselves, rather than having to help support the family. By 1944, near the end of the war, marketers noted teenage girls as a distinct demographic with buying power for the postwar world. With teenage girls as a lucrative consumer group, marketers worked hard to let them know exactly what to buy.

The daily lives of teenage girls sometimes became a source of entertainment in magazine articles and even a comic strip called *Teena*. Starting in mid-1944, the cartoon was syndicated to run in newspapers across the country. It followed a "typical" teenager in the course of her daily life, wearing the latest fashions and having fun with her friends. It became a staple of the postwar era, running for 20 years.

Also in 1944, *Seventeen* magazine was launched, aimed directly at teenage girls. Marketing companies were soon founded to help advertisers promote their products, specifically among white middle-class girls. The goal was to convince the teens that certain products would make them more popular and attractive. Feeding into each other, teen magazines and youth-oriented marketers were highly successful, dominating the marketplace they had created.

They even changed the social dynamic of womanhood. Previous generations of girls usually learned from their mothers as role models on how to enter the world of an adult female. However, Gilbert (1988) claims that postwar girls were part of their own subculture, with their world centering on teenage magazines (23).

Throughout the postwar years, publications for teenage girls mushroomed. Apart from the highly successful

American teenage girls of the postwar era generally enjoyed a great deal of freedom and prosperity. They were targeted as consumers by marketers. More than ever before, they mirrored the behavior of their peers rather than that of their parents. (Auckland War Memorial Museum)

Seventeen, other magazines of the postwar era included *Dig, Flip, Junior Bazaar, Modern Teen, Teen Digest, Teen Parade, Teen Time, Teen World*, and *Teens Today*. They regularly included advice columns and "confessional letters." Most of the content concerned dating and proper teen social behavior along with the perennially popular topic of sex. Underpinning it all were splashy ads and pseudo-articles about what hot new fashions and products to buy.

Mitchell and Reid-Walsh (2007) say that starting with the publication of *16* magazine in 1956, American girls were also linked by the shared experience of fan magazines that provided photos of teen crushes that girls could tape on their bedroom walls (284). Founded in 1965, *Tiger Beat* was a fan favorite in the later postwar years, providing a place for teenage girls to find pictures of their favorite male teen idols.

Through the rise of the mass media in the postwar era, teens no longer had to look to their family for adult role models. Postwar teenage girls, with their own set of vulnerabilities beneath their confident exterior, began mirroring the behavior of their peers rather than that of their parents.

Even when postwar teens bothered to listen to adults, young people were skeptical of what grown-ups were saying. Adults preached the "American Dream" of success through hard work and determination. With the specter of nuclear annihilation hanging over their heads, many teens of the Cold War era sought to enjoy life in the short term, while they still had the chance.

Teenage girls sought out boys with cars, which provided them the exhilaration of independence. Often, that freedom led to questionable choices. Teenage girls of the postwar era had money in their pockets and time on their hands, leading some to join the boys in what experts were calling "juvenile delinquency."

That term, which was popularized during the postwar era, referred to antisocial behavior by young people between the ages of 10 and 18. Sometimes it was chewing gum or smoking cigarettes; sometimes, burglary or vandalism. The shocking element was that girls were sometimes the culprits.

Of course, not all teenage girls were delinquents. In the postwar era, many sometimes expressed their teenage rebellion through fashion choices, such as wearing the frowned-upon blue jeans—a minor concern for parents in the big scheme of things. However, there was another form of rebellion that *was* a major concern for many parents on several levels: the rise of rock and roll music.

Postwar teens could generally afford to buy their own radio or record player. They could listen in private to the kind of music they liked, away from the scowls of disapproving parents.

With the growth of the television industry, a new element was added to the daily lives of young women in the postwar years. The teen-oriented *American Bandstand* made its national debut in 1957. It was a hugely popular television show, giving teenagers the opportunity to see their musical idols performing hit tunes. It also linked teenage girls across the country to each other. Teens in rural areas could see what "city girls" were wearing. They could also be exposed on a national scale to the products that marketers wanted them to buy.

Television also provided a role model for younger postwar adolescent girls when *The Mickey Mouse Club* premiered in 1955. Fans watched "Mouseketeer" Annette Funicello grow up before their eyes. She was able to join the pop music revolution with singles including "Tall Paul" and "Pineapple Princess."

Once she became a full-fledged teenager, Annette parlayed her television fame into hit teen-oriented movies of the 1960s. Annette's movies were relatively tame, with titles including *Beach Party*, *Bikini Beach*, and *Beach Blanket Bingo*. They spotlighted the California teenage "sun and fun" culture that teens in landlocked mid-America could only dream of.

However, Hollywood also produced teen-oriented movies that were less tame. They were centered on young people by focusing on postwar teen rebellion. Following the release of *So Young, So Bad* in 1950, such hit films of the postwar era also included *The Wild One* (1953) and *Rebel Without a Cause* (1955) as well as those that were promoted as being "ripped from the headlines" such as *Blackboard Jungle* (1955).

Filmmakers found there was a huge profit in focusing not only on male juvenile delinquents but also on the kind of teenage girls who were far from those in the old Andy Hardy movies of the 1930s and 1940s. The postwar era's "delinquent girl movies" had titles that told the story, including *Teenage Devil Dolls* (1955), *Reform School Girl* (1957), *High School Hellcats* (1958), and *Girls' Town* (1959).

The underlying theme in many of these low-budget films was, of course, sex. In the early postwar years, until the sexual revolution of the 1960s and 1970s, teenage sex was a forbidden topic. In the relative innocence of the postwar years, there seemed to be a sense that if young people learned about sex, it would corrupt teenage girls. The prevailing sentiment among adults seemed to be that if no one talked about it, teens would not be doing it.

Sex education and birth control were rarely available to young postwar women. Yet, in their daily lives, sexual content was being thrust at them through the mass media. Images of female "sex symbols" such as Marilyn Monroe were everywhere.

A 1959 film called *Blue Denim* was aimed directly at teens, purporting to show the consequences of teenage sex that inevitably resulted in the girl's pregnancy. It was a hit, due in no small part to its promotional poster that screamed, *"The lost innocence, the rude awakening to what they had done!"*

The options for teenage girls who found themselves "in trouble" by becoming pregnant were limited. They were usually forced to drop out of school. Sometimes they were sent away, (said to be visiting an out-of-town aunt or other family member) until they had the baby, which was then given up for adoption. Sometimes they went to homes for unwed mothers. Others "had to get married" to a usually unhappy teenage boy. A few underwent dangerous, illegal medical procedures that had lifelong ramifications if it did not kill them outright.

Through the mass media, the daily lives of postwar teenage girls were saturated with sexual images. At the same time, they were being told that there were severe consequences for those who indulged.

Teenage girls of the postwar era did not have to go to movies or read magazines to be surrounded by sexual images. Rock and roll music burst forth in the 1950s. It was widely condemned by parents, especially due to the pelvic gyrations of singer Elvis Presley. But rock music also contained another element that was of greater concern to many white middle-class adults: race.

Rock and roll had its origins in the rhythm and blues music of African Americans. Adults objected to the racial undercurrents as much as the rebellious-sounding music itself. They feared one of the most predominant scare tactics of the postwar era: white girls intermingling with black boys.

During the postwar era, many African Americans from the rural South migrated to northern cities for jobs. They sought the chance for their children to have better lives than they had endured amid the chronic poverty, lack of opportunity, and unrestrained violence against blacks in the Jim Crow era.

Not only did many white girls of the postwar era enjoy the music of black rhythm and blues stars such as Chuck Berry, Bo Diddley, Fats Domino, and Little Richard, they were also in much closer proximity to African Americans than in the past. In most cases, however, that proximity did not translate into white girls having close friends among their counterparts: teenage girls in the black community.

In general, the daily lives of African American teenage girls of the postwar era were often similar to whites. They wore the same kind of fashions, gathered with their friends, listened to music, and enjoyed the latest dances.

However, for some black teenage girls, the similarities in their daily lives ended there. Many attended racially segregated schools that were often old, crowded, and poorly equipped. Often, black families faced economic hardship, having limited opportunities for good-paying jobs. To help support the family, black teenage girls often worked as domestics, as their mothers did.

Other black teenage girls of the postwar era became active in fighting for their civil rights, usually through nonviolent protests.

In 1952, one of the first was an attempt to allow African Americans to be served at lunch counters in the South by staging a "sit-in." Black teenage high school and college students, both male and female, brought their schoolbooks, sitting quietly at public lunch counters all day, although they were never served. Frequently, they were harassed by white customers and the police. However, the sit-ins made news, often resulting in curtailing that particular form of racial discrimination.

In 1957, the most famous group of African American teenage girls in the world were the six young women of the Little Rock Nine. After the U.S. Supreme Court's *Brown v. Board of Education* decision in 1954 that ruled the concept of "separate but equal" to be unconstitutional, some schools began to desegregate. Television and newspapers worldwide carried disturbing images of the black teenage girls encountering vicious white mobs as they tried to attend classes at Central High School in Little Rock, Arkansas.

In later life, the women of the Little Rock Nine said their biggest concern the night before school started—like all teenage girls—was what to wear. They discovered that was not their biggest problem. Throughout the school year, they were continually tormented by whites. Just as postwar teenage girls across the country did, they laced up their saddle shoes each morning as part of their daily lives, although the girls of the Little Rock Nine essentially went into combat.

Many average teenage girls across America lived their daily lives amid unparalleled affluence, although for the most part, they were still young women caught between being children and adults. For many postwar teenage girls, daily life was a period of growth. But it was also a confusing time of mixed messages amid sexual imagery coupled with the threat of catastrophic nuclear war on top of typical adolescent angst.

ADULTHOOD

The lives of adult women in postwar America might be best exemplified in the top-rated television series *I Love Lucy*, which ran from 1951 to 1957. In real life, series star Lucille Ball was an extremely savvy businesswoman. However, on the TV show, her fictional character of Lucy Ricardo depended on her husband to bail her out of zany situations of her own making. Though Lucy Ricardo often tried, she failed at working outside the home, usually in humiliating circumstances. The ditzy housewife could not stay within a budget, and for her transgressions, Lucy was often spanked like a child by her husband.

During World War II, American women took on a variety of roles they had never played before, both on the home front and even in combat zones. Recruitment posters for women were everywhere, including the iconic image of "Rosie the Riveter," a female factory worker performing what had always been considered a man's job. Women of the World War II era built ships, drove trucks, and produced munitions. They served as nurses on the front lines and as Women Airforce Service Pilots (WASPs) who repositioned combat aircraft.

Yet, when the conflict ended, many adult women in postwar America went from "Rosie" to "Lucy." Women workers generally lost their wartime jobs, being sent back to their traditional place. And that place was in the home.

From images all around them in mass media such as television, magazines, and newspapers, messages stressed the importance of women staying at home to clean, cook, and raise the children while men were working in the outside world. Women were expected to give up any aspirations for themselves, being advised that there was no fulfillment outside the home. Elaine Tyler May (2008) states, "For some, the costs were well worth the benefits; for others, the costs were too high" (34).

Some adult women eventually started to feel a sense of unrest staying in the house with only children and appliances for company. However, many were convinced they were doing their patriotic duty with the postwar era being the height of America's involvement in the Cold War.

The Cold War was an ideologically based political hostility between the United States and Communist nations that existed from the end of World War II in 1945 to 1990. It was characterized by suspicion, threats, propaganda, international incidents, and other measures short of full-scale military action, or "a hot war," being fought with weapons.

American women were utilized to do their part. Experts claimed that if women did their jobs well at home, they would raise the right kind of children who would guarantee America's future security. If, on the other hand, women pursued careers outside the home or, even worse, turned their offspring over to outside childcare, the result would be a nation of degenerates, juvenile delinquents, crime, and chaos.

Women were told that looking attractive was not only a prime directive in keeping their husbands happy but also had a patriotic function. By looking good at all times, they would clearly show the rest of the world that the American way of life triumphed over Russia with its dowdy-looking women who were worn out from working outside the home.

Women in postwar America could take their patriotic duty one step forward by helping themselves to look attractive while bolstering the economy by shopping. To maintain America's consumer culture, someone had to do the consuming. Women could feel assured that by spending the money their husbands earned, or by persuading their men to do so, they were doing their patriotic part to win the Cold War.

If the worst happened, civil defense authorities claimed that women could protect their families against nuclear annihilation if they learned first aid, kept their fallout shelters well stocked with food, and figured out how to feed their families when supplies ran out by using some of the ingredients left in the rubble.

The role of adult American women in the postwar years was most clearly spotlighted in the famous "kitchen debate" between then vice president Richard Nixon and Soviet premier Nikita Khrushchev at the American National Exhibition in Moscow in 1959. Nixon pointed out a model home display where a woman demonstrated the wonders of push-button, labor-saving household appliances that made the lives of American women easier, thus proving the superiority of capitalism over Communism. Khrushchev, on the other hand, expressed pride in the productivity of Russia's female workers.

The message that American women's role was to be housewives and mothers was a consistent theme in one of the major forms of mass media in the postwar years: women's magazines. The concept of magazines aimed at women was not new, but it was during the postwar years when they were at their peak as tastemakers. These magazines were edited almost exclusively by men and reinforced the idea that women were fulfilled only by devoting their lives to being housewives and mothers. Conformity was key; experts agreed it was important to national security.

One popular magazine, *McCall's*, invented its own word, "Togetherness," introduced in 1954. It promoted the ideal American family where a husband and wife, within their strictly defined roles, centered their lives on home and children, all of whom enjoyed doing things together. If the husband and/or kids balked, it was the woman's fault.

These magazines were a guide to the proper role of women in postwar America, especially in mastering the new suburban middle-class ideal. Women of the postwar era often lived far from their original home. They lived lives that were different from those of their mothers, especially the generation that had endured the Depression era, which had often centered on simple survival.

Advice from their mothers was not always helpful in the brave new world after World War II. Magazines filled the void. Especially in the early postwar years before television became a common fixture in American homes, women's magazines helped to "both shape and reflect the values, habits, and aspirations of American women" (1) according to Walker (1998).

Educators also stepped in to reinforce the proper role of women in postwar America. In the age of McCarthyism, it was dangerous to veer too far from the expected norm. Teachers and administrators firmly placed women on the domestic track from elementary school onward. Adult women who took compulsory gender-segregated courses called "Homemaking" or "Home Economics" often found such training to be useful in their grown-up domestic roles. On the other hand, if something broke, many wished they had been able to attend the boys-only "Industrial Arts" class.

It was not just the public schools that perpetuated the ideal. Author Brett Harvey (1993) states that throughout the 1950s, the male president of the elite all-female Radcliffe College informed incoming "co-eds" that their education would make them "splendid wives and mothers, and their reward might be to marry Harvard men" (47).

There was a tentative path for female college graduates who were not lucky enough to get married upon graduation, which was called attaining the coveted "Mrs." (pronounced "M-R-S") degree. For educated postwar women, there were basically three career choices: nurse, teacher, or secretary. The imperative was to utilize one of those positions as a way to meet men and hopefully marry one.

If a "career woman" did get married, she was expected both by her husband and her employer to leave the job. When she became pregnant, as expected, she almost always lost her job whether or not she wanted—or needed—to keep it.

Some women gained permission from their husbands to use their education, choosing to work when they didn't need the paycheck.

Those women were usually considered selfish, putting themselves before the needs of their family, an abhorrent concept.

Lower-class women might find jobs in poorly paid clerical, assembly, or janitorial positions. In addition, no matter what their socioeconomic position might have been, women in postwar America had to keep the men in their lives happy, because so much depended on the protection of males.

Many women during the postwar years were indeed happy with their identities solely as wives and mothers. They tended to feel that any trade-off in independence was worth it for the unprecedented level of comfort and security in their lives. Many felt that as human beings, they were the same as men, just different—or, in the vernacular of that time, "separate but equal."

African American women of the postwar era heard a lot about the "separate but equal" concept. They were compelled to send their children to schools that may indeed have been separate from whites but hardly equal.

If the daily lives of middle-class white women basically took place in the home, for African American women, it was often *someone else's* home. Especially in the South, working for white women as a domestic, also called a maid, was often the only employment open to black women.

A good job for a black woman was being an elevator operator in the days before self-service. Some postwar African American women did have the chance to become professionals, such as being teachers in segregated schools. However, many who hoped to get advanced degrees were held back by a separate-but-unequal school system in the South that did not prepare them for college. It also meant going to traditionally black colleges or attending an out-of-state school that accepted African Americans.

While women in postwar America in general were discouraged from pursuing a career, African American women found doors closed to them even if it was absolutely necessary to work to provide for their family. Many left their own homes in the morning to work all day as maids in the homes of whites.

However, they too were interested in learning information that was relevant to them and their community. *Ebony* magazine was founded in 1945, soon after the end of World War II. It was a monthly publication aimed at what was then called the "Negro" or "colored" market. *Ebony*'s success led to the creation of a smaller weekly sister publication, *Jet*, in 1951.

African American women of the postwar era could read about the latest fashions as well as trends in the growing civil rights movement. As the postwar years progressed, there were small signs of change for black women. In 1950, poet Gwendolyn Brooks became the first African American to win a Pulitzer Prize. In 1954, Dorothy Dandridge was the first African American woman nominated for a Best Actress Oscar. In 1957, tennis player Althea Gibson became the first African American to win at Wimbledon and the first African American to win the U.S. Open and was also named Woman Athlete of the Year by the Associated Press.

There were two other sources of role models for women in postwar America, although blacks would be excluded for decades. The Miss America pageant was held annually, combining physical appearance with a talent that might include singing, dancing, recitation, or playing a musical instrument. There was a special award given for Miss Congeniality, which was presented to the nicest contestant as determined by a vote among the competing delegates. Although the Miss Congeniality award started as far back as 1939, only one congenial winner has ever taken the top prize of becoming Miss America.

In his study of the Miss America pageant, Riverol (1992) claims that some people cast the pageant contestants of the postwar years "in the roles of belles gone by [that] was in keeping with the times and the role of women in that time. Therefore, the pageant was merely a mirror of 1950s society" (42). Not until the late 1960s did dissent, demonstrations, and controversy cloud the pageant.

With the growing presence of television in the postwar years, women from coast to coast could watch the annual Miss America pageant. It was considered a staple of American life and a bellwether of the ideal American female. Not until 1984, with the crowning of Vanessa Williams, was an African American woman cast in that role.

Another image of women in postwar America was an improbable one, since it was arguably a toy. Mitchell and Reid-Walsh (2007) state, "There is a long-standing association between girls and dolls" (4). Throughout history, girls rehearsed their expected maternal role with baby dolls. The tradition-shattering departure in the postwar era was created by Ruth Handler, the wife of a Mattel Toy Company executive. She saw the prototype of a "model" doll on a 1959 trip to Europe and brought the idea to Mattel, naming it for her daughter Barbara. The Barbie doll had an impossibly voluptuous figure that some adult women tried to emulate to please their men. It made a huge impression on girls and was an unlikely role model for grown-ups.

While white males were clearly and unapologetically in charge during the postwar era, there were occasional attempts to pretend that women actually had any power. One film from 1954 was called *Woman's World*, an all-star movie with such popular actresses of the postwar era as June Allyson, Lauren Bacall, and Arlene Dahl. Concerning itself with three men who compete for a high-ranking corporate position, it was based on a short story in *McCall's* magazine called "May the Best Wife Win." Along with interviewing the male candidates, the company owner also studies their wives. Not too surprisingly for the era, it is the docile housewife who wins the job for her husband. The women exist as appendages to the men, summed up in the film's theme song: "It's a woman's world when she's in love / It's a woman's world, his kiss can make her glow."

Although the postwar years spurred some undercurrents of change, the daily lives of most women in that era took place in the home. A woman was someone's wife and someone's mother, no matter how well educated or capable she was in other areas as an intelligent, functioning human. As Friedan wrote after doing research for her groundbreaking postwar-era book *The Feminine Mystique*, they might be discontented but ultimately the goal of postwar women was "to get married, have four children, and live in a nice house in a nice suburb" (60).

RELATIONSHIPS WITH MEN

At the same time when some women in postwar America were attempting to reconcile themselves to the mindset that their only role in life was to stay at home and raise children, some members of an unlikely group envied them. That group was the men of the postwar era. While it seemed as though men ruled the world, many of them envied women for having a clearly defined place in it. For men, the picture was a bit unclear.

Men who were middle aged in the postwar era had gone into military service during the formative years of their late teens and early 20s. They had either been drafted or had volunteered to serve their country in the 1940s during World War II, or in the early 1950s, the Korean War.

Many had experienced unspeakable horrors they could not discuss, even with each other. Some suffered from physical disabilities that ranged from recoverable to life altering. Others ached inside but were unable to define the trouble. Some experts called it "battle fatigue" or "shell shock," precursors to the as-yet-unnamed post-traumatic stress disorder (PTSD).

Some men found the routine tasks of their daily lives after the war unable to satisfy the adrenaline-fed need for excitement that was bred during the war. Even some who never saw combat found themselves missing the masculine camaraderie of the military.

Some returned to civilian life only to discover that many jobs were held by men who had stayed home during the war and now had seniority. Many veterans were forced to accept entry-level positions. But they did accept them, because men in the postwar era generally had families to support.

Males, as well as females, believed what they were told by their government and the mass media: that it was their patriotic duty to create a strong family with a wife and plenty of children to perpetuate the American way of life. Although World War II was over, there was the threat of Communism to contend with in the Cold War of the postwar era.

Men's role was to be the breadwinner while women stayed home to handle domestic chores. Almost inevitably, tensions arose. Some women envied men for going out into the excitement of the wider world while some men envied their wives for not having to go into corporate battle every day. The strain of raising and providing for children often caused resentment between husband and wife. The *"Friday Night Blues"* found women wanting to eat out at restaurants or dance in nightclubs for a change, while their husbands wanted to stay home and relax.

Amid growing tension, some women of the postwar era might have reluctantly discussed their discontent with other women. However, men felt compelled to be stoic in their quest to "be a man about it." Many found it unmanly to discuss their dissatisfaction, even with other men. Often, they were unable to verbalize it, even to themselves. Many found solace by self-medicating with alcohol at home or in the local tavern. Some took out their anger on their wives and children.

Two distinctly different kinds of movies from the era following World War II symbolize the dilemma of men as well as their relationship with women in postwar America. In *The Best Years of Our Lives* (1946), three combat veterans return home to a small town in America to discover that they—and the women they left behind—have been irreparably changed. One man, unable to compete in the job market against more experienced workers who have not been overseas, is forced to take a low-level job as a "soda jerk," dispensing soft drinks at a soda fountain. Instead of wearing an imposing military uniform that commanded respect, the classic soda jerk outfit was an apron and little white paper cap. Another of the trio, an older man, who regains his job at a bank is reprimanded for granting relaxed terms on loans to veterans. The third man comes home after losing both hands in the war, being forced to use metal hooks. The actor playing that role actually did lose both hands in a wartime explosion, earning an Academy Award for what must have been the ultimate realistic performance. In addition to his Academy Award for Best Supporting Actor, the actor portraying the disabled veteran in *The Best Years of Our Lives* received an additional Special Honorary Oscar "for bringing hope and courage to fellow veterans."

The story hinges on how the men adjust not only to their new postwar circumstances but also how they relate to the women in their lives who had gained a newfound degree of independence during the war. Some of the women have grown but are supportive; others are not. In any case, all the women have changed.

The title has a double meaning. For many servicemen, the "best years of their lives" were with other males at war, not their civilian experiences afterward. In addition, they also *sacrificed* the best years of their lives, in terms of youthful innocence lost amid the horrors of war, becoming disconnected from domestication. The poignant, eloquent story was highly symbolic of the thousands of men who survived the war only to come home to a world that had shifted while they were gone.

The other type of film involving the role of men in the postwar era and their relationship to postwar women usually contained a degree of courage but very little hope. After the sunny patriotism of films in the war years, the postwar era brought a new, grittier kind of American movie, "film noir." The name essentially indicated a "dark movie." Film noir is marked by a pervasive sense of fatalism, pessimism, and menace, featuring flawed heroes, sometimes called antiheroes, who have often served in the war. The women in their lives are generally dangerous "femme fatales." These are not love stories, nor do they offer the promise of a happy ending. The mood is dark and shadowy. The men drink a lot, projecting a sense of doom. Two of the most notable film noir movies of the postwar era are *Double Indemnity* and *The Postman Always Rings Twice*, with both their flawed heroes undone by women.

Many postwar men felt that the earth had shifted under their feet. Part of the problem was that the standard image of what it meant to be a man had become fuzzier. Young men growing up in the past generally measured themselves against their fathers or father figures. They usually wanted to be just like their father—or his polar opposite, depending on their childhood experiences.

Many of the males in previous generations had worked with their hands on farms or in factories. While there were certainly some postwar men who did the same thing, there was a growing cohort of middle-class males with newly minted college degrees courtesy of the GI Bill. They would find themselves not in fields or factories but behind a desk, wearing a white-collar shirt and a tie that they often found constricting, literally and figuratively.

Not all men worked behind a desk in the postwar years, but many more careers in professional areas opened up during that era. Some were in new industries such as public relations, advertising, and television that had hardly been fledglings before the war.

The GI Bill offered the chance to attain college degrees, spurring a sharp increase in upward mobility. However, this often created something of a divide between fathers and sons, especially among men whose fathers were farmers or laborers in families where a college education had always seemed to be an unattainable goal. Some men struggled to find their place not only in the postwar American culture but also in their own families.

With the trend toward suburban housing, many moved with their wives and children to the booming new suburbs. Wives were besieged with constant messages from the mass media to be patriotic by building the nation's economy through buying consumer goods. Easy credit enabled them to "buy now, pay later." As debt piled up, husbands felt the pressure to keep earning more money.

With many men leaving home each morning wearing the corporate "uniform" of a gray flannel suit, some started to feel like gray men. Many felt they were trading traditional masculinity for a suit and tie in order to meet the demands of a suburban home and a new car, both of which were subject to upgrading every few years. Perhaps subliminally, they started to equate their wives with the demands society was imposing. At the same time that many women felt trapped at home, many men felt trapped at work.

After fighting corporate politics and the often unreasonable demands of bosses all day, many men felt they were expected to come home transformed into the ideal husband and father. Often, wives wanted some relief from their daily routine of dealing with children in ever-growing families. The relationship between post-war men and women often became strained.

In Sloan Wilson's 1955 novel *The Man in the Gray Flannel Suit*, the 35-year-old protagonist killed more than a dozen men in World War II, including his best friend in a grenade accident. He ponders his application form for a public relations job with a fictitious company in the new field of television, knowing he cannot truthfully answer the question of why he wants to work in public relations. The truth is that he doesn't. He recognizes his own cynicism, which he calls "cheap."

Wilson created the character based on himself and the experiences of those around him. He recognized that the daily lives of postwar-era men, as well as their relationships with postwar women, were shaped by their experiences in the 1940s.

Gilbert (2005) writes that men of the postwar years were marked by what he calls their preoccupation with masculinity, "in part because the period followed wartime self-confidence based upon the sacrifice and heroism of ordinary men" (2).

The Cold War changed the dynamics of the battlefield. Men felt obliged to fight Communism at home by being the perfect American male. However, few knew what that might consist of, and if they did, they felt themselves lacking. Such an impasse did not lead to ideal relationships with women.

Many postwar men were still coming to terms with the loss of their youth and innocence, which had been curtailed abruptly by the war. Ehrenreich (1983) states that by his late twenties, the postwar middle-class man had found a wife and was adjusting to marriage, home, family, and job. But, she states, "he knew that something was wrong" (29).

In addition to real wartime experiences that often plagued the minds of men, some felt pressured by their wives, correctly or not, to conform to an ideal image of what a family man should be. Many had joined the military just out of high school or even younger, never having had the chance to enjoy their youth. It seemed that suddenly they had wives, children, and what often felt like overwhelming responsibilities.

In addition, just as with women in postwar America, there were images aimed at men by the mass media that often left them feeling inadequate. The postwar years were the era of family shows on television such as *Father Knows Best* (premiering in 1954) and *Leave It to Beaver* (starting in 1957). With the help of good writers, the male head of the fictional households ultimately did know best.

Measuring themselves against TV fathers, many men wondered if *they* did too.

It was not just television programs that left men of the postwar era feeling confused about themselves and their relationship with women. The rise of the advertising industry in the postwar years thrust another kind of male image at American men. A particularly effective one was the Marlboro Man.

This figure was used in advertising campaigns for Marlboro cigarettes beginning in 1954, with a rugged cowboy alone on the frontier with his "manly" cigarette. The Marlboro man represented the iconic figure of America's western hero: solitary, self-sufficient, and indeed sexy, even though there were no women in sight. Ironically, back in the 1920s, Marlboros had been introduced and marketed specifically for women, even sporting a red band around the tip of the cigarette to hide a lady's lipstick stains. It was not until the 1950s that the company sought to boost sales by rebranding the product to appeal to postwar males. The craggy image of the Marlboro Man sent sales skyrocketing.

The lives of postwar American men may have centered on the conformity of their existence with their wives and, by extension, their families, home, and work. However, many family men nurtured inner spirits that were closer to the Marlboro Man.

MARRIAGE

According to writer Karen Karbo (2018), a woman who reached age 22 in the postwar years was considered to be an old maid if she was not married or at least engaged. Karbo states, "You were probably living at home and working in one of the lady-approved jobs—teacher, nurse, secretary—while looking forward to a life of caring for aging parents and being a beloved auntie. Maybe you were saving your virtue for the husband who would give your life meaning, but who'd failed to materialize as yet" (137).

In the postwar years, the average age of an American woman to wed was 20. After marriage, the lack of safe, reliable contraception often meant giving birth to numerous children. With many postwar couples moving to affordable housing in sprawling suburban developments, women often met other young housewives like themselves. It all appeared to be an ideal world for married women. Everybody seemed so happy, especially in magazines and on television.

Therefore, when a housewife felt the first stirrings of discontent, she tended to think that she was the only one with such feelings, reproaching herself for having such an ungrateful attitude. Many grew up in the poverty of the Great Depression, so they knew how good they had it in an era of prosperity. Still, spending all day, every day, with gleaming appliances and bickering children for mental stimulation was, for many, not the best of all possible worlds.

After World War II, some people returned to the area of the nation where they had grown up. However, many others settled in the new suburban developments that were springing up from coast to coast. These would prove to be communities that were very different from those of their parents. For women, alone in the house all day except for children, their daily lives could prove to be very isolated.

Despite the general prosperity, there was often one car in the family, which the husband drove to work. It was not the norm for most women to drive, with jokes about "female drivers" becoming fodder for comedians despite their accident rate being the same or better than that of males. With no transportation, women often felt stranded in new developments that rarely had shopping centers or other destinations except schools and houses of worship.

Some female friends might have expressed their frustration, but many kept it to themselves. With everyone appearing to be happy, a woman did not want to appear different in such an age of conformity.

In the past, a newly married woman might have sought guidance from trusted family members. But for many in the postwar years, far from their traditional home, there were other primary sources of information: the mass media.

To women's magazines and television programs, a woman was not a reader or viewer; she was a consumer. The media reinforced their advertisers' message; that was how they made money. The images women saw in the mass media were smiling models posing as housewives who looked overjoyed to be using their new electric floor waxer.

In the postwar years, especially before the widespread advent of television, women's magazines were big business. Edited almost exclusively by men and intended to sell products promoted by their advertisers, magazines such as *Good Housekeeping*, *Ladies' Home Journal*, and *McCall's* carried articles on how to have a successful marriage. The way to do that was to keep men happy, emphasizing that it was the wife's duty to make their marriage work. During the postwar era, male dominance and female sacrifice signified the prevailing pattern.

This was reinforced with the arrival of television, which became the predominant communications medium in American life. It appeared to set the standard for a successful marriage. Women saw fictional couples who solved their problems in 30 minutes or less, usually with a hug and a good chuckle at the end.

The most popular situation comedy of the 1950s was *I Love Lucy*, which premiered in 1951 and remained at the top of the ratings until it ended its run in 1957. With a hilariously zany new situation each week, the program could be said to bear little resemblance to reality. Lucille Ball had been a glamorous MGM starlet, but for *I Love Lucy*, she cast glamour aside. Her willingness to do messy sight gags created scenes that are still stamped on people's minds: lighting her fake nose on fire, stomping grapes with her feet, stuffing assembly-line chocolates in her mouth.

However, there were some underlying truths about postwar marriage in *I Love Lucy*, with its title written from the husband's point of view. The fictitious Lucy always yearned to be more than a housewife, rebelling in episode after episode against the constraints of her role. She sought employment, although her husband was so opposed to her working outside the home that she often had to do it in secret. She schemed to make her own money and frequently disguised herself to perform in show business. When she got caught or overspent her "allowance," she was spanked by her husband. Most people understood it was simply for laughs, although the plots directly underscored the restrictions placed on the role of housewives in the postwar era.

If, for example, episodes had ended with Lucy defeating the gender stereotypes in postwar marriages by succeeding in what she undertook outside the home (and not getting spanked for her efforts), the show might have been seen as controversial. Instead, Lucy returned to her "domestic containment" as a housewife, at least until the next episode. Audiences understood that the irrepressible Lucy could not be contained. She would emerge with a new screwball plan to make them laugh the following week.

Other taste-making television programs of the postwar era were presented as being a bit more realistic. In shows such as *Father Knows Best* starting in 1954 and *Leave It to Beaver* in 1957, the housewife showed patience, understanding, and wisdom, although she never overstepped her role where her husband was concerned. If he was the one who found himself in a mess, she could sort it out behind the scenes to preserve his ego. Everyone had their role to play: the man left for work in the morning, and when he returned at night, the woman served his supper. While there might be complications such as the wife burning dinner, for the most part, TV marriages hummed along splendidly.

Discontent among real-life couples of the postwar era often sprang from media images where fictional marriages all seemed so happy. "Togetherness" was a phrase coined by *McCall's* magazine in 1954 to promote the concept of the ideal marriage with its strictly defined roles, centering on children and home, where everyone enjoyed doing things together. It did not help togetherness when the daily lives of the marriage partners were often lived in two different worlds. Men went to work, women stayed in the house. Each partner sometimes fantasized about how much better the other had it: men enjoying an exciting workplace, women "taking it easy" at home. They also often had differing needs on nights and weekends, with the wife wanting to get out of the house for a change of scene while the husband hoped to stay in and relax.

Couples struggling with differences often found themselves frustrated, assuming it was just *their* marriage that was plagued with problems. Everyone else seemed so happy. If other couples were unhappy, they weren't talking about it.

Often the element of patriotism deterred people from discussing their problems honestly, even between a husband and wife. Marriage was promoted as a significant way for average Americans to fight the Cold War. The appearance of millions of stable families in the United States was a solid endorsement of the American way of life.

In postwar society, it went without saying that marriage was virtually the only option. As Stephanie Coontz (2016) points out, a 1957 survey reported that four out of five people in the United States believed that anyone who preferred to remain single was "sick," "neurotic," or "immoral" (246). Any departure short of widowhood—whether due to divorce, late marriage, non-marriage, single motherhood, or even delayed childbearing—was considered deviant.

Regarding deviance, with the postwar climate of McCarthyism, a person of appropriate age who was unmarried stood a good chance of being considered to be a homosexual. Along with Communists, the McCarthy investigations sought out individuals who were suspected of being homosexual (the term "gay" was not yet being used). They were compelled to "name names" of other people who might be Communists to avoid being publicly labeled as a homosexual, which usually resulted in the loss of their job, or worse.

If unmarried postwar women found jobs in the approved fields as nurses, teachers, or secretaries, they were expected to quit after getting married. In some areas, teachers could not keep their jobs after marriage even if they wanted to.

"Career gals" were the subject of a 1958 book by Rona Jaffe and a 1959 movie of the same name, *The Best of Everything*. The story line concerns three young women who work together in an office as they encounter romance, often with married men. A cautionary tale is their bitter boss, an older woman who is miserable because she chose a career over marriage.

Therefore, women had to work hard for that all-important husband. There were numerous guides to finding a man and enticing him to propose marriage. It was also vital to find the *right* man according to community standards. Nancy Cott (2002) states that while marriage represents personal love and commitment, it also part of the perceived public order. She states that marital status was vital to a person's standing in the community, adding that, "entry to the institution [was] bound up with civil rights" (4).

In states across the nation during the postwar era, following statutes that were in place since before the Civil War, there were laws that prohibited people from marrying the person of their choice. In various regions of the country, whites were prohibited from marrying nonwhites such as African Americans, Asian Americans, Native Americans, and so on. Even among whites, some religions banned intermarriage between those of different faiths.

Before *I Love Lucy* took to the airwaves, television executives balked at showing a "mixed marriage" between the fictitious Lucy Ricardo and her husband, a fictional Cuban named Ricky Ricardo. Lucille Ball was told that American audiences would neither believe nor accept it, whereupon she informed them that she was married in real life to the proposed actor playing the part, the Cuban Desi Arnaz. The program aired, and the rest was broadcast history.

There were other "mixed marriages" that were not always resolved as happily or comedically: war brides. They were women, usually from battle-torn countries, who married military personnel and came with their husbands to the United States. The War Brides Act of 1945 allowed American servicemen who married women abroad to bring their wives home after World War II. Most estimates place the number of postwar-era war brides at about 350,000.

Those women adjusted to both their marriage and to American society with varying degrees of success.

Some came from countries that had been American allies. For example, more than 15,000 Australian women and about 70,000 war brides came from the United Kingdom. They spoke the same language and had grown up in a similar culture. Others came from countries such as France and Italy. Women from those groups usually faced little, if any, hostility in America.

About 20,000 German war brides came to the United States by 1950. Although Nazi Germany had been the enemy, German women physically resembled their American counterparts and faced little overt hostility as they went about their daily lives.

Another group of war brides was not as fortunate. Between 30,000 and 35,000 Japanese women married American soldiers. They came to the United States to face an uncertain future based on their race and the way they looked. Most of them had left the devastated country of Japan amid angry resentment by their families, who did not have warm feelings about daughters and sisters marrying their nation's former enemies.

Things did not go much better when they arrived in the United States to meet their new in-laws. Some would not call their daughter-in-law by her Japanese name, substituting something "American" such as the name "Susie." Beyond their new families, many faced opposition for literally being the face of the enemy, especially in small towns where families had lost loved ones at Pearl Harbor or in the ensuing battles that were fought in the Pacific. Although some Japanese war brides married for love, others married out of desperation. Some of their marriages were reasonably happy; others were not. All the Japanese war brides faced a strange new world in the United States after their marriage: American culture, English language, Western food.

The status of these foreign women was satirized in the 1949 Cary Grant movie, *I Was a Male War Bride*. No doubt there were more laughs in the movie than in many marriages. Even beyond foreign nationals, during wartime many American couples had married in haste, leaving them to repent in leisure during the postwar years. At the breakfast table, they often realized they hardly knew the person sitting across from them.

If things did not appear to be working out, options were limited. Divorce was frowned upon in the postwar years, even in cases of alcoholism, abuse, or extramarital affairs. The burden was usually placed on women. It was the wife's duty to make sure her husband didn't stray and up to her to make the marriage a success. Celello (2009) states that consistent messages in the media of the postwar era asserted that to keep America strong, marriage was the only route for acceptance, companionship, and intimacy. However, that did not always end up being the case. One or both marital partners might be miserable, but to the outside world, "a successful marriage was, quite simply, one that did not end in divorce" (3).

The common perception of married women's roles might be summed up with a line from the television comedy, *Leave It to Beaver*. In it, the namesake boy, worried about an upcoming test, tells his mother, "Girls have got it lucky . . . They don't have to be smart. They don't have to get jobs or anything. All they gotta do is get married."

FAMILY

One example of the daily lives of American women during the postwar era is this: Waking up before the rest of the family, she bathes, puts on makeup, dons a pretty dress, and makes breakfast for her husband and children. She lovingly gives them each a kiss as they head out the door to work or school, with the children carrying a lunch she has made. After cleaning the house, she does her baking, sewing, and perhaps a bit of volunteer work, followed by meal preparation for dinner. After the children come home from school, they might be served milk and cookies to tide them over until dinnertime, as long as there is no danger of "spoiling their appetite." When Dad gets home from work, the whole family sits down together for a large home-cooked evening meal. After dinner, Mom cleans up the kitchen and does the dishes before joining the family in front of the television. Together, they watch the same program on one of three television networks. Without remote controls to conveniently change channels, the entire family usually sits through commercials, getting ideas on what they might buy to make their family home even better. The ads make an impression because the people in the commercials look just like themselves— white, middle-class, attractive, happy families—whose daily lives are improved after buying the advertiser's product.

In these families, there are no juvenile delinquents, alcoholic fathers, or unhappy wives. Mothers are self-sacrificing saints. If Dad sometimes seems to be a well-meaning bumbler, Mom quietly steps in to restore order without damaging the male ego. Although the children are often wise beyond their years, they still struggle

In the postwar era, a woman's place was said to be in the home. Her special domain was the kitchen, making hearty meals for her family. Images of idealized American mothers, like the one pictured here, were presented in women's magazines and on television. (Lightfieldstudios prod/Dreamstime.com)

with childhood issues such as fear of an upcoming test or a dateless prom. Those anxieties can be assuaged by Mom's calm reassurance. Any awkward family problems that crop up can be solved together, with love and humor, in less than 30 minutes.

Those families existed in one place: television. The postwar airwaves teemed with situation comedies about white middle-class suburban families. Popular family comedies that ran throughout the postwar era include *I Married Joan* and *My Little Margie* (both debuting in 1952), *Father Knows Best* and *December Bride* (both 1954), *The Life of Riley* and *Mama* (both premiered in 1949 and ran throughout the 1950s), *Leave It to Beaver* (1957), *The Donna Reed Show* (1958), and *Dennis the Menace* (1959).

The most popular of all was *I Love Lucy*, which topped the ratings charts through the postwar years. When it first aired in 1951, *Lucy* seemed to be an outlier since it originally concerned a married couple with no children. But that was resolved on January 19, 1953, when the title character, Lucy Ricardo, gave birth to a son. Twelve hours before the broadcast, series star Lucille Ball had given birth to her real-life son. Audiences had been able to watch the fictional Lucy from the time she announced that she was "expecting" to the birth of the baby, which most Americans knew coincided closely with reality. Almost 75 percent of viewers in all American homes with television sets tuned in, setting a record for its era.

A few novelty programs of the postwar era focused on a wacky, single career girl. All of them had a central theme: her attempts to snare a husband, which was the first step in creating the perfect family. These included *Our Miss Brooks* (1952), *Private Secretary* (1953), *The Gale Storm Show* (1956), and *The Ann Sothern Show* (1958).

Departing from the white Anglo-Saxon Protestant norm, the short-lived *Beulah Show* ran in syndication from 1950 to 1952. It was the first television situation comedy to star an African American woman, centering around a maid who is able to resolve family problems that her white employers cannot. However, being a postwar woman, Beulah states in the opening credits that she is "in the market for a husband."

Arguably, the most significant situation comedy of the postwar era in terms of presenting the perfect American family was *Ozzie and Harriet* (1952). It blurred the line between fiction and reality by starring the real-life Nelson family as themselves. Viewers knew that the Nelsons were a real family. America watched sons David and Ricky grow up before their eyes. To many, it was a precursor to later "reality" shows, giving viewers a peek at the daily life of the Nelsons in which Harriet spent her life taking care of her husband and sons. Actually, later studies of the program point to a dictatorial, dysfunctional atmosphere, far removed from the ideal existence being portrayed. But postwar-era viewers only saw a perfect family and wondered why their own was not quite as ideal.

The exciting new phenomenon of television exploded in the postwar era. Every family had to have one, awarding it a central spot not only in their living rooms but also in their lives. "TV Moms" became the standard by which real-life women were measured. Much of our image of postwar families—and women's place in it—comes from the television programs of that era. Two of the most prominent females were the "TV Mom" characters of June Cleaver on *Leave It to Beaver* and Donna Stone on *The Donna Reed Show*. When not dispensing sensible advice to family members, those female characters kept their suburban homes spotlessly clean while wearing attractive dresses, often topped off with a pearl necklace. Postwar viewers saw them wearing high heels while they cleaned the house, as if that was just what real-life women were expected to do. However, later interviews with the actors revealed that the TV Moms wore high heels so they could appear taller in the camera frame with their TV kids, who were constantly gaining height as they grew up.

In addition, TV homes had sparkling labor-saving appliances. Families that did not have them often felt woefully behind the times. As it happened, sponsors often provided the appliances for the TV families.

With television ads reinforced by women's magazines, the post-war years marked a historic boom in consumer spending, specifically in household goods, the arena most often controlled by women. With easy credit—"a dollar down and a dollar a week"—American women could make sure their families were not left behind.

Even facing a constant barrage of messages urging them to buy the advertisers' products, most women were not gullible or greedy. They believed it was their patriotic duty, as the keepers of the domestic front, to keep the American economy strong.

Labor-saving devices did in fact help with work that was often backbreaking for women. Electric washing machines were a blessing to many housewives. Similarly, they could economize. Purchasing a large freezer meant being able to buy meat and other products in bulk, cutting down on both food costs and trips to the supermarket.

Pollsters reported that Americans consistently claimed that home and their nuclear family—mother, father, and children—were the wellsprings of their happiness and self-esteem. Most probably truly felt that way. After the Great Depression and a cataclysmic global war, it was comforting to have a cozy personal retreat at the end of the day. However, even in "confidential" polls, in the age of McCarthyism, many people may have been inclined to say what they felt they were expected to say, in order not to appear "different."

They may not have been wrong. Coontz (2016) cites the prevailing wisdom surrounding the domestic version of American diplomat George Kennan's containment policy toward the Soviet Union. An All-American family with its vigilant mother became the front line of defense against treason in the Cold War era with its ever-present nuclear threat: "Anticommunists linked deviant family or sexual behavior to sedition. The FBI and other agencies instituted unprecedented state intrusion into private life under the guise of investigating subversives" (34).

It is ironic that American women's daily life in the postwar era was centered on two uses of the word "nuclear." First was the reality of the atomic age in which the word conjured images of nuclear bombs, nuclear power, and nuclear warfare, referring to the nucleus, or center, of the atom. Though often unspoken, the threat of nuclear annihilation was a standard part of people's daily lives, with many women fearing for their children's futures.

The other use was in reference to the nuclear family, derived from the Latin words *nucleus* or *nux*, meaning "core." It was defined as a father, mother, and dependent children living in one household. Its first known usage was popularized after World War II when the "core" family was held up as America's basic social unit.

In the past, economic necessity often compelled several generations to live under one roof. Sometimes this was still true during the postwar era in rural regions or among African American families. But in the general affluence of postwar America, there were fewer extended families as well as those with single parents.

Having a perfect nuclear family with "vigilant" mothers was a key element for how women in postwar America could help fight the Cold War. With the government's encouragement, women had a role to play, as clearly defined in the mass media. For example, in referring to American values versus Communism, Douglas (1995) claims, "Our women had to be different from *their* women. *Their* women worked in masculine jobs and had their kids raised by state-run daycare centers" (47).

Douglas states that there were newspapers and politicians who proclaimed daycare to be a "Communist plot" that would brainwash children into becoming socialists. "Therefore," adds Douglas, "our kids had to be raised at home by their moms if we were going to remain democratic and free" (47).

While boys were encouraged to find their place in the wider world, girls were taught homemaking by their mothers as well as through courses in school. During the postwar years, college was not considered the norm for girls. Many young women remained in their parents' home until they got married.

Whatever frustrations postwar women might have felt in their familial role, many knew it was a step up from what their own family experience had been when they were growing up during the poverty of the Great Depression in the 1930s.Most postwar women were determined to make their children's lives better than their own had been.

Still, although women in many postwar families enjoyed a life that was better than in previous generations, watching a latter-day television comedy such as *Happy Days* (1974–1984) can be deceiving. Some families had less to do with keeping Communists out than keeping secrets *in*.

Later memoirs from adult baby boomers reveal tensions within the family that were kept concealed in postwar families. Housewives were said to be "restless" for no apparent reason. Battered women usually blamed their injuries on falling down since the conventional wisdom dictated that if a wife was beaten, she had probably goaded her husband into the attack. Alcoholism, infidelity, and venereal disease transmitted to the wife were dirty little secrets kept hidden. A future Miss America later revealed that within the confines of her respectable postwar family, her father had sexually violated her from the time she was five years old until she left home at 18. Some women drowned their problems in alcohol; others used tranquilizers commonly called "Mother's little helpers."

If women or children faced abuse in their daily lives, divorce was frowned upon. Apart from the social stigma of divorce in the postwar years, job prospects for women were grim if they had to provide for their children. On top of societal pressures, there was therefore an economic incentive for women to keep the family together.

Even if there were two parents in African American families, according to statistics, about 40 percent of black women had to work outside the home to help support their family. Often, she worked as a domestic servant for a white family. The poverty rate among two-parent black families was 50 percent. Since African American males were usually limited to low-level jobs, the family could stay afloat financially only if both parents worked.

Women in postwar America were encouraged to root their identity and self-worth in their family. If they failed to measure up, the lack of a suitable wife and family could result in the husband's job loss or at least being passed over for promotion.

To give them an idea of what was expected, postwar women looked to the mass media, especially television, for role models in a world that was often quite different from the one in which they had grown up. Most women understood that television characters were fictitious, but seeing them week after week in their own living rooms often made the characters appear to be part of the family. In programs such as *Ozzie and Harriet*, where everyone knew that Ozzie, Harriet, David, and Ricky Nelson were a real-life family who were playing themselves, the line was further distorted.

Being exposed to perfect TV families who solved problems in 30 minutes led to a disquieting blur between what women saw on television and what was happening in their own lives. It was hard for many to remember, as Stephanie Coontz (2016) puts it, that *"Leave It to Beaver* was not a documentary" (31).

SEXUALITY

The daily lives of women in postwar America centered on a fact of life that has always been the case for females: biology is destiny. From the beginning, women were the ones who conceived a child, carried the developing baby in their bodies, and gave birth. Many other facets of the female existence also surround their sexuality: development of breasts, their monthly period, menopause, and so on.

Despite stunning advances in most other fields during the 20th century, women's roles when the postwar era began continued to be limited due to their gender. Basic contraceptive devices that women could control, such as the diaphragm, were often only available by prescription and solely with permission from the husband. With few options for safe, reliable female contraception, a woman who had an unprotected sexual interlude only once could well be pregnant the next morning.

The arrival of children meant job loss if she was employed. It also effectively tied her to the home, devoted to childcare for much of the rest of her life.

During the postwar era, women who were desperate not to become pregnant used a variety of methods for birth control, with varying side effects. Some used a strong household disinfectant internally that was rumored to be useful as contraception but was in fact damaging to women. The disinfectant's manufacturer declined to discourage its use inside the female body, using coded language in ads that promoted its use beyond scouring sinks and toilets. It did not prevent pregnancies but led instead to genital burning, blisters, and several deaths.

Some women also used mixtures containing baking soda, iodine, or vinegar. Rumors persisted throughout the postwar era that using Coca-Cola in the genital tract was an effective contraceptive. Some religions only permitted abstinence as well as a system involving body temperature and expected ovulation dates, which became known as the "rhythm method," providing fodder for 1950s-era comedians.

The issue was that throughout the postwar era and as late as the 1970s, American laws were inhospitable to the idea of birth control. There were statues on the books in a majority of states prohibiting or restricting the advertisement and sale of contraception, or even making accurate information available. These laws stretched back to what were called the Comstock Laws of 1873, passed by the U.S. Congress during the presidential administration of Ulysses S. Grant.

With state legislatures following suit, the Comstock Laws reflected the position by lawmakers (all male) that contraception was lewd, immoral, and promoted female promiscuity. The statutes made it a crime to use the U.S. Postal Service to send information on contraceptives, termination of a pregnancy, and even personal letters with sexual content or information. Although some portions were later struck down, a few portions of the Comstock Laws still remain on the books.

Printed material concerning birth control was held to be obscene. The subject was not often discussed among female relatives and friends. If women needed advice, they were often reluctant to see doctors, who, during much of the postwar era, were primarily male.

However, a change was coming for females of the postwar years. Several major factors contributed to a sexual upheaval among American women.

The first factor pertained to a man named Alfred C. Kinsey, who can best be described as a "mild-mannered scientist." Reumann (2005) states that Dr. Kinsey was responsible for the United States being rocked by response to his work. Observers compared it to the impact of an atomic bomb. Popularly known as the Kinsey Reports, the publication of *Sexual Behavior in the Human Male* (1948) and *Sexual Behavior in the Human Female* (1953) were as groundbreaking as an earthquake. Reumann states that the findings of the studies shocked experts and the public alike, as Kinsey demonstrated that "the majority of the nation's citizens had violated acceptable moral standards as well as state and federal laws in pursuit of their sexual pleasure" (1).

Kinsey's field was entomology, the study of insects. With a specialty in gall wasps, he collected thousands of specimens. That endeavor might not seem connected with the sexually related works that made him a household name. However, Kinsey became intrigued by the work of playwright Tennessee Williams who wrote such dramas as *The Glass Menagerie* (1944) and *A Streetcar Named Desire* (1947), many of which concerned facade versus reality. According to Halberstam (1993), Kinsey felt that he and Williams were interested in something very similar, "tearing away the façade that Americans used to hide their sexual selves" (272).

Although Kinsey released his findings through a scientific publishing house, his statistics in some areas such as homosexuality in *Sexual Behavior in the Human Male* and data on female libido in *Human Female* caused an uproar. Much of the outrage was due to the fact that Kinsey presented his findings without moral judgments. His grant from the Rockefeller Foundation was withdrawn, leaving him in dire financial straits. After being publicly condemned, Kinsey died in 1956 at age 62.

The second groundbreaking development in sexuality among women in postwar America came via another mild-mannered man, Hugh Hefner. Although accused of exploiting women, Hefner launched a new magazine that he called *Playboy* as something slick and sophisticated, not cheap and crude in the manner of the "girlie" magazines of the day. If not always entirely respectful of women, *Playboy* acknowledged them as human beings. The magazine included tips for men on everything from autos to wine and contained stimulating articles by renowned authors, the reason many gave for buying it. Some housewives may have also enjoyed *Playboy*'s stimulating literary articles by sneaking a peek at their husband's latest issue. Within its relatively tasteful format, some may have learned things they were embarrassed to ask about.

The magazine featured stylish photos of beautiful women in various states of undress. Hefner's first issue in 1953 featured up-and-coming starlet Marilyn Monroe in a pose she had taken for racy calendars because, as she said, "I was hungry." Monroe received no payment for *Playboy*'s use of the photos although sales of the magazine skyrocketed. Luckily for her financial status, Monroe shot to stardom as the postwar era's leading female sex symbol, validating Hefner's prescient eye.

Playboy also led directly to a magazine aimed at women. It dealt explicitly with female sexual matters and also became a cultural phenomenon. Previously a literary publication, *Cosmopolitan* was relaunched in 1965 as a women's magazine. Its editor was Helen Gurley Brown whose 1962 advice book, *Sex and the Single Girl*, was a bestseller. Under Brown's editorship, a post she held until 1996, the magazine set itself apart by frankly discussing sexuality from the point of view that women could and should enjoy sex without guilt. Brown championed career women and sexual openness, taking direct aim at the notion that an unmarried woman was an "old maid" while an unmarried man was a "swinging bachelor." In July 1965, the first issue of *Cosmo* ran a cover story on the birth control pill, which had gone on the market five years earlier.

It is difficult to overstate the impact of birth control pills, or simply "the Pill," the next factor that influenced sexuality among women in postwar America. In the most basic sense, it provided a woman with a safe, effective, affordable method that she could control to avoid pregnancy. Since the dawn of time, it was something even Queen Elizabeth I might have traded her crown jewels to have.

The first oral contraceptive was developed in 1951, partly due to women's rights activist Margaret Sanger who raised $150,000 to fund its development. The much-maligned and often-arrested Sanger had such "revolutionary" ideas as giving females accurate information about their bodies and reproductive systems. In a 1917 pamphlet, she summed up the lives of women for whom biology was destiny: "burdened down with half a dozen unwanted children, helpless, starved, shoddily clothed, dragging at your skirt, yourself a dragged out shadow of the woman you once were."

Beyond the realm of sexuality, in the daily lives of women in postwar America, the Pill had an impact in other areas of her existence. Prior to the Pill, many women did not seek higher education or aim for a long-term career knowing they would lose the job as soon as they became pregnant and be out of the employment market for years. If they worked outside the home at all, they accepted low-level jobs, which impacted their economic status throughout life, including in old age when they had little Social Security savings to rely upon.

Before the Pill, if a woman who was not married became pregnant with an unwanted child, her options were limited. Terminating the pregnancy was dangerous, expensive, and illegal. Going to a "home for unwed mothers" brought shame to her and her family. Giving the baby up for adoption often left lifelong emotional scars. And raising a child on her own was difficult at best.

In 1965, the U.S. Supreme Court established the right of married couples to use contraception. However, millions of unmarried women in 26 states were denied access to birth control until 1972.

One more factor regarding sexuality in the daily lives of women in postwar America was tied to the era's political climate, specifically McCarthyism and the Cold War. McCarthyism was named for Joseph McCarthy, the U.S. senator (R-Wisconsin), who led congressional hearings with the stated purpose of exposing alleged Communists during the early 1950s.

A major component of McCarthyism was what was called the "Lavender Menace," or the accusation that homosexuals were as much of a threat to the American way of life as Communism. Men and women were questioned about their sexual nature, with the threat of causing them to lose their jobs unless they "named names" of acquaintances who might be homosexuals or Communists. The investigators were aided by the nation's laws, making acts such as homosexuality a felony in every state, punished by a heavy fine and a lengthy prison term.

Same-sex attraction was considered deviant as well as illegal. With little accurate information available to them, many people fearfully concealed their sexuality and felt themselves to be abnormal.

Although the country was in the midst of one of its most conservative periods, gay and lesbian rights organizations emerged in the early postwar years. In 1950, the Mattachine Society, founded in Los Angeles, became America's first known major organization for gay males (although the term "gay" was not yet in use).

In 1955, during a time when most people refused to believe that females had same-sex tendencies, the Daughters of Bilitis (DOB) was founded as a leading organization for lesbian women. By 1959, the group had chapters in New York City, Los Angeles, Chicago, and Rhode Island along with the original chapter in San Francisco. In 1960, the DOB held a convention in San Francisco, attracting about 200 women. Since cross-dressing (women clad in men's clothing) was illegal, police arrived on the scene only to find all the women wearing dresses, stockings, and high heels. Among the speakers was a clergyman who informed the audience they were sinners, to which they listened politely.

Nor was the early postwar era a particularly happy time for many heterosexual females. Some women were condemned for "frigidity," the inability to achieve sexual arousal and climax, which was said to diminish pleasure for the male. Even in cases of domestic abuse or mistreatment, many experts of the day placed the burden on the wife. Some suggested psychotherapy. Men were reassured that they were not to blame, being told that the woman would have the same problem with another partner.

In addition, women who "faked" arousal or climax were also condemned for deceiving the male.

On the other hand, women had to appear to enjoy sex, but not *too* much. It was said that male impotence could be caused either by female frigidity or, at the other extreme, a woman being a "nymphomaniac" (having excessive sexual desire). It was up to postwar women to find some middle ground.

In the course of their daily lives, most women in postwar America could hardly avoid the sexual realm. Magazines, newspapers, television, and movies all confirmed the axiom that "sex sells." Along with Marilyn Monroe, the latest sex symbols of the moment, such as Brigitte Bardot and Jayne Mansfield, were heavily promoted. Sexual themes were referenced by "edgy" comedians of the 1950s and 1960s including Lenny Bruce, Redd Foxx, Dick Gregory, Mort Sahl, and most shockingly, a risqué *female* comic named Rusty Warren.

The works of Tennessee Williams, who had influenced Alfred Kinsey, received a lot of publicity. Along with plays of the postwar era with sexual themes such as *Summer and Smoke*, *Cat on a Hot Tin Roof*, and *Suddenly Last Summer*, Williams also wrote the screenplay for the film *Baby Doll*, which was released in 1956 and condemned by the Catholic Legion of Decency.

Other movies of the postwar era included "naughty" comedies such as *The Seven Year Itch* (1955) with Marilyn Monroe. Many films contained saucy double entendres (suggestive words or acts open to two interpretations, one of which is usually sexual in nature). *The Moon Is Blue*, released in 1953, used language that was not often found in polite conversation, including one that referred to women who had not yet had sexual intercourse. If controversy erupted over what were then considered sexually explicit films, the furor did not hurt one bit at the box office.

For those who preferred to stay at home and read, a bestseller that women sometimes carried home from bookstores in a plain-brown wrapper was the steamy *Peyton Place* by Grace Metalious, published in 1956. It focused on the hypocrisy of small-town America, centering around women seeking fulfillment. The book shocked the nation by presenting females as sexual beings. It became one of the best-selling works in publishing history.

By 1960, with the approval of the birth control pill, the sexual life of women in postwar America was in for a big change.

RITES OF PASSAGE

Like humans in all known cultures since the dawn of time, women in postwar America often pursued their daily lives by adopting customs that are known as rites of passage.

Rites of passage are defined as culturally oriented rituals marking the transition from one stage of life to another. In most cultures, the predominant rites of passage often center around the shift from childhood into adulthood. Some of these rites of passage are triggered by physical changes that take place in young people and some by marriage or childbirth. Others come at a specific point in time such as the Jewish religion's bar mitzvah for boys and bat mitzvah for girls, which is held when they reach the age of 13.

In postwar America, modern rites of passage for girls might include purely secular events such as getting a driver's license, graduating from high school, owning a car, or reaching the legal age to purchase alcohol. There were celebrations including the debutante ball, sweet sixteen party, and the *quinceañera* for 15-year-old girls in Hispanic cultures. For many young postwar women, it was marriage, followed by becoming the head of her own household that was the defining rite of passage in her life.

In addition, there were religious rites of passage that were common in American society. Many postwar women participated in the milestones of Christian denominations including confirmation, first communion, first Eucharist, and first confession.

All of those events are very tangible points of transition. As Ronald Grimes (2000) puts it, "Even a single rite of passage can divide a person's life into 'before' and 'after'" (5).

Although the postwar years stood firmly in the modern era, in rural America, rites of passage for girls often took the form of labor that had been the norm for generations. This was particularly true with Southern sharecroppers, on family farms, and among Hispanic migrant workers. At a relatively young age, a girl in those cultures might assume the general adult duties of childcare, cooking, cleaning, and sewing so her mother could work in the fields.

Among white middle-class Americans during the prosperous postwar era, rites of passage among young women took a different form. As teenagers, they might have helped around the house by doing the dishes or assisting with the ironing but often had time on their hands and money in their pockets. Their labor was not needed to help support the family. As magnified by the lens of the mass media, rites of passage for teenage girls during the postwar years were often influenced by consumer culture. With the national reach of television, teenage girls from coast to coast knew what was happening with their peers on the other side of the country and were anxious not to be left behind.

For young women, common rites of passage during that era included starting to wear lipstick and other cosmetics, embracing consumerism by keeping up with the latest fashions, getting the first bra, and attracting a steady boyfriend.

In the same manner as teenage boys, girls of the postwar era transitioned from their parents to their peers as the major source of influence on their daily lives. Teenage girls might have lived much of their daily lives under adult control at home or in school, but they spent a lot of time trying to escape it by asserting a newfound sense of rebellion.

After school, many teenage girls exhibited one of the rites of passage by gravitating to malt shops or drive-in eateries where they could meet their peers instead of having milk and cookies served at home by Mom.

On weekends, there were rites of passage such as joining friends for a movie instead of going out with the family as they did in their younger years. A significant rite of passage was a girl's first date and then her first love, often followed by her first heartbreak.

Graduating from high school was another rite of passage for a postwar girl. At that point, she had to get serious about how the rest of her life was going to evolve. Reflecting the postwar culture, significant amounts of a girl's time and energy were spent trying to attract a husband before age 20. If not, without a ring on her finger, she would be on her way to becoming an "old maid."

To paraphrase an old expression that is applicable to the postwar years, first came love, then came marriage, then came women with a baby carriage. A major rite of passage for women in postwar America was becoming a wife and mother. For most, it was a major adjustment. She had to quickly learn how to run a household, cook for a family, raise her children, and please her husband. While situation comedies on television utilized time-worn devices such as burning dinner or shrinking a man's suit by putting it in the washing machine, it was not always funny at home.

Once a woman transitioned from bride to wife to mother, it was time for most to pass on their acquired knowledge to their daughters. For many, a girl's mother offered advice beyond proper techniques for cooking and cleaning. One rite of passage for teenage girls was the point at which her body began to change. For example, her mother might help buy her first bra when her breasts began to develop.

A teenage girl might have noticed confusing ads in magazines for products that never quite specified what they were for. Many featured elegantly dressed models with the tagline, "Modess . . . *because.*" This particular rite of passage was tied to the fact that for a woman, once again biology was destiny. The point at which she began to have her monthly "period" was a significant turning point, indicating that she had entered the years in which she could bear children.

Some girls who were lucky were prepared by their mothers. In some school districts, girls and boys were separated into gender-specific groups and told by teachers what to expect as their bodies changed. However, in keeping with the conservatism of the postwar era in which such topics were deemed better left unsaid, some girls were completely unprepared, terrified that they were bleeding to death.

That particular topic was one of the few that were not advertised down to the tiniest detail in the postwar era. This was especially true of the most critical rite of passage for a postwar American woman: getting married. Howard (2006) writes that advertisers, wedding professionals, and the media successfully transformed the ritual of a wedding into a consumer rite of passage (143). The wedding gown itself symbolized that rite of passage as well as a socioeconomic status symbol. For upper- and middle-class girls of that era, the white dress was alleged to be symbolic of her "purity." It also showed the assembled multitudes that she could afford a princess moment in a frothy, frilly gown that was usually completely useless after that day.

Those who could not afford such an emblem often made do with a nice dress they had handy and which might be worn in the future. But many scrimped and saved for this rite of passage, impractical though it may have been. They were finding their place in postwar American society. As Burger (2012) states, "White-clad brides walked down the aisle girls, but would walk back American housewives" (8).

As the postwar years wore on and the advent of the birth control pill revolutionized society, white wedding dresses prevailed although the notion of "purity" became fluid. A rite of passage during the late postwar years was the moment when a girl began taking "the Pill," marking her potential for entry into sexual activity. It was usually followed by a rite of passage for a woman that almost all cultures traditionally took very seriously: her loss of virginity. Giving birth to her first child was another.

As a postwar woman aged, there were additional rites of passage along the way. Her first gray hair was one. Many had grown up during the 1930s and 1940s when a woman who had her hair dyed was considered disreputable. But in 1956, Clairol launched an at-home version that became a household name as well as a classic in the advertising industry. Ads featured wholesome women often pictured with children having the same golden hair color, and asked the question "Does she . . . or doesn't she? Only her hairdresser knows for sure." No one was confused; the message was perfectly clear. Within a few years, almost three-quarters of women in postwar America were coloring their hair.

For postwar women, there was a good reason. As she aged and had no resources of her own, she grew even more dependent on her husband. Ads for hair color products began to ask another question: "What would your husband do if suddenly you looked ten years younger?" Others stated, "The closer he gets, the better you look." Women had to stay young-looking to keep from being "traded in" on a newer model, similar to postwar-era cars.

The advent of Social Security provided some financial relief for older people after they retired from the workplace. However, women who had been homemakers and unable to enter the workforce often found there was no financial safety net at all. As Dora Costa (1998) states, in the postwar era, more than half of women over age 64 were widowed, and "many of them were dependent on their children for support" (5).

Most women, never having worked outside the home, did not have access to resources including pensions. Medicare, the national healthcare insurance program, did not exist until 1966. In the postwar era, the husband usually handled the money, so any savings would be dependent on him. In an age when Americans were encouraged to spend their money freely to help keep the economy strong, many women found that in old age, when she most needed security, there were no savings at all.

Even those women who had managed to have a career in the postwar years often found it difficult to make ends meet after they were forced to retire. One retired schoolteacher was appalled to find a woman who was a fellow former teacher living in an abandoned chicken coop after retirement. The woman had no healthcare and no one to care for her as she declined. After seeing her friend in such dire conditions, Ethel Percy Andrus founded the American Association of Retired Persons (AARP) in 1958 to fight for struggling retirees, especially women of the postwar years who had few other resources.

Thanks to medical science, the final rite of passage could be postponed in some cases. Kübler-Ross (2014) pointed out that as the 1950s came to an end, medicine was advancing greatly (1). In the postwar years, there were improvements in living standards, public health, and technology. Life expectancy rose, with statistics showing that average white men and women could expect to live significantly longer than they had in the year 1900. Although African American men and women had a shorter life expectancy compared to whites, their life expectancy too was increasing.

Perhaps because it was not as much a common part of their daily lives in the postwar years as it had been during the Great Depression and World War II, references to death were softened somewhat. John Canine (1996) states that friends "might make vague references to the loved one 'going on to a better place,' or might deny death with such expressions as 'departed,' 'passed away,' 'expired,' and 'just passed'" (7).

In the consumer-driven atmosphere of the postwar years, even death was becoming a burgeoning industry. Because husbands had a tendency to die sooner than their wives, women often found themselves having to deal with his death in the final rite of passage.

In her landmark book *The American Way of Death*, author Jessica Mitford (2000) noted a trend that mirrored the consumer culture of the postwar years, even after the consumer in question was dead. Among her findings, she stated that "sellers of funeral services have, one gathers, a preconceived, stereotyped view of their customers. To them, the bereaved person who enters the funeral establishment is a bundle of guilt feelings, a snob, and a status seeker" (20). That guilty bereaved person was quite often a woman.

The ideal client for funeral services reflected the values of the postwar era in which people were encouraged to buy major items such as cars, televisions, and furniture on credit. According to Mitford, her research showed that steering the grieving widow toward high-priced caskets, vaults, and even vehicles in the funeral procession would be evidence of how much she cared for the departed and how she would be judged.

FURTHER READING

Bentley, Amy. *Inventing Baby Food: Taste, Health, and the Industrialization of the American Diet*. Oakland: University of California Press, 2014.

Burger, Tarin. *As Advertised: Depicting the Postwar American Woman from Bride, to Wife, to Mother*. Tallahassee: Florida State University Libraries Press, 2012.

Canine, John. *The Psychosocial Aspects of Death and Dying*. New York: Appleton & Lange division of McGraw Hill, 1996.

Celello, Kristin. *Making Marriage Work: A History of Marriage and Divorce in the Twentieth-Century United States*. Chapel Hill: University of North Carolina Press, 2009.

Coontz, Stephanie. *The Way We Never Were: American Families and the Nostalgia Trap*. New York: Basic Books, 2016.

Costa, Dora L. *The Evolution of Retirement: An American Economic History, 1880–1990*. Chicago: University of Chicago Press, 1998.

Cott, Nancy F. *Public Vows: A History of Marriage and the Nation*. Cambridge, MA: Harvard University Press, 2002.

Douglas, Susan J. *Where the Girls Are: Growing Up Female with the Mass Media*. New York: Three Rivers Press, 1995.

Ehrenreich, Barbara. *The Hearts of Men: American Dreams and the Flight from Commitment*. New York: Anchor, 1983.

Friedan, Betty. *The Feminine Mystique*. New York: Norton, 50th anniversary edition, 2013.

Gilbert, James. *A Cycle of Outrage: America's Reaction to the Juvenile Delinquent in the 1950s*. New York: Oxford University Press, 1988.

Gilbert, James. *Men in the Middle: Searching for Masculinity in the 1950s*. Chicago: University of Chicago Press, 2005.

Grimes, Ronald L. *Deeply into the Bone: Re-inventing Rites of Passage*. Berkeley: University of California Press, 2000.

Halberstam, David. *The Fifties*. New York: Villard, 1993.

Harvey, Brett. *The Fifties: A Women's Oral History*. New York: HarperCollins, 1993.

Howard, Vicki. *Brides, Inc.: American Weddings and the Business of Tradition*. Philadelphia: University of Pennsylvania Press, 2006.

Johnson, Claudia Durst. *Daily Life in Colonial New England*. Santa Barbara, CA: Greenwood, 2017.

Karbo, Karen. *In Praise of Difficult Women: Life Lessons from 29 Heroines Who Dared to Break the Rules*. Washington, DC: National Geographic Books, 2018.

Kübler-Ross, Elisabeth. *On Death & Dying*. New York: Scribner, reprint edition, 2014.

"Live Births, Birth Rates, and Fertility Rates, by Race: United States, 1909–2000." *Centers for Disease Control, National Center for Health Statistics, Vital Statistics*. http://www.cdc.gov/nchs/data/statab/t001x01.pdf.

May, Elaine Tyler. *Homeward Bound: American Families in the Cold War Era*. New York: Basic Books, 2008.

Mitchell, Claudia, and Jacqueline Reid-Walsh, eds. *Girl Culture: An Encyclopedia* (2 volumes).Westport, CT: Greenwood, 2007.

Mitford, Jessica. *The American Way of Death Revisited*. New York: Vintage, 2000.

O'Rourke, P. J. *The Baby Boom: How It Got That Way (And It Wasn't My Fault)*. New York: Atlantic Monthly Press, 2014.

Reumann, Miriam. *American Sexual Character: Sex, Gender, and National Identity in the Kinsey Reports.* Berkeley: University of California Press, 2005.

Riverol, A. R. *Live from Atlantic City: The Miss America Pageant Before, After, and In Spite of Television.* Bowling Green, OH: Popular Press, 1992.

Walker, Nancy A. *Women's Magazines, 1940–1960: Gender Roles and the Popular Press.* Boston, MA: Bedford/St. Martin's, 1998.

Wilson, Sloan. *The Man in the Gray Flannel Suit.* 4th ed. Cambridge, MA: Da Capo Press, 2002.

2

ECONOMIC LIFE

Apart from the devastating loss of life and the massive social upheaval of World War II, another major effect of the conflict was that the global economic system was left reeling in its aftermath. During the postwar years, countries in many parts of the world were still struggling to rebuild their economy from the wreckage of the war.

America, however, had been blessed. Although there had been a Japanese attack on Pearl Harbor in the American territory of Hawaii, the United States mainland was left untouched by the brutal hand of war. During the 1940s, assembly lines in the United States churned out the airplanes, ammunition, battleships, guns, jeeps, parachutes, and tanks that brought victory to America and her allies. After the conflict ended in 1945, those same assembly lines were quickly retooled from wartime production to generating a vast array of consumer goods. While other countries struggled, the war provided a positive effect in the United States, as average postwar Americans could easily afford to purchase those consumer goods.

In the Great Depression of the 1930s, America had suffered an economic meltdown. However, after factories geared up for wartime production in the 1940s, there was almost full employment. With so many men serving in the armed forces, American women were recruited to fill much-needed positions in war industries. It was the first time many women had money of their own, to spend any way they pleased.

Most women left the workplace when the war ended, willingly or otherwise. They were guided by the government and mass media onto a path that led to a woman defining herself by being someone's wife and someone's mother.

A postwar housewife may not have had the chance to earn her own money, but many women did experience a sense of economic security in their daily lives. The educational benefits of the Servicemen's Readjustment Act of 1944, popularly called the GI Bill, gave returning members of the armed forces access to college or vocational training. Educational benefits generally led to the kind of well-paying employment for white middle-class American men that delivered a comfortable existence for their families. The GI Bill helped individual American families as well as stimulating long-term economic growth for the nation.

For nonwhites, the economic situation was different. Along with education, the GI Bill provided low-cost mortgages to buy a home, plus low-interest loans for returning servicemen wanting to start a business. However, African American veterans often found that they were denied many of the law's benefits.

For example, African Americans were unable to join their white counterparts by purchasing homes in the quickly growing suburbs that were restricted to whites only. The value of suburban homes rose steadily in the coming years, creating new wealth for those who had bought them early. But due to restrictions and neighborhood "covenants" that kept certain kinds of people out, many minority groups were barred from buying those homes and often remained in rentals.

Banks often declined to approve loans for African Americans, citing their alleged financial instability that would then presumably hinder blacks from paying the money back.

In addition, after the war, businesses and industries retained their traditional practice of hiring blacks only for low-paying jobs such as janitors. Those bottom-tier wages were often well below the average subsistence level in the booming economy of the postwar United States. It forced many African American women to seek jobs outside the home, although these too were usually limited to low-paying positions such as maids.

The postwar economic picture was as stark as black and white, literally and figuratively. As quoted by Halberstam (1993), historian

Robert Payne's postwar *Report on America* stated, that for whites at least, "there never was a country more fabulous than America. . . . Half the wealth of the world, more than half the productivity, nearly two thirds of the world's machines are concentrated in American hands" (116).

Soon there came a more critical look at the United States during the postwar era. In *The Other America*, a book that was originally published in 1962, Harrington (1997) studied the plight of those American citizens who he claimed had become "invisible" during the postwar years. They included women, minorities, unskilled workers, migrant farm laborers, the elderly, "and all the others who live in the economic underworld of American life" (2).

Harrington saw struggling African American women in urban inner cities who lived just a short drive from suburbia but who were unseen by the white middle classes. He cited black female hospital workers in the late 1950s, who were often the main support of their families, earning about $30 a week (the equivalent of around $262 a week or $13,624 a year in 2019). Harrington found that their paychecks often contained a mandatory deduction for food costs, whether they ate at the hospital or not. He saw it as a case of hospital management, consisting of the community's "best" people, exploiting the helpless women.

Many white Americans assumed that the title of John Kenneth Galbraith's 1958 book, *The Affluent Society*, was a glowing testimonial. However, Galbraith (1998) underscored the great inequality between different classes of American citizens, stating that race acted "to locate people by their color rather than proximity to employment" (238), producing a ghetto environment. Groups such as women, poor whites, African Americans (in the inner cities of the North as well as in the Jim Crow South), and other minorities were not attaining the good jobs that were hallmarks of the nation's postwar prosperity. Galbraith stated that the result was the "disintegration of family life in the slums that leaves households in the hands of women" (238). The economic chasm between blacks and whites impacted all areas of daily life and was often most severely felt in the daily lives of women.

One other important factor in the daily economic life in postwar America was the connection between its financial and its political climate in what essentially became "Consumerism versus Communism." Consumerism is defined as a socioeconomic system that encourages people to buy material goods in ever-increasing amounts. The message drummed into women in postwar America was that they could help keep the country strong by purchasing more and more consumer goods to bolster the national economy. In the fight against Communism, shopping was considered the patriotic thing to do.

Although women had little money of their own, they were seen as the ones who made decisions regarding purchases for the family. As such, women in postwar America became a prime target in the age of consumerism.

ADVERTISING

Mara Einstein (2017) notes the shift in advertising that moved away from focusing on the features of a product, swinging toward how the product would allegedly make the consumer *feel*. She cites the growing trend of postwar advertisers to sell products by appealing to emotions. And as male advertising executives of the postwar era firmly believed, women were *highly emotional*.

According to Einstein, advertisers also leaned toward repeating their message over and over and then over again: "This concept was fundamental in the 1950s at the time of the rise of mass media and its concomitant mass marketing" (27).

Often, messages were repeated to women in terms of making life more "convenient" for them. Hill (2002) uses the example of frozen meals, known in the postwar era as TV dinners in which "women surrendered all control of meal preparation" (61). It was the manufacturer, not the housewife, who determined what and how much the family would eat.

Hill also notes that women were told repeatedly by advertisers how they *should* feel. That directive was impressed upon women "in issue after issue of magazines and in daily TV commercials" (63). If women were lacking in sensitivity as well as cleanliness, they could be saved by buying a certain product, as in the ad that read, "Housewives are mortified by 'ring around the collar.'" The implication was that if women weren't mortified, they certainly *should* be.

Television became a permanent part of the daily life of many women in postwar America. For those who felt isolated in suburbia, television was often their only companion during the day when children were in school and husbands were at work. When small children lived at home, television personalities were often the only adult voices that women heard all day. There were plenty of opportunities for advertising that was aimed squarely at females, repeating the same messages over and over and over. Pioneering adman Rosser Reeves was widely quoted saying that advertising on television was like shooting fish in a barrel.

Apart from television's capability to disseminate commercials to a huge audience nationwide, its sheer novelty benefited postwar-era advertising. It was new, and it was exciting. People would watch virtually anything, even test patterns if there was no programming being broadcast at the moment.

When a family brought their first television home, it was given a central spot in the living room like an honored guest. Moreover, it fit into the concept of family "togetherness" being aimed at postwar women.

In the days before television, women who listened to the radio had only been able to hear descriptions of products. Knowing that their audience was primarily women, manufacturers such as those selling cleaning products were major advertisers on radio during the daytime. There were so many continuing daytime dramas on radio being sponsored by detergent companies that the programs themselves became known as "soap operas."

When the daytime drama format was carried over from radio to television, advertisers found daily soap operas, or simply "soaps," to be even more successful spots in which to place ads for their products. Television was visual. Women could *see* the product at work.

Television could also hammer away at viewers with repetitive visual messages. One of the most successful ad campaigns of the postwar eras was for a pain reliever that featured hammers pounding inside a human head. Everyone claimed to hate it for being so annoying. Yet after the ad started running on television, sales of the product quadrupled.

Another ad for a pain reliever featured a tagline that became so widely known, it turned into a punch line for comedians as well as being used in average conversations of the postwar era. In the commercial, a suburban housewife was cooking dinner when an older woman suggested it might need more salt. Snapping back, the younger woman's irritated response was, "Mother, please! I'd rather do it myself!" After taking the pain reliever, the headache disappeared as generational harmony and respect for elders were restored.

Advertising to American women in the postwar era was primarily aimed at the average white suburban housewife as depicted in "Mother, please!" This was the case in television commercials as well as in magazine or other print ads.

However, many marketers understood that there were other potential purchasers in the postwar era. *Ebony* magazine, aimed at African Americans, was launched in 1945, soon after the end of World War II. In 1951, it was joined by a sister publication, the smaller weekly digest called *Jet*. Two other popular publications aimed specifically at black women in the early postwar era included "Home Magazine" in *Tan Confessions* (1950–1952) and *Aframerican Woman's Journal* (1935–1954).

By 1967, 80 of the top 100 national advertisers were using *Ebony* to promote their product lines. Advertisers recognized that while African Americans in general may not have possessed the massive purchasing power of their white counterparts, they still bought things.

Sutton (2009) states that the advertising logo depicting fictional "Aunt Jemima" (63) was the most well-known African American woman's face in advertising. However, in 1955, the real-life Mary Alexander was chosen as Coca-Cola's first female African American model in an ad campaign for *Ebony*. Alexander was dressed professionally, evoking a clerical position, holding paper and pencil while enjoying a soft drink at the workplace. In 1957, Coca-Cola added an attractive black family for Alexander in her ads. During her successful campaign for Coke, Alexander's face was seen in traditionally black magazines and newspapers as well as on billboards in predominately African American areas.

In 1963, Lever Brothers, which was one of the largest TV advertisers at the time, announced that it would show more blacks in its commercials. Television spots for All detergent featured popular white entertainer Art Linkletter talking with a black housewife about her laundry issues.

Despite a trend toward depicting African American women of the postwar era as part of the upwardly mobile mainstream, authors such as Noliwe Rooks (2004) maintain that the majority of the advertisements in publications aimed at blacks were for skin lighteners and hair straighteners. According to Rooks, she used advertisements to support her argument when she asked her mother's permission to straighten her hair, joining "African American women in earlier periods [who] would have used advertisements as they struggled to define their relationship to the culture in which they lived" (10).

Ads aimed at African American women of the postwar era indicate that advertisers felt black women ought to emulate white society, with a multitude of ads for hair straighteners and skin lighteners. But advertisements targeting African American women also utilized the same techniques that were used on white women: insecurity, vulnerability, and fear.

Along with ads for skin lighteners and hair straighteners directed at black women in traditionally African American publications, there were also those for "Nu-Nile Smokeless Curl Crème" and the cure for a shiny nose (under a headline reading, "How embarrassing!") They addressed conditions from which African American women may not have known they suffered.

But for all women, regardless of race or socioeconomic class, advertising messages of the postwar era were all around them due to the tremendous growth of the mass media, especially television. The message women heard was: "Your house isn't clean, your laundry looks dirty, your floors have ugly wax buildup, you don't cook well, you are a bad hostess, you are unrefined, unsophisticated, behind the times." One advertisement informed women that "your husband thinks the girls at the office make better coffee" (leaving some wives who saw that ad to wonder what *else* the girls at the office did better).

As for the women themselves: "You are too fat, you are too thin, you smell bad, you look old, your body hair is disgusting, your skin is too dark (lighten it with our product), your skin is too light (tan it with our product), your natural hair color is unattractive, your eyelashes are too short, your un-manicured fingernails look lower class, your cellulite is hideous." Incidentally, the word "cellulite," specifying a fatty buildup under the skin, was apparently unknown in males and was said by some social observers to have been invented during the postwar era in order to sell products to deal with it, as if women didn't have enough to worry about.

As for females of the postwar era who ignored advertising messages about how inferior they were, Peiss (2011) refers to author Naomi Wolf whose verdict was: "Women who are beautiful or achieve beauty according to imposed standards are rewarded; those who cannot or choose not to be beautiful are punished, economically and socially" (269).

Marketers wanted to be sure the selling cycle would continue by being passed along to the daughters of women in postwar America. Sivulka (2008) cites a 1966 magazine ad headlined "Who is Suzy Homemaker?" It features an attractive adult housewife holding a delicious-looking confection while exclaiming, "I baked this cake in my new oven!" Beside her is a pigtailed preteen girl (presumably her daughter) holding a smaller version, equally proud to proclaim,

"I baked this cake in my new Suzy Homemaker oven!" Both look absolutely blissful. According to Sivulka, "This ad portrays a common stereotype, the dedicated homemaker who sacrifices all her aspirations to dote on her family and teaches her daughter to do the same" (229).

It was not just in the Eisenhower era of the 1950s that such messages to women were prevalent. The Suzy Homemaker ad was published in 1966, the same year that the Beatles played their last concert and was one short year before 1967's countercultural "Summer of Love."

Like the publishers and editors of women's magazines, ads for women in postwar America were written almost exclusively by men. Maas (2013) claims that one leading ad agency published a guide called *How to Create Food Advertising That Sells* including tips such as "Tell her how and when to use your product" and "Don't forget to tell her it tastes good" (13).

Lears (1994) maintains that from the earliest days of the advertising industry, "only a few women rose to prominence in national advertising despite frequent observations in the trade press about how well suited they were for the work" (209). He adds that there was a "tacit assumption that women's minds were vats of frothy pink irrationality" (209).

However, there was a small handful of postwar-era females who, one way or another, rose through the ranks of advertising agencies, and were assigned to "women's" accounts. They were considered experts on what all women want, or at least want to buy.

One of the most famous is Shirley Polykoff who wrote hugely successful campaigns for hair color products in the 1950s such as "Does she or doesn't she?" and "Is it true blondes have more fun?" as well as "If I've only one life to live, let me live it as a blonde." According to Maas (2013), it was Polykoff who substituted the word "color" for "dye" since the latter was traditionally considered to be something used by lower-class hussies (51).

Hirshey (2016) cites the experiences of Helen Gurley Brown, another one of the very few successful adwomen of the postwar era. One male ad manager who was Brown's superior came to meetings armed with a Smith & Wesson gun, firing ear-shattering blanks. Brown learned to shriek bloody murder: "The louder she screamed and carried on, the more he seemed to like her" (156).

Brown recalled that when two other women copywriters were hired, all three were forced to share a small office that had been part of a dental clinic, complete with sinks and basins. They also had to share the same assignments, "with the expectation that [they] would simply claw it out" (157).

One of their assignments was for a cosmetics account. Some of the names for lipstick that were to be pitched at women in postwar America, many of whom had helped win the war, included "Kiss Kiss," "Ssshhhh," "I Like Men!," "If You Can't Be Good Be a Little Wicked," "Love in the Morning," "Pyro Pink," "Timid Temptress," "Vice 'n' Virtue," "With My Eyes Open," "Who's That Girl," and "Yes Darling" (157).

Maas (2013) states that although their campaigns brought in hundreds of millions of dollars, "women in advertising were earning about half of male copywriters" (52).

However, the advent of television in the early 1950s created the first TV advertising celebrity, and it was a woman. Betty Furness served as the on-air spokesperson for Westinghouse appliances during her decade-long tenure on television during the postwar era.

Furness performed the commercials live, changing her fashionable outfit repeatedly for spots that ran up to 20 times a day. It was felt that female viewers would watch in order to see what she was wearing. Known as "The Lady from Westinghouse," Furness was a welcome visitor in people's homes as part of their daily lives. They stopped her on the street as if she was an old friend. In an interview with Halberstam (1993), Furness would later say she sensed her role was to keep as many people as possible from going to the bathroom during commercials (499). But whatever the case, Westinghouse kept introducing new products and Betty Furness kept selling them—with spectacular success.

Furness and the sponsor knew they were selling what people wanted, not what they needed. American women did not need a new refrigerator since the one they bought a few years earlier worked just fine. But television commercials in the postwar era enabled them to repeatedly see a shiny newer version, persuasively described by someone they liked and trusted, until they feared being left behind.

One reason that television advertising in the postwar era was so successful was because many of the women who were isolated in suburbia kept the television on all day for company. Effective advertising succeeded by playing on women's vulnerability repeatedly and consistently. Marketers were aided by the overall prosperity of the era, which generated buying power.

Advertisers certainly had to vie with competitors for business, but the predominant mood of the decade's "Affluent Society" was on their side. It was not difficult to convince women to buy what they didn't actually need, especially with easy credit and the security of a husband with a steady, well-paying job.

That same husband was also used as a stealth weapon in advertising aimed at postwar women. In his groundbreaking book *The Hidden Persuaders*, Vance Packard (1957) stated that advertisers felt women had the ability to "do a tremendous job of exerting pressure on a man to make him dress right" (146).

Postwar men's fashions did not change as frequently as women's, so something had to spur increased sales of male clothing. Advertisers convinced wives to mold her husband's image to improve his socioeconomic status. She did that by convincing him to regularly buy new clothes that advertisers declared to be more stylish. In doing so, she believed she was aiding his ability to advance at work and therefore to better provide for the entire family. The welfare of the family unit was the prime directive for a woman of the postwar era, the one she felt was her ultimate responsibility.

CONSUMERISM

The affluent postwar era is often synonymous with a massive onslaught of consumerism, which is defined as a socioeconomic system that encourages acquiring material goods in ever-increasing amounts.

Consumerism is opposed to simple consumption by going beyond what people need in favor of what they *want*. The implicit goal of consumerism is to convince people that by purchasing more material items, they will feel better about themselves as well as impressing others.

In an important addendum during the postwar years, American women could also feel better about themselves by believing they were practicing *patriotism*. The message from the government and mass media was that the more things American people bought, the more they were making their country stronger against Communism.

It was made clear in the 1959 "Kitchen Debate" between then vice president Richard Nixon of the United States and Soviet premier Nikita Khrushchev at the American National Exhibition in Moscow. The exhibition was said to be part of a cultural exchange to promote understanding. Some saw it as an attempt for America to show off its cornucopia of consumer goods to deprived Russians, particularly items utilized in the daily life of the average postwar housewife.

In 1959, a debate took place between U.S. vice president Nixon and Soviet premier Khrushchev (left, in white hat) at a trade show displaying a model American kitchen filled with labor-saving appliances. The exhibit was meant to demonstrate the superiority of U.S. capitalism. Nixon said the daily life of an average postwar American housewife was better than that of Russian women. (Library of Congress)

At the exhibition, there was a replica of what was said to be a typical house in the United States that any average American worker could afford. It was filled with dozens of the latest labor-saving appliances and entertainment devices provided to the U.S. exhibit free of charge by American companies. They were meant to represent the success of capitalism and the consumer market in the United States.

In general, the replica was upper middle class. The exhibition did not feature the average home of poor whites or African Americans in either the inner city or in the Jim Crow South.

In the exhibit, an attractive model who represented the average white American housewife was surrounded by labor-saving appliances. The point was that American women lived a glamorous stay-at-home daily life, purchasing consumer goods at will, overseeing lovely suburban homes, and having their time freed by labor-saving devices to rear their young into good citizens of the future. Soviet women, on the other hand, were portrayed by

America's mass media as unattractive, worn down by hard work, and forced to leave their children at state-run daycare centers.

Soviet premier Khrushchev praised Russian women for contributing to their country after the devastation of the war, rather than being ladies of leisure. Nixon maintained that American women had better lives. Nixon did not acknowledge that there were few alternatives for women in postwar America for things such as economic independence, professional achievement, and personal fulfillment.

Women in postwar America were guided by the government and the mass media to find financial security and social standing in their daily lives through marriage to a successful man. Many women took their job as housewives seriously, considering the role of wife and mother to be deserving of respect. In the 1960s and 1970s, however, it turned out that many postwar women (and their daughters) did not necessarily find fulfillment in their domestic role, regardless of how many appliances they bought.

The good news for consumerism was that in the course of their daily lives, many women were in a position to buy a lot, and they eagerly did so. Halberstam (1993) paints a picture of the postwar American culture as being ripe for mass consumerism. He claims that in the 1950s, "the number of families moving in to the middle class—that is, having more than $5,000 in annual earnings after taxes—was increasing by 1.1 million a year" (587). Those annual earnings would equal about $47,000 in 2018. By 1959, conservative estimates projected 20 million such families, virtually half the families in America. Halberstam wrote that *Fortune* magazine called it an "economy of abundance" (587).

Halberstam noted that no one was paying very much attention to what consumerism, specifically all the labor-saving devices for the home, was doing to postwar women: "The new culture of consumerism told women they should be homemakers and saw them merely as potential buyers for all the new washers and dryers, freezers, floor waxers, pressure cookers and blenders" (589).

Women were seen more as a target demographic than as human beings. They represented an important market segment. Women influenced about three-quarters of all consumer purchasing, either by suggestion or by the power of the veto. Each woman also represented multiple markets in one, since she was the primary purchasing agent for the home, children, husbands, and sometimes aging relatives, in addition to buying items for her own personal use.

However, even with her husband's steady paycheck, a woman could sometimes find that a buying spree could stretch the family budget to its limit. The attitude of retailers was "No money? No problem!" In the heady atmosphere of postwar American consumerism, the magic words were "Charge it!"

The Diners Club credit card was introduced in 1950 as the first independent credit card company in the world. Its original purpose was to avoid embarrassment at restaurants if the dinner check ran higher than a patron's cash on hand. In 1958, American Express launched the first all-purpose credit card that could be used at gas stations, hotels, restaurants, and stores. Other credit card companies joined in during the postwar years, emphasizing *convenience* to people rather than spending money they didn't actually have. Some American women were old enough to remember the disaster of the Great Depression in the 1930s when they lost the household goods they had bought on credit during the prosperous 1920s. Promoting credit for convenience was a safer strategy.

The promotion of convenience worked. Between 1950 and 1959, American consumer indebtedness virtually tripled, soaring to almost $200 billion (about eight times that amount in 2018 dollars). With all the new appliances pouring into American homes, the use of electricity also tripled during the decade. Easy credit made instant gratification the norm. Many American women, far from their traditional homes, were building a new kind of lifestyle.

Yet even with a woman's acknowledged power of the purse, the name on the credit card was usually not hers. Cohen (2003) states that as credit purchasing increasingly became more common, women found themselves at a disadvantage: "Store credit cards, national credit cards like Carte Blanche and American Express, and mortgage lenders all discriminated against women" (147). When Carte Blanche solicited a household, "the card always bore the husband's name, although 'a special HERS card to give your wife all the credit she deserves'—in shocking pink—was offered to wives" (147).

Divorced, separated, and widowed women found themselves at a significant disadvantage. Cohen writes that when a marriage ended, the husband took all the credit standing with him, leaving widows and ex-wives "with no credit rating of their own, 'poor risks' in the eyes of lenders who, to make things worse, usually refused to consider alimony and child support as income" (147).

Consumerism in the postwar era also had a subtext. Sutton (2009) looked at skin care ads featuring famous socialites who claimed to use the product. The women in the ads were white, and the context emphasized social class. Sutton states that "the depiction of all the women appearing in the ads as white implies that 'this is just the way it is.' To the millions of women reading the ad, including groups of African American, immigrant, and working class women, the ad might appeal to their sense of social ambition" (95). Sutton adds that "immigrant and African American women were all encouraged to become modern"—to join the white mainstream—through consumption (63).

Rooks (2004) notes that like whites, postwar African American women were also being studied for their consumerist potential. What they "wore, bought, read, cooked, ate and did at home with their families were all fair game" (5).

During the era when women in postwar America of all kinds were being encouraged by the government and the media to pursue consumerism, it was called "patriotism." It was also called "keeping up with the Joneses." In the postwar years, that often meant outdoing others of their social circle in any way possible. Doing so involved two additional phrases: "conspicuous consumption" and "planned obsolescence."

Although it was perfected on a large scale in the era following World War II, the concept of consumerism came to light before the dawn of the 20th century. So did its critics. In 1899, economist Thorstein Veblen published his book, *The Theory of the Leisure Class*. With the United States booming as it embraced the industrial age at the turn of the 20th century, average people who had traditionally produced necessary items for themselves moved beyond simple survival. They soon became accustomed to purchasing goods from manufacturers. In doing so, they also discovered that luxuries were more fun than necessities. Impressing other people made it even better.

Although Veblen (1994) did not use the word "consumerism," he saw that sort of purchasing as a display of status, not as the need or usefulness of material items. He did not specifically criticize the spending patterns of women, but he did not excuse them either. Discussing women's clothing, voluminous skirts, and high-heeled shoes, he was ahead of his time in calling a woman's tight corset "substantially a mutilation, lowering her vitality and making her unfit for work" (106).

But that was the point of the turn-of-the-century version of consumerism. "Dress must not only be conspicuously expensive and inconvenient; it must at the same time be up to date. No explanation at all satisfactory has hitherto been offered of the phenomenon of changing fashions" (Veblen, 106).

During the post–World War II era, no explanation was even remotely felt to be necessary. Changing fashions were integral to consumerism as well as patriotism. Facing the Communist threat, it was important that *"our"* women looked better than *"their"* women.

Soon after Veblen discussed the concept of rampant consumerism, the idiom of "keeping up with the Joneses" was popularized nationwide. The phrase refers to the accumulation of material goods in order to compete with friends and neighbors as a benchmark of social class. Although it was serious business in the postwar years of the 1950s, it was popularized in a comic strip that originated before America's entry into World War I.

Created by Arthur Momand in 1913, *Keeping Up with the Joneses* was a comic strip parody of American life that ran in several hundred newspapers across America until 1945, ironically just before the beginning of the post–World War II era of consumerism, where it would have been right at home. The comic strip depicts the struggles of a social climbing family to improve their societal rank by trying to impress their unseen neighbors, a family named Jones.

In the 1920s, the comic strip embraced all the essential elements of the post–World War II consumerist age to come. Under consumerism, the purchase of material goods must be conspicuous, or visible for all to see.

However, amid the widespread poverty of the Great Depression of the 1930s, people rarely had the money to consume anything, conspicuously or otherwise. During the war years in the 1940s, consumer goods were limited and rationed as factories produced the implements of war.

But manufacturers knew that someday World War II would end. Advertisers promised exciting consumer products that would be available when peacetime arrived, often giving potential buyers a sneak preview through their advertisements of goodies to come. That marketing strategy led to a ready-made cohort of eager potential customers just waiting for the merchandise to roll off postwar assembly lines.

In addition, Americans would have the money to buy them. Without many consumer goods available for purchase in the 1940s, average Americans had saved their money. When they found good jobs with rising incomes in the 1950s, along with dazzling consumer goods that finally reached stores, the stage was set for the rampant consumerism of the postwar years.

Advertising agencies had also had a few years to determine their consumerist strategy when the war ended. As soon as American industries retooled from wartime production to consumer goods, ad agencies were enthusiastically prepared to promote them. In addition, the new goods on the shelves were hardly warmed-over items from before the war. Postwar goods were new, and they were exciting. In the consumerist climate, the shiny new products virtually sold themselves.

However, consumerism was not without critics. Patterson (1997) claims that intellectuals and social observers were repelled by much of postwar American society, with its attendant "vulgarity of runaway materials and consumerism, and the deterioration of traditional American values" (333). Ironically, many people today point to the postwar years of the 1950s as the era most symbolic of those same "traditional American values."

In the 1940s, U.S. President Franklin Roosevelt had stressed America's "Four Freedoms": freedom of speech, freedom to worship, freedom from fear, and freedom from want. During the postwar era of the 1950s, "freedom from want" was stretched to become the touchstone. American women received the message that more consumption more meant more freedom and thus was superior to Communism.

African American women and the females who were classified as poor whites also wanted to participate in mass consumption. Many did. Girard (2009) states that amid the postwar atmosphere of consumerism, many unlikely people had more material goods. He cites figures from the depressed coal-mining community of Harlan County, Kentucky, in which "88 percent [had] washing machines" (51). It was not by chance that in Harlan County there were more washers, an appliance used by women, than cars and telephones.

Cohen (2003) believes that "African Americans and women used their influence in the consumer market to assert themselves" (403), not just by purchasing items such as washing machines but also by boycotting stores and manufacturers that angered them for offenses including racial discrimination and selling inferior meat.

While that side of women's involvement in the consumerist culture bore some positive results, Cross (2000) points to a darker side that went beyond mere materialism. He maintains that consumer culture was a response to the world that average Americans experienced, an environment where social mobility coincided with divisions of class, race, and gender. "Just as the privileged used commodities to distance themselves from and humiliate their inferiors, so the humiliated used them to imitate others and salve their wounds" (248).

The influence of television in the postwar era cannot be overstated. It not only carried commercials for new products aimed at women but also disseminated the news about boycotts or other consumer actions. Patterson (1997) states there is no doubt that television reinforced the already rising consumerism that was such a prominent feature of the 1950s, citing female-oriented companies such as Revlon with its "striking increase in sales" (353).

Back among the poor whites in Harlan County, Kentucky, Girard (2009) states that "67 percent [had] TV sets" (51). Some sources state there were more television sets in the poverty-stricken region of Appalachia than homes with indoor plumbing.

Apart from television's capability to sell products on a massive national scale, TV sets themselves were a consumer commodity. Every year, the lure to buy a new TV set was "bigger, better, improved!" There were even enticements for women to be good mothers, with one ad proclaiming, "Protect your children's eyes against television eye strain [with a] television eye filter."

The concept of planned obsolescence was a critical factor in postwar consumerism. It led to perfectly good products being perceived as obsolete by being outdated. Women's clothing companies did this on a large scale by introducing the "latest fashion trend" every season, making last season's perfectly usable garments appear old fashioned. Many an American woman was afraid she could not keep up with the Joneses if the Joneses thought she was a rube who was hopelessly oblivious to what was "in."

In the age of consumerism, marketers had other tools targeting women. Packard (1957) cites a marketing executive who stated that women will pay 10 times more for a jar of skin cleaning cream than an equally sized bar of soap that does the same thing due to the implication that the cream will make them beautiful, not just clean. According to Packard, the executive put it succinctly: "The women are buying a promise" (5).

Packard notes another expert in the field of postwar consumerism who advised his sales staff, "To women, don't sell shoes—sell lovely feet!" (25).

Miles (2006) states that "while consumption is an act, consumerism is a way of life" (1). It virtually defined the daily lives of women in postwar America.

RACE

As the 1950s began, many white middle-class American women lived their daily lives as if race were not an issue. For those who lived in the affluent suburbs, where nonwhite people were kept out by restrictive covenants, most chose not to think about racial matters. In cities and rural areas as well as suburbs, if white people thought about racial issues at all, the subject was considered in simple terms such as "that's the way it's always been." But as Kendi (2017) writes, there was nothing "simple or straightforward or predictable about racist ideas" (4).

In the booming economy of the postwar era, racism was inextricably entwined with economics. If minorities had to compete with each other for the few relatively well-paying jobs available to them, it was often an enticement to accept lower wages. There was always the underlying implication that if one applicant didn't want the job at substandard rates, there were others who would jump

African American seamstress Rosa Parks (at right) was taken to jail in 1955 for refusing to give up her seat on a city bus in Montgomery, Alabama, to a white man. Her arrest spurred protests and helped the civil rights movement gain momentum. (Library of Congress)

at it. The same held true for minority employees who were often reluctant to apply for a better-paying job, knowing they might lose the one they had.

Similarly, property owned by minorities was often rezoned or acquired at bargain rates by eminent domain, a governmental entity's right to seize private property for public use. If a minority owner objected, the option was to hire a lawyer and submit the case for a lengthy lawsuit, an economic option few minorities could afford. There are numerous examples of land appropriated from minorities in this way for baseball stadiums, country clubs, and oil fields.

The relationship between race and economics was nothing new in the postwar era. Racial matters were an underlying part of America's prosperity since the time of its birth. August 2019 marked exactly 400 years since the first Africans were transported to the English colonies in 1619. Beyond the appalling lack of morality, according to historian Kelley Deetz (2019), this was a line of demarcation that sent racial shock waves through the nation all the way to the current day.

Slavery existed around the world for thousands of years as a testament to the darker side of mankind. Historically, enslaved people had usually been abducted from their homeland as prisoners of war, notably by ancient Rome. However, Deetz claims that in cultures of the past, "slavery was not permanent nor was it inherited" (89). In past eras, the children of slaves did not automatically become enslaved themselves; they could actually be socially mobile.

But slavery was transformed in the Americas. In 1619, about 20 captive Africans were brought to the ironically named Port Comfort in Virginia. They were the first recorded African slaves brought to an English colony. These 20 survivors had begun their harrowing journey across the Atlantic months earlier as part of 350 Africans who were kidnapped from their homes and shipped to the New World. None of the other men, women, and children survived the trip.

With their dark appearance starkly different from white indentured servants, the Africans were listed in official records under "race." This, claims Deetz, marked the beginning of racial caste. It was formalized into law as slaves became taxable property. By the 1660s, "the enslaved status of African women was written into Virginia law, as their children automatically inherited their status and were enslaved at birth, regardless of the father's identity" (86). Thus, slavery became a permanent condition, hereditary for successive generations. According to Deetz, these slave codes "cemented racism firmly in the DNA of the United States" (86).

In 1619, the first known enslaved female was brought to America. She was listed in official records as "Angela," no doubt renamed by her owners.

Even after the Emancipation Proclamation and the end of the Civil War, enslaved blacks found their lives severely restricted in the United States. Some of that was due to the preconceptions held by both Northerners and Southerners. Beginning in the 1830s, stage performances called minstrel shows were some of the most popular forms of American entertainment. With white performers in blackface, they claimed to represent the African American culture, caricaturing blacks as ignorant, lazy, and superstitious, but always portrayed as entertainingly happy-go-lucky. African American women in the minstrel shows were stereotyped as a maternal mammy or a lusty wench.

One stock character gave a label to an entire era. In 1828, Thomas "Daddy" Rice, a white man in blackface, first performed a routine as a carefree black slave singing, "Wheel about and turn about and do jus' so/Eb'ry time I wheel about, I jump Jim Crow."

Jim Crow laws were post–Civil War state and local regulations that governed the lives of black people, in matters from schools to water coolers. The laws were utilized primarily in the South to keep blacks at the bottom of the racial hierarchy, although Northerners frequently practiced discrimination even if it was not codified as in the South.

Through much of the 1950s, African Americans were relegated to second-class citizenship in the United States. The Jim Crow system stressed the notion that whites were superior to blacks in all respects. In the South, African Americans were separated from whites in areas including movie theaters, schools, and public transportation as well as enduring daily indignities such as drinking fountains labeled "whites only" and "colored."

A huge portion of Jim Crow laws involved women. Sexual relations between black men and white women were strictly forbidden. Violence, including death for the alleged offender, was used for enforcement. Some sources claim that up to a third of lynchings took the lives of black men who were falsely accused.

The alleged "crimes" could be minor. In 1955, the torture and murder of 14-year-old Emmett Till by white men for allegedly whistling at a white woman in Mississippi caught the nation's attention. Till's mother insisted on having an open casket, a horrifying image for many women of all races who saw the brutalized remains of the boy in news photos.

On the other hand, since the earliest days of slavery in America, the incidence of white males impregnating black women was generally categorized as "boys will be boys." Ardent white segregationists in public office were sometimes found to have fathered children by women of the race they denigrated.

Throughout the postwar era, there was widespread segregation of blacks from whites in both the North and the South as well as discrimination in education, employment, housing, jobs, lending, and social structure. During the postwar years, average American women found racial issues becoming a more visible part of their daily lives.

In what was called the Great Migration, millions of African Americans moved to urban areas of the North and Midwest in search of jobs to escape the oppressive Jim Crow South. African Americans often moved to traditionally black neighborhoods in cities such as Chicago, Detroit, and New York City.

For many middle-class white American women, the black people they encountered in their daily lives were found in what were frequently the only jobs available to blacks: janitors and maids.

But in the 1950s, the times were changing. In 1954, school segregation was declared unconstitutional by the U.S. Supreme Court in the landmark *Brown v. Board of Education* decision.

But as some black families strove for better living conditions, Woodward (2001) states that in the postwar era, "there were indications that the Southern Way was spreading as the American Way in race relations" (115). Lorraine Hansberry's 1958 play *A Raisin in the Sun* dramatized the resistance to African Americans moving into white neighborhoods.

Women in postwar America, even the most insulated white suburbanites, started hearing new race-related phrases: "blockbusting," "Negro invasion," and "white flight." A real estate agent might sell a nearby house to an African American family and subsequently circulate rumors that a "Negro invasion" was coming that would cause property values to plummet. In a practice called blockbusting, the agent would buy white-owned homes cheaply in the ensuing panic and then sell those same homes to African Americans at highly inflated prices. In the resulting "white flight," the same broker might relocate the fleeing Caucasians to an upscale "whites-only" development that the real estate company was promoting.

Women in postwar America were, of course, caught up in the aftereffects of practices such as this. But many, black and white, also courageously took a stand against what they saw as injustice.

They included African American seamstress Rosa Parks who was jailed in 1955 for refusing to give up her seat on a city bus in Montgomery, Alabama, to a white man. They also included six young women in the "Little Rock Nine," black students seeking to lawfully integrate the city's previously all-white Central High School in 1957.

Both events were broadcast nationwide by the unblinking eye of television cameras. Fellow Americans saw the dignified Mrs. Parks standing for her mug shot. They saw white demonstrators spewing hate at a lone black girl, Elizabeth Eckford, as she tried to survive the mob in Little Rock. These were not one-dimensional photographs in a newspaper or magazine. The visceral power of television brought African Americans to life as human beings.

More than ever before, American films were bringing race to the forefront in the daily lives of postwar women. *Pinky* (1949) was about a light-skinned black woman passing for white. Although the noted African American actresses Lena Horne and Dorothy Dandridge hoped to play the title role, they were passed over for a little-known white. In 1951, there came a sanitized remake of the movie *Showboat* concerning interracial marriage between a white man and light-skinned African American woman. Once again, light-skinned African American actress Lena Horne was interested in the role, and once again she was passed over for a white.

Yet in postwar daily life, it was a time when women who considered themselves "ordinary" did extraordinary things. Along with Rosa Parks and the high school girls of the Little Rock Nine, a number of women stepped forward, often in the face of danger and usually without widespread recognition.

One, Ella Baker, was inspired by young black college students who refused to leave a lunch counter in Greensboro, North Carolina, where they had been denied service. In 1960, she organized a meeting for the student leaders of the sit-ins, from which the Student Nonviolent Coordinating Committee (SNCC) was born.

Daisy Bates and her husband ran a weekly African American newspaper, the *Arkansas State Press*. As president of the local chapter of the National Association for the Advancement of Colored People (NAACP), she became known for coordinating the high school students called the Little Rock Nine who attempted to integrate that city's Central High School.

Septima Clark, often called the "Mother of the Movement," participated in a class action lawsuit filed by the NAACP that led to pay equity for black and white teachers in South Carolina. In 1956, when South Carolina passed a statute that prohibited city and state employees from belonging to civil rights organizations, she refused to resign from the NAACP, thereby losing the teaching job she had held for 40 years. When the Southern Christian Leadership Conference (SCLC) established their Citizenship Education Program, it was based on her model.

Fannie Lou Hamer helped register blacks to vote in Mississippi and was instrumental in organizing Mississippi Freedom Summer for SNCC. In 1964, after attending the Democratic National Convention, her use of spiritual hymns and fervent belief in the Biblical righteousness of civil rights gained her a reputation as an electrifying speaker. Hamer was cofounder of the National Women's Political Caucus to train women of all races to seek elected office. In Mississippi, she was harassed and threatened and was assaulted by police and white supremacists for trying to register to vote.

Anna Pauline "Pauli" Murray fought for human rights as far back as 1938 when she unsuccessfully attempted to enter the all-white University of North Carolina. In 1940, Murray sat in the whites-only section of a Virginia bus to avoid the broken seats in the back but was arrested for violating state segregation laws. Determined to become a civil rights lawyer to fight such injustices, when she was awarded a prestigious Harvard Law School fellowship, she was rejected from the all-male institution because of her gender. By 1960, her work as a human rights activist and scholar was well known enough for President John F. Kennedy to appoint her to his Committee on Civil and Political Rights. Murray worked closely with Martin Luther King and other civil rights leaders but was critical of the way men dominated the leadership, coining the phrase "Jane Crow." In honor of her work for human rights, future Supreme Court justice Ruth Bader Ginsburg credited Pauli Murray as coauthor of Ginsburg's brief for a landmark Supreme Court decision based on equal protection under the law regardless of race or gender.

During the Montgomery Bus Boycott of 1955–1956, which followed the arrest of Rosa Parks, a number of average women of both races joined together to fight injustice. Their efforts in Montgomery were dramatized in the 1990 movie *The Long Walk Home*, starring Whoopi Goldberg and Sissy Spacek.

Following the highly publicized events in 1957 surrounding the mobs that harassed the nine black students, the Women's Emergency Committee to Open Our Schools (WEC) was formed by a group of Little Rock matrons. They advocated for the integration of the Little Rock public school system. Because of their respected position in the white community, they proved to be an obstacle to the governor's efforts to prevent racial integration by closing the schools. The women lobbied the Arkansas General Assembly, which was attempting to pass segregationist bills (where the women were told to "please shut up") and demanded a special election to remove segregationists from the Little Rock school board. The Women's Emergency Committee was the first white organization to speak out against segregation in Little Rock. The story of those events, as well as courageous Little Rock schoolteachers, can be seen in the 1981 movie, *Crisis at Central High* starring Joanne Woodward.

There were many other unsung women in postwar America who fought for racial justice as well as those who saw inequity based on people's ethnicity. Whether by law or social customs, there were rights and privileges in the United States that were traditionally enjoyed by white Anglo-Saxon Protestants but denied to African Americans, Asian Americans, Hispanic Americans, and Native Americans. Even European Americans who practiced Catholicism such as those from Ireland, Italy, or Poland faced a struggle as did Jewish people and those from the Middle East.

Hispanics, with origins in Mexico, Central America, Latin America, and the Caribbean islands, also experienced racial bias. When the United States annexed much of the current Southwest from Mexico after the Mexican-American War (1846–1848), the Mexican citizens who resided there found themselves subject to Anglo discrimination.

The U.S. government sponsored what was called the Mexican Repatriation program during the Great Depression of the 1930s. It was intended to remove Mexican Americans to Mexico. Although it was said to be a voluntary move, many were forcibly uprooted against their will. Up to a million persons of Mexican ancestry were deported; well over half were U.S. citizens.

In the postwar era of the 1950s, many businesses and homeowners' associations had official policies to exclude blacks and Hispanics. In areas such as the western United States, Mexican American children were subjected to segregation in public schools.

Dolores Huerta, a grammar schoolteacher in the postwar era, noticed that many of her students showed up for class hungry, sick, or in need of shoes. She began a crusade to correct the kind of injustice against Hispanics that she saw all around her, especially against migrant farmworkers. In 1955, Huerta helped start the Stockton, California, chapter of the Community Service Organization (CSO), which fought for economic improvements for Latinos. In 1962, she cofounded America's first successful union for migrant laborers, the United Farm Workers. Due to her activism, Huerta was targeted for assault. Once, while peacefully and lawfully demonstrating in San Francisco, an attack by police left her hospitalized with critical injuries. Winning a large judgment, she donated the proceeds to the farmworkers.

Native Americans found themselves in the same continuing pattern of racial discrimination and marginalization that had been in existence in America for hundreds of years. By the 1950s, many had been segregated by the federal government's Bureau of Indian Affairs in arid regions of the West. The Indian Relocation Act of 1956 offered vocational training to Native Americans who moved off the reservation into urban areas. About 30,000 Indians did so but found discrimination, high living costs, low-paying jobs, segregated schools, and undesirable housing. With their former reservations being dissolved after being cut from federal funding, many Native Americans found themselves scattered and isolated during the late 1950s.

In a traumatic event for many Native American women, some families even lost their children under the Indian Adoption Project starting in 1958. The federal program removed hundreds of Native American children from their families to place them with white parents, allegedly to help them assimilate into mainstream culture.

Some Native American women became activists for their people during the postwar years. Ada Deer saw injustices to her native Menominee tribe in Wisconsin but found few local services for Native Americans living in urban settings. Trying to meet with federal authorities on their behalf, she was ignored by elected officials in Congress. Persevering, she ultimately became the first Native American woman to head the Bureau of Indian Affairs.

In the Pacific Northwest, Catherine Troeh became the only woman to join the Chinook Tribal Council, beginning in 1952. To engage her people, she wrote a Native American–focused newsletter that was distributed at least once a month during her lifetime.

Annie Dodge Wauneka had been sent as a child to an Indian school in Albuquerque, New Mexico, where native culture and language were discouraged. Returning to her Navajo tribe, in 1951, she became only the second woman to be elected to the Tribal Council, after activist Lilly Neil was injured in an automobile accident. In 1953, Annie Wauneka's husband ran for the position that she herself held. She felt he was not a good candidate. In a nod to Navajo matriarchal tradition, she ran against him and won. In 1960, Annie Wauneka began hosting a public affairs radio show completely in the Navajo language.

During the postwar era, Asian Americans experienced a strange phenomenon. In World War II, racial discrimination against Japanese American people led to them being forcibly removed from their homes, losing their businesses and property, and being placed in desolate internment camps. Many say that it was the incarcerated women who kept their families and culture together, stepping away from their traditional submissive role. After the war, Japanese Americans were recast in the 1950s as hard-working, upstanding citizens, even if they were still seen as different from whites. They were portrayed in the postwar era as a minority group that was "pulling themselves up by their bootstraps."

In 1963, Japanese Americans received the ultimate cultural accolade when the recording "Sukiyaki," sung entirely in Japanese, hit the top of America's pop music charts, something that would have been unthinkable only a few years before. Although they enjoyed the jaunty tune, few Americans understood the lyrics about looking up and whistling so no one can see your tears. Some might say that was applicable to many women's racial issues in the postwar years.

RURAL LIFE

Writing about American women living in rural areas of the nation during the postwar era, Wuthnow (2011) states that magazines in the 1950s portrayed country life as idyllic, with bountiful crops and "happy housewives preparing luscious meals on modern kitchen appliances for grateful husbands and children" (10).

Some rural women of the postwar era may have experienced that adjective-laden lifestyle, but by no means all. Wuthnow states that many families in rural America during the 1950s were still recovering from the Great Depression of the 1930s, adding that many lacked even the paved roads and electricity that other parts of the nation had enjoyed for decades (10).

Rural areas, as defined by the U.S. Census Bureau, are communities of fewer than 2,500 people. In 1953, there were 54 million

The daily lives of rural women in the postwar era included tending to farm animals, chopping wood, and sometimes helping in the fields. In addition, they processed farm products such as milk into butter and did the cooking, cleaning, laundry, and sewing while caring for children. Sometimes they could barter eggs, handmade quilts, or other items to obtain necessities. (Library of Congress)

people categorized as rural in the United States, about a third of the nation's population.

Agriculture has been a central component of American life dating back to colonial times. Daman (2018) writes, "It is impossible to understand American history unless you understand agricultural history" (51). Most of the English colonies were founded on their ability to grow crops for trade as well as for the colonists' own survival. Even in cold, rocky New England, farm families were usually able to grow enough fruit and vegetables to feed themselves. The Middle Colonies cultivated grains such as barley, corn, oats, rye, and wheat. Cotton and tobacco were the cash crops on large Southern plantations. Farmwives everywhere were expected to grow a "kitchen garden" to feed the family with a variety of vegetables. In colder climates, farmwives would preserve these products by canning them to help ensure the family's survival through the winter.

The Industrial Revolution, which began in the United States during the late 18th century, transformed the nation as more people moved to larger towns for factory work. In the 19th century's age of invention, the coming of the cotton gin, electricity, and transcontinental railroads permanently changed American society. In the 20th century, technological advances arrived with dazzling regularity, especially during the postwar era.

But even after the coming of the industrial age, farm families grew or made most of what they needed. Women's chores included hauling water by hand from a nearby stream or helping to dig and maintain a well. If a farm family had surplus crops, milk, or eggs, women might sell or barter them in nearby towns. These traditions extended well into the postwar era.

Since farmers needed plenty of land to grow their crops, rural life was extremely isolated. Farm families generally had to become self-sufficient units. A prime source of their outside social contacts came from going into town on Saturday to shop at the general store or attending church services on Sunday.

Well into the postwar era, daily life for rural women consisted of hard physical labor and ceaseless work year-round. Women cleaned the house, cooked, and processed their farm's commodities such as milk into butter or apples into cider. Often, they chopped wood, tended to farm animals, and helped the men by working the fields, especially at harvest time. They reared the children and usually continued with their daily chores while pregnant with another.

Women were responsible for kitchen gardens close to the back door in which various vegetables such as tomatoes and green beans could be grown and canned for later use. The canning process required hours spent over a hot woodstove in summertime for winter provisions. In addition, beef and pork needed to be butchered, salted, and smoked.

In the course of their daily lives, rural women also baked bread, made soap from bacon fat, sewed and mended clothing, and swept the constant drift of dust from the house. Washing clothes by hand was an especially backbreaking task, with farmwork generating a huge amount of dirty clothing. The laundry also had to be dried, thus a challenge during wintertime and the rainy season. It was women's task to figure out how.

Depending on whether the family had children old enough to do so, farm women might also clean the chicken coop, feed livestock, fill the woodbox, gather eggs, harness horses or mules, milk cows, and take care of the outhouse.

Women cooked three hearty meals a day on a woodstove for the family and as well as farmhands in residence. After supper, farm women might knit, quilt, sew, sing songs, and/or read the Bible by firelight with the rest of the family.

For many rural women, daily life on a farm or ranch went on as it had done for generations. However, by the postwar era, some farm families also enjoyed many 20th-century advances such as appliances, radio, and television as well as mechanized farm equipment.

Electricity had come to many of America's urban locations in the early 20th century. However, it was slow to arrive in rural areas because it was not profitable for privately owned power companies. Still, many farm families had a system of generators and batteries to provide lighting, bring power to water pumps, and enjoy conveniences such as an "ice box" if they could afford it in order to keep food cold.

For many rural women, listening to a battery-charged radio was their window on the world. When they went to town, they could sometimes enjoy films if there was a local "movie house" or "picture show." Such amusements offered women a bit of entertainment and a glimpse of what other kinds of lives were like.

The huge distances between homesteads often led to extreme isolation for rural women. Risjord (2013) states that even with improvements in technology, nothing could help ease the daily drudgery and isolation of farm life. This was especially the case on the wide-open spaces of the West before the coming of modern conveniences such as the telephone. According to Risjord, "Farmers' wives in particular often suffered from loneliness and despair" (142). There was a name for the depression rural women sometimes suffered: "prairie madness."

Mental health facilities, along with hospitals and other rural healthcare providers, were usually few and far between. Midwives or neighboring women were often the only help available for childbirth.

For rural women, their church became an especially important source of socialization as well as spirituality. Roth (2017) describes the sight of young mothers lining up babies on blankets along the wall while they met (92).

Some rural women of the postwar era had actually seen more of the wider world by serving as military nurses, taking government jobs, or working in defense plants during World War II. Some were city girls or foreign "war brides" who had married soldiers from rural America. They knew that the postwar consumer culture provided all sorts of items to make rural life more pleasant. All they needed was electricity.

Many rural areas were still without electricity through the 1950s. Power companies were often privately owned, and the owners felt it cost too much money to build electrical lines to scattered families in rural areas with too little promise of profits.

The creation of the Rural Electrification Administration (REA) in 1935 had changed matters somewhat. Local cooperatives, subsidized by the federal government, were organized to build transmission systems to outlying rural homes. However, in the political climate of the 1950s, rural Americans found themselves in the middle of the Cold War. Privately owned power companies and conservative politicians condemned entities like the Rural Electrification Administration as "socialistic."

Postwar Americans were told that socialism was the enemy of the United States during the Cold War. Certainly, farmers were patriotic. But they also wanted electricity. By the mid-1950s, electrical power came to most parts of rural America.

In Arkansas, for example, about two-thirds of the state's farms had electricity by 1950, although another third continued to remain without it for several more years.

Most rural women were thrilled with the coming of electricity to their farm homes, although there are anecdotal reports that some women feared it. Not knowing what it was or how it worked, some women blocked the electrical outlets in their home, afraid that electricity would "leak out."

But for most, electricity raised the standard of living for postwar rural women immensely. Electric-powered pumps carried water to the house, enabling indoor plumbing. A healthy variety of food could be stored in refrigerators. Vacuum cleaners and washing machines replaced brooms and washtubs. Electricity could be used to grind corn and milk cows. It powered electric lights, radios, and television. In short, it brought rural women into the modern world.

However, electricity could not solve all the problems of rural women in the postwar era. There were rural areas that did not share the bounty of the "Affluent Society." Women whose families were sharecroppers, for example, lived daily lives after World War II that were very similar to the lives of their ancestors just after the Civil War.

Duncan (2015) cites two regions mired in poverty during the postwar years. Rural communities in the Mississippi Delta remained impoverished, including broad swaths of Arkansas, Louisiana, and Mississippi that had large African American populations. "Poor whites" could be found in the Appalachian Mountain region, which contained rural portions of Georgia, Kentucky, North Carolina, Tennessee, and West Virginia (10).

Ironically, as the postwar world generally became more electrified and mechanized, many urban and suburban Americans sought to escape to remote rural areas for vacations. Communities in places such as the Ozark Mountains in Arkansas and Missouri maintained their traditional rustic lifestyle. The natural beauty attracted vacationers who enjoyed camping, fishing, hunting, and relaxation, just as similar rural regions did across the nation.

But for rural women who lived year-round in those regions, the luxury of a vacation or even an extended trip to town seemed unlikely. For them, there were other rural women who proved to be a godsend: "Cooperative Extension Ladies."

In 1914, the U.S. Congress created a system of Cooperative Extensions through each state's land-grant university to educate rural people about current developments in agriculture and home economics. As part of the U.S. Department of Agriculture, the Cooperative Extension Service (CES) offered—and continues to offer—programs providing information on agricultural production, consumer issues, protection of natural resources, public affairs education, rural community development, and youth programs through 4-H clubs.

With offices in each county, female Cooperative Extension agents traveled their region to bring rural women programs such as canning, gardening, nutrition, and sewing in what were called Home Demonstration Clubs. "Cooperative Extension Ladies" showed rural women how to make their families' lives better through home improvements, labor-saving devices, innovative techniques, and a general enhancement of the family's living conditions.

One major project was showing rural women how to make mattresses out of surplus homegrown cotton. Unpaid volunteers joined the agents in providing training for thousands of farmwives, giving rural women—both the trainers and the women they trained—not only the means for much-needed socialization but a way to feel useful and fulfilled.

During the postwar years, more families left their farms, sometimes selling their land to neighbors. Sometimes they were bought out by large industrial agricultural companies. According to the Cooperative Extension of Arkansas, a state with a relatively small population, about 17,000 families left Arkansas farms soon after World War II.

After rural electrification, there came a slow, steady climb toward an improved standard of living in rural areas. But during the postwar era, the daily lives of many rural American women would have been instantly recognizable to their grandmothers and great-grandmothers.

SUBURBAN LIFE

New York is home to many unique distinctions, but there is one that many residents could do without. According to the U.S. Department of Agriculture, a tiny worm called a golden nematode that infests potato fields is found domestically only in New York State. After World War II, the microscopic creature was instrumental in a major upheaval for American society, including revolutionary changes in the lives of many women in postwar America.

In 1946, following World War II, builder William "Bill" Levitt (1907–1994) had a name in mind for his new housing development on Long Island, about 20 miles from New York City. He intended to call it Island Trees. According to Ferrer and Navarra (1997), Levitt bought farmland from its owner for a relatively cut-rate price. His development would be constructed atop potato fields, "1200 acres of farmland devastated by a fancifully named parasite—the Golden Nematode" (7). For Levitt and suburban developers to follow, the Golden Nematode turned into a gold mine.

Symbolic of the Island Trees name that Levitt attached to the ultra-flat land, he planted two small trees at the front entrance of his new development. Soon, both the saplings and what they were meant to represent became a footnote to history. The name that stuck was the one that propelled Bill Levitt into immortality: "Levittown."

His development, and those to follow, initiated the postwar rise of the suburb, or a small community that is neither urban nor rural, located within commuting distance of a larger city. Documented evidence on a clay tablet indicates that the concept of the suburb existed at least as far back as ancient Babylon, more than 500 years before the birth of Christ.

In postwar America, two great success stories of the 20th century were linked. Cars made suburbs possible; suburbs created a demand for cars. There had been previous suburban areas across the landscape of America, scattered communities where residents could ride trains or streetcars to their place of employment in the city. But the boom in auto sales during the postwar years added privacy and independence for car owners as they traveled to and from work.

When Bill Levitt returned home to New York after World War II, he saw the critical shortage in housing for fellow veterans and their young families. General prosperity and low-interest home loans through the GI Bill enabled veterans to purchase their own home. They could leave rental apartments in the crowded city as soon as they could find a place in the suburbs to live. Some affordable new housing was being built, but not fast enough.

It was Levitt who solved the problem. He understood the art of quickly building homes and, just as quickly, selling them. Kushner (2009) states that while some suburbs had been in existence already, Levitt's company "mastered something dazzling . . . an inexpensive home with state-of-the-art gadgets in a seemingly perfect storybook town" (13).

The aforementioned gadgets were aimed at housewives. Brand-new appliances such as refrigerators, stoves, and washing machines were installed while Levittown homes were still in the process of being constructed. They were identical houses that essentially became part of an assembly line of residential building.

Because the top priority was speed, Levitt's houses were all the same, thus becoming the target of detractors who criticized Levittown, citing the conformity of both its housing and its inhabitants. Levittowners didn't care. They liked their homes, their communities, and Levittown founder Bill Levitt.

What the cynics didn't quite comprehend was the gratitude felt by new homeowners to purchase a home of their own. Critics may not have known too many people like the postwar bride cited in Ferrer and Navarra (1997): "[Bill Levitt] was a wonderful man. We were living in a two-room apartment in Queens with my mother. When Levitt called to say he had a home for us . . . we jumped at the opportunity and bought it sight unseen" (42).

In the past, many people married other people very much like themselves. Often, brides and grooms had known each other since childhood, with their extended families also acquainted with each other. During the upheaval of World War II, however, men and women were married after knowing each other for only a short time, often coming from quite different backgrounds. Some young brides, living with their new husband's family, dealt with in-laws who never quite approved of the stranger in their midst.

Some young postwar couples sought rentals, although they were at the mercy of a landlord who could raise the rent at any time or evict them at will. Some were paying top dollar for apartments like the couple whose "shower" was cold water through a garden hose that had to be attached to the landlord's outside faucet two floors down.

Certainly, some returning veterans and their wives preferred to rent; many did not. In suburban developments like Levitt's, single-family residences gave them privacy, security, and pride of owner-ship. Suburban women could have a home of their own.

Suburban developments were generally populated by white middle-class World War II veterans and their wives who may have come from different prewar backgrounds but in the postwar years were remarkably similar. In the suburbs, women met other women very much like themselves, with a sameness of population that was not often seen in 20th-century America.

When criticizing the suburbs for their sameness, most detractors did not attack a darker fact: most developments prohibited non-whites. Therefore, young white middle-class women met other young white middle-class women.

At gatherings, while their husbands talked about work, politics, or crabgrass, the women talked about how to keep their husbands happy or new ways to cook chicken. Most of all, women talked about children.

In the postwar years, the concept of "domestic containment," so labeled by author Elaine Tyler May (2008), centered almost exclu-sively around children. Men left the house each day to go to work in the outside world. Women cleaned the home and cooked the meals. But mostly, women dealt with their children.

The postwar baby boom was a result not only of young cou-ples finding the security and desire to start their own families but was also encouraged by both the American government and the nation's popular culture. Women were expected to have babies—lots of them. It was considered their patriotic duty during the post-war years to raise a lot of upstanding All-American kids in order to make the country safe from Communism.

Thus, the overwhelming majority of women's daily lives involved children, even down to the design of suburban homes. Developers constructed houses with mothers in mind, having the kitchen cen-trally located so they could be near the rest of the family at all times. Suburban homes were built with a large expanse of glass, called a picture window, so that women could keep an eye on their children playing in the yard.

The daily lives of suburban women took on a virtual sameness, much like the houses they lived in. Having babies was the prime directive, so a woman often had school-age children along with toddlers in the house while expecting yet another "bundle of joy." On an average weekday, she would get up early to start breakfast before waking the rest of the family and supervising their morning routine. After husbands left for their job and school-age children for class, women stayed home. They cleaned, they cooked, and they waited for the others to come back home. After supper, women tidied the kitchen before joining the rest of the family for an evening of television and then off to bed.

Many women in postwar America had grown up during the deprivation of the Depression in the 1930s. At first, they loved their new lives as well as the feeling that they were doing something useful and patriotic in raising strong All-American families. Sometimes, the efforts of suburban women prompted community projects such as ball fields, playgrounds, libraries, and swimming pools.

Newspaper and magazine articles reported that in interviews, most suburban women claimed to be very happy. In one respect, considering the political climate of the postwar years, it would have been unsafe to express unhappiness at doing what was considered their patriotic duty: having babies, raising children, taking care of their men. Any woman who began to harbor doubts usually kept them to herself. Everyone else seemed happy, so individual women who began to feel restless and unfulfilled simply assumed it was just their own selfishness and ingratitude, leading to enormous feelings of guilt.

A growing sense of restlessness was not something suburban women discussed with each other. Everyone else *seemed* so happy. Husbands could not often be sympathetic, sometimes envying their wives for women's ability to stay home while men had to go out each day and face the jungle of the workplace.

In the suburbs, many women were often physically removed from their birth family. In addition, when suburban women did have the chance to talk with their mothers, it was often difficult for the two to relate since their daily lives were so different. It was hard to argue with the rationale that past generations did not have it as easy as the average postwar suburban housewife. In the past, many had cooked over a woodstove, drawn water in buckets, and washed clothes by hand. The mothers of suburban women had often faced hardships during the Depression, when survival took precedence over restlessness.

Postwar suburban women did feel they had one resource to help them navigate the new lifestyle of the 1950s, but that source turned out to be a false prophet: the woman's magazine. Often being far from their original family after the war, housewives looked to women's magazines as their guide to success in mastering the new suburban middle-class ideal.

The concept of magazines aimed at women was not a new one. *Godey's Lady's Book* was popular in the United States around the time of the Civil War. But magazines really rose to prominence during the early postwar years, before television became the predominant means of communication. Walker (1998) states that as the postwar era began, television was not a common fixture in homes, so "magazines thus assumed more importance than they do today in helping to both shape and reflect the values, habits, and aspirations of American women and their families" (1).

Women's magazines were edited almost exclusively by men, reinforcing the standard postwar notion that women were fulfilled only by devoting their lives to being housewives and mothers.

In addition, postwar women were considered not so much readers as consumers. From cover to cover, the magazines became vehicles to hawk advertisers' products. Thinly disguised articles bolstered the concept that women could only reach the white middle-class suburban ideal by purchasing the products that advertisers were selling.

In the magazines, everyone appeared to be so happy. Of course, they were models. But the message was clear, so when the first stirrings of discontent began to occur, individual women thought they were the only ones with such feelings. Women's magazines reinforced their advertisers' messages, so the only kind of images readers saw were smiling women who appeared overjoyed to be using a new electric floor waxer.

In addition, the women's magazines guided young mothers in teaching their daughters to lead the same kind of life as theirs. In suburban homes and schools, boys were steered toward learning work skills; girls were guided toward becoming housewives.

There was often one car in the postwar suburban family, which the husband drove to work. Many women felt stranded in new developments that did not yet have shopping centers. There were fewer opportunities for any type of job, even in the limited fields available to women. Many employers openly refused to hire married women.

Some suburban housewives joined the Parent Teacher Association (PTA) at their children's school, although top positions were often taken by men. The same male-oriented leadership structure existed in local politics or property owners' associations. Suburban housewives could join a sewing group or some type of women's club, but they had to make sure to be home in time to have dinner on the table for their family's evening meal.

In the limited space between ads, women's magazines cautioned housewives to freshen their makeup and hair before the husband arrived home, to be cheerful and interesting, speak softly, and to generally create a haven for their family within their suburban home.

Some suburban women recognized that for them, staying home all day with appliances and bickering children led to feelings of emptiness. Many began to feel as if they didn't exist apart from being someone's wife and someone's mother. They often felt like shut-ins, implied even by the word "housewife."

If they were educated, their lives felt out of sync with their training. Some experts responded by stating it was not a good idea to admit women to college. If women had previously lived in the city, suburban life began to feel like a barren landscape. As more women became open about feeling restless and unfulfilled, male humorists said the problem could be solved by taking away women's right to vote since women obviously had too much to think about.

Many women felt guilty for having the feelings they had. They knew that they had it better than women of the past whose lives centered on survival and trying not to die during multiple childbirths. Some turned themselves over to religion. There, they were often told that the husband was master of the house and that the wife should submit to him in all things.

Some women had worked in factories or other kinds of positions during World War II, when they had been needed. They found a sense of independence and even had the chance to earn their own paycheck, to do with as they pleased. But most lost their jobs when the men came back home. According to Halberstam (1993), "in the two years after the war, some 2 million women lost their jobs" (589).

Jobs for suburban women were strongly discouraged—a woman mustn't take a job away from a man who might need it to feed his family. This mindset could have disastrous consequences if a woman found herself widowed or divorced. She had no skills if she needed a job to feed her children. Nor had she accrued social security savings, not having been employed.

Some women thought about the greater possibilities available in urban areas. The city offered more and better jobs for educated women. There were cultural centers including great libraries and museums. There were more volunteer organizations, and there were nursery schools or other kinds of child daycare. But for many women, staying in suburbs was necessary for the sake of the children.

Some suburban women found that although confined to their neighborhood, they could often find both socialization and fulfillment along with an independent income while not being seen as neglecting their home or family. One of those ways was selling Avon cosmetics. Another was Tupperware.

Invented in 1946, Tupperware containers kept food fresh longer. Under a company saleswoman named Brownie Wise, women could become authorized dealers, utilizing a direct marketing strategy of selling the plastic products to women at "Tupperware Parties" in their homes. Many "Tupperware Ladies" developed confidence, professional skills, and personal satisfaction along with earning their own income. The plan developed by Brownie Wise was so successful that in April 1954, she became the first woman to grace the cover of *Business Week* magazine. Sadly, getting all that attention might have been her downfall. In 1958, with the Tupperware company earning millions, owner Earl Tupper fired Brownie Wise.

Especially after Betty Friedan's book *The Feminine Mystique* became a bestseller in 1963, more women challenged the belief that their only place in life was in the home, specifically the nursery, kitchen, and bedroom. In addition, some began to wonder if it was really enough in life to be somebody's wife and somebody's mother with no identity of their own.

Indeed, many women felt it was more than enough. To them, being a wife and mother was the highest calling. Their daily lives might have reflected honorably on the sentiments of Beecher and Stowe (1869), just after the Civil War: "The family state, then, is the aptest earthly illustration of the heavenly kingdom, and in it, woman is the chief minister. Her great mission is self-denial" (n.p.).

In the course of their daily lives, a number of suburban women in postwar America found themselves in the large middle range. Although they may have sometimes felt discontented, they were proud of taking good care of their homes and families. They noticed that men sometimes had a workshop or den, the postwar era's equivalent of today's "man cave." In most suburban homes, women did not often have a space of their own in which to occasionally read or simply be alone. For some suburban women, a room of their own might have been enough.

URBAN LIFE

In 10 short years during the postwar era, the pendulum swung for American cities. With that transition came a change in the daily lives of many urban women. As the decade of the 1950s began, major cities such as New York, Boston, Chicago, and Philadelphia could still flaunt their glitter. Michael Johns (2004) claims, "America reached its peak as an urban society in the 1950s" (1). During the early part of the decade, city women could enjoy the culinary delights of legendary restaurants, the cultural wealth of world-class museums, and the cutting-edge glamour of downtown shopping.

However, as the 1950s came to a close, America's great cities were struggling. The decline of urban centers came down to several interrelated factors, most having to do with the concurrent rise of suburbia.

A suburb is defined as a small community that is neither urban nor rural, located within commuting distance of a larger city. After World War II, housing developments sprang up in suburban areas like the crops on the farmland they replaced. Returning veterans took advantage of educational benefits, finding plentiful jobs away from the cities. Low-interest home loans through the GI Bill made suburban housing affordable. Many could buy cars or find convenient transportation including commuter rail lines. Therefore, even if people had city jobs, they were not limited as to where they could live their daily lives. Rather than remain living in a cramped apartment in crowded cities, families could move to the fresh air and wide-open spaces of the sparkling new suburbs.

The relative rise and fall of city life had an effect on gender roles. Up until the rise of the urban centers following the Industrial Revolution, farmwives gave birth to numerous children. In part this was due to having little access to birth control, but on the whole, a large family was desirable because it provided a source of free, accessible labor. In 1800, the average size of the American family was seven children, not counting those who died soon after birth.

But by 1900, more families were moving to urban centers. While a farm child was added agricultural labor, a city child was basically an extra mouth to feed. With greater educational opportunities in the city, women slowly became more educated and independent. Throughout the postwar years, the three main jobs that were open to educated women were teacher, nurse, and secretary. But even being limited to those three, there was more potential for average postwar women than being a farmwife.

The rural population of America remained in the majority until the 1920s, which was when cities grew. One source of urban growth was the Great Migration, African Americans who sought to escape the hostile environment of the Jim Crow South. Many migrated to northern cities where, although they enjoyed more freedom, they were usually restricted to housing in certain neighborhoods, such as New York City's Harlem.

After World War II, the white middle class began migrating to the suburbs. Armed with an education courtesy of the GI Bill and propelled by the scare tactics of real estate developers who trumpeted the city's rising crime rate, whites who could afford to move to new suburban housing developments often did so.

Suburbanites could commute to jobs in the city and come home to fresh air at night. The racially tinged movement by America's middle class from the city to the suburbs became known as "white flight."

With many middle-class families leaving for the suburbs, the tax base for urban areas decreased. Cities were unable to pay for infrastructure improvements, resulting in a steady deterioration through the late 1950s. This in turn spiraled into still more "white flight" to what was promoted as affluent, clean, safe suburbia. As millions moved to the suburbs, shopping malls sprang up, so postwar suburbanites did not have to go into the city to shop.

Wealthy urban residents created separate, secure enclaves for themselves, which often led to American cities becoming home to the very rich and the very poor, with little in between. Therefore, according to Hendricks (2019), the daily life of a postwar American woman who was a city dweller "might include shopping at nearby exclusive stores, lunching at a renowned restaurant, visiting a world-class museum, and ending the day with exciting nightlife. Or it could mean waking up amid noise and dirt in a cramped airless slum, dodging violent gangs on the street, and going to sleep at night hoping not to hear the sound of a break-in" (79).

The daily lives of many women who were African American or Hispanic often included working in the homes of urban white employers and then returning home to their lower-class neighborhood at night to care for their own family. Levenstein (2009) states that as they sought to support their families, "poor black women faced distinct challenges in postwar cities. They suffered not only from racial discrimination in housing and employment but also from sex discrimination" (5). Their daily lives included a lack of childcare, lack of employer-provided benefits, and lack of healthcare. According to Levenstein, what they *did* have was dilapidated housing that contributed to health problems, domestic violence, and being portrayed as criminals and "welfare cheats" (6).

One black woman, Dr. Mamie Phipps Clark, conducted landmark research that played a central role in the civil rights movement, influencing the 1954 *Brown v. Board of Education* decision ordering racial integration in public schools. However, Clark found it difficult to find work as a psychologist in New York City, repeatedly being passed over for white males. Noting that there were virtually no mental health services for African Americans in Harlem, she and her husband created the Northside Center for Child Development after World War II. But for many postwar women who were African Americans or other minorities, there was little in the way of any healthcare in their neighborhoods, mental or otherwise, and even less in the way of health insurance.

Some average urban white women recognized the inequity that other women suffered in their daily lives. Some city women, such as those described by Curry et al. (2002) in *Deep in Our Hearts: Nine White Women in the Freedom Movement*, left their daily lives to work for civil rights, both in the rural South and in urban environments.

Roger Guy (2007) describes another group of women on the move. He studied "poor whites," migrants from America's Appalachian region who moved in the postwar years to cities such as Baltimore, Chicago, Cincinnati, and Detroit. There, they were perceived as "hillbillies," receiving what he sees as adverse treatment as an underclass. Following the postwar collapse of the coal industry, Appalachian migration to northern cities increased significantly, with women taking a significant role in settling their families into a new and often hostile place.

From his research, Berry (2000) concurs, calling poor whites "Southern migrants, Northern exiles." In the postwar era, more Southerners believed that opportunity in the "Affluent Society" did not exist in the South. Berry calls it "The Great White Migration," as thousands of Southerners found that "the solution to problems in the South was exile" (18).

Berry claims that for many Appalachian women, the move north was not intended to be permanent. While their poverty-stricken Appalachian communities were more like those of a past century than the space age, women had enjoyed a sense of fellowship in their daily lives there that was often lacking in the North.

Upon arrival in the North, they often found that locals accused them of taking away jobs by accepting work for less pay. This was frequently true, as poor whites were played off against poor blacks.

Summing up the negative feelings of some urban northerners to having Appalachian migrants in their midst, Berry cites a 1959 letter to an Ohio public service commission regarding "The Southern mountaineer in Cincinnati." The letter writer claims, "They respect no authority. [They are] unschooled, unskilled. . . . The simplest solution to the problem would be to encourage these people to go back to their home states. Why unload their problem children on us?" (172).

Even with negative perceptions, white Southern migrants were often able to blend in with the general population. Black Americans did not have that luxury. Most were barred from living anywhere but in inner-city black neighborhoods. Many entry-level jobs that might have traditionally gone to blacks were lost to automation or by companies leaving the city to build sprawling complexes or "office parks" on less expensive land in suburban industrial zones. Fewer jobs for blacks and other minorities meant less of a tax base. Infrastructure—public transportation; sanitation; and, in some places, law enforcement—crumbled.

As the 1950s progressed, suburbia rose as cities declined. Tochterman (2017) claims that in postwar New York, "fear of crime transformed the metropolitan political economy, as . . . industry and white-collar firms joined the suburban exodus" (16). People followed jobs, and jobs were steadily moving to the suburbs, making a commute into the city unnecessary.

One American city, however, actually became synonymous with commuting as much as for its glamour and postwar population boom. Buntin (2009) writes that before it was a city, Los Angeles, California, "was an idea" (12). While other cities grew based on geographical features such as the ports of New York or San Francisco, "nothing about the arid basin of Los Angeles other than its mild weather suggested the site of a great metropolis" (12). However, that is exactly what it became in the postwar years.

Part of the growth was attributed to women from all over the country who had volunteered for war work and were sent to work in the defense plants of Los Angeles. In the postwar years, many of the women, called "Rosies" (as in "Rosie the Riveter"), returned to their home states. But according to Redman (2017), many others stayed in California, transitioning from wartime work in defense industries to other occupations. He states that the Los Angeles area offered more progressive social conditions and a wider range of opportunities for women than could be found in many other parts of the country during the postwar era. Many Rosies claimed they stayed because they fell in love—not just with local men but with having the ocean and palm trees as part of their daily lives, something most had never seen.

For African American and Hispanic women amid the postwar urban sprawl of Los Angeles, things were not quite as rosy as for the "Rosies." Many Hispanics were confined to living their daily lives in "barrio" neighborhoods such as East Los Angeles. Hispanic women often helped support their families by working in garment factories or other similar industries as well as serving as maids for white people. Many African American women were limited to similar types of work, residing in traditionally black neighborhoods of Los Angeles including South Central and Watts.

For many urban women of the postwar era, large cities represented opportunity. Some minority women found work in food service as well as in domestic jobs. Educated African American and Hispanic urban women were often able to find work as teachers in public elementary schools in neighborhoods that reflected their racial group, although they were underrepresented in urban high schools. Other educated women from minority groups were able to find clerical jobs, often with city or state government and usually far below their educational level. Some women could find jobs advertised in the classifieds of major newspapers that, during the postwar years of the 1950s and 1960s, were listed as "Help Wanted-Female," emphasizing that a job requirement was to be attractive and "well groomed."

The urban landscape reflected the kinds of transitions taking place in postwar America across the board. For women and minorities, they would be played out amid the upheavals of the coming decades.

FURTHER READING

Beecher, Catharine Esther, and Harriet Beecher Stowe. *The American Woman's Home, or, Principles of Domestic Science: Being a Guide to the Formation and Maintenance of Economical, Beautiful and Christian Homes*. New York: J.B. Ford and Company, 1869.

Berry, Chad. *Southern Migrants, Northern Exiles*. Urbana: University of Illinois Press, 2000.

Buntin, John. *L.A. Noir: The Struggle for the Soul of America's Most Seductive City*. New York: Three Rivers Press, 2009.

Cohen, Lizabeth. *A Consumers' Republic: The Politics of Mass Consumption in Postwar America*. New York: Vintage Books, 2003.

Cross, Gary. *An All-Consuming Century: Why Commercialism Won in Modern America*. New York: Columbia University Press, 2000.

Curry, Constance, Joan C. Browning, Dorothy Dawson Burlage, Penelope Patch, Theresa Del Pozzo, Sue Thrasher, Elaine DeLott Baker, Emmie Schrader Adams, and Casey Hayden. *Deep in Our Hearts: Nine White Women in the Freedom Movement*. Athens: University of Georgia Press, 2002.

Daman, Glenn. *The Forgotten Church: Why Rural Ministry Matters for Every Church in America*. Chicago: Moody Publishers, 2018.

Deetz, Kelley Fanto. "African Odyssey: The Epic Journey of Virginia's First Africans." *National Geographic History*, July/August 2019, pp. 76–89.

Duncan, Cynthia. *Worlds Apart: Poverty and Politics in Rural America*. New Haven, CT: Yale University Press, 2015.

Einstein, Mara. *Advertising: What Everyone Needs to Know*. New York: Oxford University Press, 2017.

Ferrer, Margaret, and Tova Navarra. *Levittown: The First 50 Years*. Charleston, SC: Arcadia Publishing, 1997.

Galbraith, John Kenneth. *The Affluent Society*. New York: Mariner Books, 40th anniversary edition, 1998.

Girard, Jolyon, ed. "Daily Life in the United States, 1940–1959." *The Greenwood Encyclopedia of Daily Life in America*. Westport, CT: Greenwood, 2009.

Guy, Roger. *From Diversity to Unity: Southern and Appalachian Migrants in Uptown Chicago, 1950–1970*. Lanham, MD: Lexington Books, 2007.

Halberstam, David. *The Fifties*. New York: Villard, 1993.

Hansberry, Lorraine. *A Raisin in the Sun*. New York: Vintage, reprint edition, 2004.

Harrington Michael. *The Other America: Poverty in the United States*. New York: Scribner, reprint edition, 1997.

Hendricks, Nancy. *Daily Life in 1950s America*. Santa Barbara, CA: Greenwood, 2019.

Hill, Daniel Delis. *Advertising to the American Woman*. Columbus: Ohio State University Press, 2002.

Hirshey, Gerri. *Not Pretty Enough: The Unlikely Triumph of Helen Gurley Brown*. New York: Farrar, Straus and Giroux, 2016.

Johns, Michael. *Moment of Grace: The American City in the 1950s*. Berkeley: University of California Press, 2004.

Kendi, Ibram X. *Stamped from the Beginning: The Definitive History of Racist Ideas in America*. New York: Nation Books, 2017.

Kushner, David. *Levittown: Two Families, One Tycoon, and the Fight for Civil Rights in America's Legendary Suburb*. New York: Walker Books, 2009.

Lears, Jackson. *Fables of Abundance: A Cultural History of Advertising in America*. New York: Basic Books, 1994.

Levenstein, Lisa. *A Movement without Marches: African American Women and the Politics of Poverty in Postwar Philadelphia*. Chapel Hill: University of North Carolina Press, 2009.

Maas, Jane. *Mad Women: The Other Side of Life on Madison Avenue in the '60s and Beyond*. New York: St. Martin's Griffin, 2013.

May, Elaine Tyler. *Homeward Bound: American Families in the Cold War Era*. New York: Basic Books, 2008.

Miles, Steven. *Consumerism: As a Way of Life*. Thousand Oaks, CA: Sage Publications, 2006.

Packard, Vance. *The Hidden Persuaders*. New York: Pocket Books, 1957.

Patterson, James. *Grand Expectations: The United States, 1945–1974*. New York: Oxford University Press, 1997.

Peiss, Kathy. *Hope in a Jar: The Making of America's Beauty Culture*. Philadelphia: University of Pennsylvania Press, 2011.

Redman, Samuel. "During World War II, Thousands of Women Chased Their Own California Dream." *Smithsonian Magazine*, November 29, 2017. https://www.smithsonianmag.com/history/during-world-war-ii-thousands-women-chased-their-own-california-dream-180967357/#RuEB2XwI40kQjtTL.99.

Risjord, Norman. *Dakota: The Story of the Northern Plains*. Lincoln: University of Nebraska Press, 2013.

Rooks, Noliwe M. *Ladies' Pages: African American Women's Magazines and the Culture That Made Them*. Piscataway, NJ: Rutgers University Press, 2004.

Roth, Brad. *God's Country: Faith, Hope, and the Future of the Rural Church*. Harrisonburg, VA: Herald Press, 2017.

Sivulka, Juliann. *Ad Women: How They Impact What We Need, Want, and Buy*. Amherst, NY: Prometheus Books, 2008.

Sutton, Denise H. *Globalizing Ideal Beauty: Women, Advertising, and the Power of Marketing*. New York: Palgrave Macmillan, 2009.

Tochterman, Brian. *The Dying City: Postwar New York and the Ideology of Fear*. Chapel Hill: University of North Carolina Press, 2017.

Veblen, Thorstein. *The Theory of the Leisure Class: An Economic Study of Institutions*. Mineola, NY: Dover Publications, 1994.

Walker, Nancy A. *Women's Magazines, 1940–1960: Gender Roles and the Popular Press*. Boston, MA: Bedford/St. Martin's, 1998.

Woodward, C. Vann. *The Strange Career of Jim Crow*. New York: Oxford University Press, commemorative edition, 2001.

Wuthnow, Robert. *Remaking the Heartland: Middle America since the 1950s*. New York: Oxford University Press, 2011.

3

INTELLECTUAL LIFE

As with many elements of the postwar era, its intellectual life often seemed to be a mix of the comfortable past versus the uncertain future, cultural criticism versus popular preference, and romanticism versus reality.

While many people today think of the 1950s as a sleepy, uneventful time, seeds were being sown that laid the groundwork for the world as we know it, especially for women. In the course of their daily lives during the 1950s, women could occasionally come across harbingers of the revolutionary events that came in the decades to follow.

The consistent underpinning of intellectual life during the postwar years found its basis in three Cs of the era: Conformity, Communism, and Children.

Most women believed the messages that were communicated by the news media and their government in the Cold War era—that their duty was to be mothers who raised patriotic, All-American children in the fight against Communism. They could help fight Russia's Communist menace in the 1950s just as they had done against the fascism of the Nazis during World War II in the 1940s.

Many average women in postwar America accepted their daily life as housewives in order to conform to the status quo. Others pondered the pronouncements of cultural critics who were rebelling against it.

People who were labeled as intellectuals (sometimes derisively called "eggheads") were able to communicate their opinions nation-wide via the new mass medium of television. They had much to say about such postwar issues as civil rights, conformity, consumerism, crime, the Cold War, the Korean War, and the fight against Communism at home under McCarthyism.

Average postwar women in the United States might pay particular attention to issues in their daily lives that affected their children, such as the coming of racial integration in the public schools and the alleged inferiority of American education in the space age. Many critics claimed that U.S. schools trailed behind the Soviet Union, but others saw the tremendous American advances in medicine and science as evidence that the United States lagged behind no one.

One area of concern by intellectuals was their belief that American schoolchildren spent more time watching television than doing their homework. Indeed, the nation's popular culture in the post-war years exploded with the coming of television. With very few choices—three networks plus some local television stations in larger cities—most people basically watched the same things and often discussed them with each other the next day, spreading the culture of the era.

Some women were concerned about the effect on their children as television grew in popularity until almost every American home had one by the end of the 1950s. Articles in women's magazines brought up such issues as asking whether watching television caused eyestrain in youngsters as well as tendencies toward violence. Television was also discussed in its role as an "electronic babysitter," keeping baby boom children occupied while women did other things, such as preparing dinner. Intellectuals pondered whether the impact of television contributed to a general decline in American society.

In 1952, three elements of American life collided: current events of the postwar era, the popularity of the emerging television industry, and the realities of the marketplace. It was a highly publicized real-life incident about which few women in postwar America would have been completely unaware.

During the reign of McCarthyism in 1952, Lucille Ball, star of television's hit comedy *I Love Lucy*, was accused by the House Un-American Activities Committee (HUAC) of Communist ties. Such an allegation might have proven disastrous even for a top-rated program such as *I Love Lucy*, which at the time was going into its second year. Kanfer (2003) notes that costar Desi Arnaz stood before the show's studio audience, saying that his wife Lucille Ball was as American as FBI director J. Edgar Hoover and President Dwight Eisenhower. Referring to the familiar shorthand for Communism, Arnaz said that the only thing "red" about Lucy was her hair, "and even that is not legitimate" (170). Ratings held firm, and profits for the show's advertisers were undented. HUAC lost interest when both the American public and the program's sponsors showed that they still loved Lucy.

Much of the intellectual life of the postwar era was accessible in the daily lives of American women via the literature of the era. One of the best-selling books in 1950 was directly related to their role as mothers. *The Pocket Book of Baby and Child Care* by Dr. Benjamin Spock offered a "how-to" guide about what was said to be their primary role, housewives who raised their children well. *Baby and Child Care* continued to be a mainstay on bestseller lists throughout the postwar era.

But by the end of the 1950s, thought-provoking books criticizing the era also became bestsellers, such as *The Ugly American* by Eugene Burdick and William Lederer, which cast an unflattering light not only on newly affluent American tourists abroad but also the entire scope of the nation's postwar international policies. "Ugly American" became a phrase that entered the language, defined as a citizen of the United States in a foreign land whose behavior is offensive to the people of that country.

During the postwar era, books by anthropologist Margaret Mead made Americans aware of the significance of "primitive" societies around the globe. While Mead was spotlighting the value of cultures around the world, many intellectuals found a culture being undervalued right in the United States—that of African Americans.

A number of works by black writers became a mainstay of postwar intellectual discussions. Greater interest in black authors by the intelligentsia was stimulated in 1949 when the Pulitzer Prize was awarded to an African American poet, Gwendolyn Brooks. She was the first black writer to win a Pulitzer.

Some intellectuals pointed out that even though the United States was the world's richest country in the postwar era, there were pervasive pockets of poverty in Appalachia and in the inner cities as well as overt racial abuses in the Jim Crow South.

However, the social issue cited most often by the intelligentsia was the lack of individuality in postwar American society. Amid the dangers of McCarthyism, many American women felt there was safety in conformity.

Against that backdrop, the intellectual life of women in postwar America took shape as they lived their daily lives.

COMMUNICATION

In 1957, the same year that the Sputnik space satellite was launched, a full-page ad appeared in major magazines. It featured Bernard Gimbel, chairman of Gimbel's Department Store in New York City, endorsing the Western Union Company by stating, "Nothing gets things done like telegrams." It featured a photographic effect that was innovative for the era, with the telegram that Gimbel held being printed in a golden color while the rest of the ad was black and white.

In the postwar era, Western Union was expanding in terms of its corporate technology. In 1959, it introduced promotions such as the candygram, a box of chocolates accompanying a telegram. The telegraph company recognized that communications in the postwar years were changing.

Still being used at the dawn of the space age, telegrams had been a familiar form of communication in America from the time of the Civil War.

According to Coe (2003), in 1865, most Americans learned that the Civil War ended via telegrams sent from a telegraph office near Appomattox, Virginia, where the surrender took place (51). During World War II and the Korean War, many American women dreaded the sight of a Western Union boy delivering the news that a father, son, or husband had been killed in action.

Telegrams were also used in the postwar era to quickly notify far-flung relatives of news such as the death of a family member. But more and more often during the postwar era, despite Mr. Gimbel's endorsement, such news was being communicated by telephone.

Starting in 1876, when Alexander Graham Bell was the first to be granted a U.S. patent for an instrument that transmitted the human voice, the telephone grew in popularity and sophistication. By the postwar era, it was something many American women found they could not do without in the course of their daily lives.

After World War II, America's telephone technology rapidly expanded to become a prime means of communication. During the early postwar era, telephones had a rotary dial on heavy desk models that were always black. Long-distance calls were costly and usually had to go through an operator. Overseas calls might take hours for the operator to make the connection.

But as the postwar years progressed, phones started to become available in various colors as well as those that could be mounted on a wall, with the kitchen being a popular spot for one to be installed. Wall-mounted telephones were often promoted to women, allowing them to cook while chatting on the phone. Extra-long phone cords allowed a housewife to move around the kitchen in the course of her daily life as she used her shining new postwar-era appliances.

Females, especially teenage girls, were seen as a prime group of consumers of the Princess telephone, which was introduced in 1959. It was a sleek model that came in many colors, had a light-up dial, and was designed for convenient use on a bedside table. For many young women of the postwar era, the Princess phone was a staple of their daily lives.

A push-button system called "touchtone" rather than rotary dialing was introduced to help accommodate an all-numerical system of phone numbers that was introduced in 1958. All-numerical dialing replaced the previous combination of words and numbers that was exemplified in a 1961 hit song called "Beechwood 4–5789."

However, while communicating by telephone was perfect for local calling, the cost of long-distance service remained high. For many women in postwar America, the U.S. Postal Service remained a prime means of communicating. Throughout most of the postwar era, a stamp to mail a standard letter or holiday card cost $0.03. According to sources tracking inflation, $0.03 in 1957 had the same purchasing power as $0.27 in 2019. When the cost of a stamp moved up to $0.04 in 1958 (or $0.36 in 2019), some people were annoyed at the additional expense, but most found that mailing a letter was a convenient way to communicate.

In many parts of the United States during the postwar era, mail was delivered twice a day. American women often wrote friendly letters filled with family news, mailed postcards from vacations, and sent thank-you notes for a gift. In December, with greeting cards arriving daily from family and friends, the Christmas season was a highly anticipated time of year. Usually, the task of writing holiday cards fell to the woman of the household.

Young women often corresponded with pen pals across the country as well as around the world. Some women received subscription newspapers though the mail, perhaps from a now-distant hometown after they moved to the suburbs. Many postwar women subscribed to magazines. Gallagher (2017) notes that while postwar-era women had many ways to communicate, and "as much as they loved their radios, telephones and televisions . . . they devoured [magazines such as] the *Saturday Evening Post* and *Woman's Day*" (239).

In the course of their daily lives, women in postwar America did indeed enjoy their radios. For many housewives isolated in suburban homes, it was similar to having the voice of a friendly visitor around the house. Rader (2012) states that postwar radio executives "realized they had a captive and potentially enormous audience in housewives" (54), feeling that radio had an advantage over television where women were concerned. Rader quotes Pat Weaver, president of the National Broadcasting Company (NBC), saying that "radio [is] more like a companion" (54). Radio did not demand attention to be focused on a television screen, making it easy for women to cook, clean, and take care of their daily household tasks while listening to radio broadcasts.

Still, as the postwar years went on, times were rapidly changing for the radio industry. According to Ramsburg (2012), "radio's audience was moving out of the home and into cars" (216) as people listened in their automobiles on the way to work or to go shopping. However, Ramsburg adds that during the postwar era, daytime radio programming still "had millions of listeners and was highly profitable" (21).

But as in the movie industry, radio found itself struggling against an unstoppable force, the powerful new communication medium of the postwar era called television.

Even though daytime television required some level of attention while housewives were taking care of daily tasks around the home, television was a growing means of communication for women during the postwar years.

To attract a female audience, some television broadcasters sought to build on the success of NBC TV's popular *Today* show by producing daytime programming with more of what was seen as a woman's angle. In 1954, a program called *Home* began airing in the midmorning hours. Charles L. Ponce de Leon (2015) states it was aimed at middle-class housewives, offering a mix of "fashion, cooking, decorating, childrearing, and travel" (34). Although the cohost was a male, *Home* boasted female TV personality Arlene Francis as its "femcee" (34). According to de Leon, Francis persisted in also bringing viewers harder news topics such as divorce and juvenile delinquency. The show was cancelled in 1957.

Other daytime programming aimed at postwar housewives aimed higher than what many considered to be lowbrow entertainment. Cassidy (2005) states that the question was whether television was to be a mere extension "of radio's designated feminine sphere, replicating soap opera, audience participation shows, game shows, and sob shows, or [whether it would be] a site for superior programming that offered women cultural uplift" (215).

Televised communication to women included top-ranked daytime programs such as *Arthur Godfrey Time* and *Art Linkletter's House Party*, both variety shows. They joined innumerable soap operas, many of which stayed on television for decades.

The culturally uplifting *Matinee Theater*, debuting on NBC in 1955, was a daily anthology show featuring original material as well as adaptations of literary classics. The midafternoon show, with serious presentations such as *Wuthering Heights*, was usually performed live. It featured major stars as well as performers on their way up. The culturally uplifting *Matinee Theater* was cancelled in 1958.

Some television programmers sought to communicate with the growing Hispanic population in the United States. "Telenovelas," which are dramas or soap operas produced primarily by Latin Americans, combine the word "tele" (for television) and "novela" (a story). In 1957, Mexico produced a drama serial in the telenovela format called *Senda Prohibida* ("Forbidden Path") that could be seen in the Southwestern United States.

Singer Hazel Scott was the first African American to host a television program in the United States. *The Hazel Scott Show* premiered on the DuMont Television Network in 1950, but Scott, an outspoken civil rights activist, came to the attention of House Un-American Activities Committee (HUAC) during the McCarthy era. She was blacklisted, and her show was cancelled after only a few months on the air.

Communication to black audiences via television was limited in the postwar era. Apart from Hazel Scott, the few female African American television performers were generally those who portrayed servants, such as on the situation comedy *Beulah*, which premiered in 1950.

As in the previous cases, some niche programming attempted to communicate with women in American society who lived daily lives that were different from white middle-class suburban housewives. However, it was white suburban housewives at whom a major portion of the postwar communications media was aimed.

One example is the "woman's magazine," a prime means of communication with women in postwar America in the course of their daily lives. Although there had been a few such publications throughout American history such as *Godey's Lady's Book* dating back to 1830, women's magazines became extremely popular in the era following World War II.

In most suburban homes, there was some combination of *Better Homes and Gardens, Family Circle, Good Housekeeping, Ladies' Home Journal, McCall's, Redbook, Woman's Day,* and *Woman's Home Companion.* Women's magazines, edited almost exclusively by males, reinforced the idea of female Americans devoting their lives to being housewives and mothers.

Many women, ill at ease with the changing world and unsure of the new suburban lifestyle of the postwar era, found women's magazines to be handy instructional guides. Ogden (1986) states that after "the image makers in the magazines, on the radio, and on television guided girls toward their wedding days and their tidy houses in the suburbs" (174), women's magazines continued communicating information to shape them as wives, mothers, and especially consumers in their daily lives.

The information being communicated by a typical woman's magazine of the postwar era usually included items on fashion and hairstyles as well as entertaining at home. Recipes for hearty family meals and mouthwatering desserts were followed by items on how women could lose weight. There might also be poems, short stories, or condensations of books.

An average issue might even include an item on a semi-controversial subject, often something to do with sex, such as how a woman could overcome her "frigidity." There might be an advice column, often regarding how a woman could cure problems in her marriage. Above all, there were advertisements. The overriding message to be communicated in most women's magazines, both through ads and articles, was that women could improve their daily lives by purchasing advertisers' products.

Some publishers recognized that there were other groups of women in postwar America beyond white middle-class suburbanites. *Ebony* magazine, aimed at African Americans, was launched in 1945, joined in 1951 by a smaller weekly digest called *Jet. Hue* began publication in 1953, the same year as *Copper Romance.*

Two publications were aimed at communicating specifically with black women. "Home Magazine" in *Tan Confessions* ran from 1950 to 1952, with *Aframerican Woman's Journal* running from before World War II until 1954.

The message that seemed to be communicated to an average African American woman of the postwar era strongly suggested that black women should aim to be like whites. They could do this by purchasing the same products as whites, along with those aimed directly at blacks such as hair straighteners and skin lighteners.

Communication aimed at women in postwar America was also included in daily newspapers, especially the Sunday edition. With articles presumed be of interest to women, they were called the "Style Section," "Women's Pages," "Women's Section," or some combination such as "WomaNews." In newspaper parlance of the postwar years, these were the "4-F" pages: family, fashion, food, and furnishings.

But the postwar era had an added dimension that previous decades did not: a few daring female reporters who had covered World War II. These women returned home to find their only employment in journalism to be in the women's pages. As the post-war era wore on, some tried to ease the women's section toward including what they felt were more substantive issues.

This new breed of female journalists wanted to write news stories that they felt were important to communicate to average women who were being transformed as the postwar era wore on. They tried to convince their editors to allow them to move beyond trivial topics by also including exposés of such issues as domestic abuse and the movement toward reproductive rights.

One woman did not have to ask approval from any editor. Doro-thy Buffum "Buff" Chandler's family owned the *Los Angeles Times*. Referring to the way Buff Chandler transformed the newspaper's Style section, Halberstam (1979) states, "The importance of what she did in the women's pages should not be underestimated in the history of contemporary Los Angeles" (272). Under Buff Chandler in the 1950s, the women's section in the *Los Angeles Times* began to change as Chandler "featured a new kind of woman, a doer, an activist who was a community leader" (273). Chandler's influence communicated the idea of women leading daily lives that were not confined to the home.

Of course, there was another time-honored means of communi-cation for women of the postwar era, one that dated back to the dawn of human culture: women talking with each other. In urban environments of the postwar era, female conversation often took place on the "stoop," a short flight of steps leading to the front door of residential buildings such as apartment houses. Especially in the era before air conditioning, city women could congregate outside on the stoop as part of their daily lives to communicate (usually called "gossiping" by males) with each other.

In the suburbs, women could interact as they hung laundry out to dry on clotheslines or chat over the back fence. Even amid the sparse population in rural areas, women could communicate with each other at church or on market day in town.

Some modern advances in the postwar era, such as air conditioning and automatic clothes dryers, put a dent in such personal means of communication among women. But for many postwar women, with all the communication choices available to them, there was often nothing better in the course of their daily lives than communicating face-to-face.

EDUCATION

In the daily lives of women during the postwar years, there were two issues regarding education that were of concern to many, especially the mothers of school-age children. One looked back, and one looked forward.

The 1954 Supreme Court decision, *Brown v. Board of Education*, mandated racial desegregation in America's public schools. It addressed past race-related standards in the nation that dated back to before the Civil War. Some postwar communities reacted strongly against desegregation, closing their public schools rather than admit African American children, who had been attending all-black schools that were often substandard. There were white families who were able to send their children to private schools or newly founded "segregation academies," but many average women could not. They were concerned about their children's education if the public schools were closed indefinitely.

The other issue involving education in the postwar years was grounded in the futuristic era of the space age. There was concern among observers that American schools were not keeping pace with the Russians, especially in science and technology. Alarming books and articles were being written, claiming that the nation was at risk of its children falling behind, barely able to read. In 1958, Congress passed the National Defense Education Act to provide scholarships in the areas of science, engineering, and math, although those fields were not generally open to females.

Some African American women were able to attend college, generally at a historically black institution. Many became teachers, often limited to working in segregated schools for African American children, such as the one pictured here. In 1954, the *Brown v. Board of Education* decision directed America's public schools to integrate. (Library of Congress)

In the past, there were many generations of American women for whom educational issues did not exist. That was because there was little education of any kind for a woman. The postwar years of the 1950s would start to change that, but there was a lot of history to overcome.

In colonial New England, girls were provided with a rudimentary education in the town's public school. They were taught to read on an elementary level so they could study the Bible and read it to their children. Few girls went beyond that.

In the Southern colonies, there were not many public schools. Instead, there were a few small private academies, often religiously based. Individual families who were wealthy enough to afford it often hired private tutors to provide home schooling. Many girls in the Southern colonies were at least taught to read the Bible. However, they generally did not receive the same type of classical education as boys. Girls were taught by their mothers or other female relatives in how to run a home.

Between the American Revolution and World War II, the population of the United States continued to grow along with a trend toward more education for its citizens. Women made some gains by demanding the right to greater educational opportunities. However, the degree of education often depended on the individual's gender and race.

Throughout the 20th century, more public schools were built in large cities. Isolated rural areas often had a local one-room schoolhouse where children of both genders and various age groups were taught at the same time. Girls rarely progressed beyond what would today be considered an eighth-grade education.

After World War II, continuing the general trend in 20th-century American education, girls were steered into coursework designed for females such as home economics. There they learned things such as cooking, sewing, and proper cleaning techniques. It was assumed that a woman would marry and spend her daily life as a housewife. However, unless a girl was able to find a husband who would provide for her and her children for the rest of their lives, she was often left without marketable skills apart from entering domestic service.

Some secondary schools offered classes available to girls in vocational areas such as secretarial skills so they might find work in the clerical field. However, women were expected to quit when they married. It was compulsory for most to lose their jobs when they became pregnant, once again rendering the woman dependent on a man to provide for her and her children.

Throughout much of American history, college for women seemed a remote possibility at best. Founded in 1833, Oberlin College in Oberlin, Ohio, was the first college in the United States to accept both women and African American students.

A huge step forward for the potential of college education of women took place in 1862 with the Morrill Land-Grant Colleges Act. It provided for the creation of universities to educate both men and women (henceforth called "co-eds," referring to the coeducational facilities that admitted them). However, courses for women were generally focused on the fields of home economics and social work. By the year 1870, still only about a third of American colleges accepted women.

As the 20th century wore on, more women attempted to better themselves by going to college. There, they might be able to join one of the three acceptable career paths for educated women: secretaries, teachers, or nurses.

Well into the early 20th century, doctors and other male authority figures claimed that higher education for women would render females unfit for bearing children. The end result for women who attended college, they warned, would be malformed outsized skulls containing monstrous brains that were affixed to feeble, barren bodies.

Even in the mid-20th-century world of the postwar years, the negative term "bluestocking" was applied to college-educated women who were perceived as intellectuals, being dubbed "frumpy." In the postwar years, there was a common perception that college-educated women were less likely to marry, being branded as "too old" or "set in their ways." Even more dangerous under the McCarthyism of the postwar era was the slur that college-educated women were "man-haters," which was a coded phrase regarding their sexuality.

To avoid those labels, some women went to college specifically to find a husband. Well into the 1950s, with many times more men on college campuses than women, there was a good likelihood of that happening.

There was often an economic factor that hampered average women who sought to attend college. Many families did not have the financial means to send their daughters. Some young women were expected to work in order to help pay college tuition for a brother. Many college scholarships were limited to males only.

For a great number of African American women, a college education was out of the question. However, some aspired to a field such as teaching, often limited to finding a job in a segregated public school for African American children. Bennett College, a historically black college for women in Greensboro, North Carolina, was founded in 1873. Spelman College in Atlanta, also a historically black college for women, was established in 1881.

Women of all racial backgrounds who lived in rural areas often found their educational opportunities to be more severely limited than those of city women. Many attended a local one-room schoolhouse, although it was generally felt that education—certainly higher education—for a female was unnecessary.

But some, including future Senator Hattie Caraway, the first woman elected to the U.S. Senate, found a way. According to Hendricks (2013), Caraway was "aware that a lack of education, especially for women, meant being trapped on the farm" (19). As farm families struggled to make a living amid the vagaries of weather and fluctuating crop prices, a woman could expect to repeatedly bear children along with enduring constant backbreaking physical labor. Caraway's only female role model for a different kind of life was the young woman who was her teacher at the one-room schoolhouse, and she was determined to become an educator herself. With financial help from a "maiden aunt," Caraway was able to attend college. She found education to be her ticket out of poverty on the farm.

By the post–World War II era, some young women had their own financial resources based on their earnings for performing war work in the 1940s. Many who been hired by defense industries during World War II had saved enough money to provide for their college education during peacetime.

Still, even in the 1950s, some women encountered resistance on college campuses. In an oral history shared with this author, a postwar-era woman who enjoyed mathematics went to college, hoping to work in a field where she could use her math skills. One professor who taught an entry-level math class believed that women had no place in mathematics, pelting female students with chalk until they left the room and dropped the course. His hostility toward women students and habit of bombarding them was well known on campus. Yet he was never disciplined; in fact, the school named its college library for him.

There were other kinds of incidents suffered by postwar women who sought higher education. Future Supreme Court justice Ruth Bader Ginsburg entered Harvard Law School in 1956 as one of nine women in a class of over 500 men. She and the other women were invited to dinner at the dean's home with several of their professors. According to Hope (2003), after dinner, the women were told to justify why they were at Harvard Law School "taking the place of a man" (105).

As related in Gilbert and Moore (1981), Justice Ginsburg said that women students during her time at law school had to be on their guard constantly for the so-called Ladies Days when the few female law students in class were asked complex questions that were designed to humiliate them in front of all the men.

Still, women of the postwar era persevered. While many acceded to the messages from the government and mass media to live their daily lives at home by being housewives, others sought to carve a new path for themselves through education. According to DuBois and Dumenil (2008), in 1950, American women received

23.9 percent of bachelor's degrees and 9.7 percent of doctorates. By 1960, those numbers had risen to 35 and 10.5 percent, respectively. While the numbers still lagged behind males, the trend for women's education was on the rise.

For some postwar women, it was too late for their own education, but as the years progressed, there was greater hope for their daughters. One major milestone directly involving education for women in postwar America did not take place until the 1970s.

Arguably, no breakthrough was more significant for women's education in the late postwar era than the passage of Title IX of the Education Amendments Act of 1972. This federal law outlawed discrimination against anyone based on their gender in federally funded educational programs in America. An early draft was authored by Representative Patsy Mink with the assistance of Representative Edith Green. When the bill was passed in 1972, there were two women serving in the Senate and 13 in the House of Representatives, most of whom had come of age during the postwar era of the 1950s.

Many of the young women who enrolled in college during the 1950s often did so to earn what they called the Mrs. degree (pronounced "M-R-S"); in other words, they were hoping to find a husband. With a national average of about nine men to every woman on college campuses in the early postwar era, the odds appeared favorable.

Some women, either by intention or default, slowly began entering career paths in the 1950s that had traditionally been the exclusive domain of males.

Future Supreme Court justice Ginsburg was one of those. However, even after she graduated at the top of her law school class at both Harvard and Columbia, no law firm would hire her, openly stating that it was because she was a woman. Another future Supreme Court justice, Sandra Day O'Connor, was also a top student who attended law school in the 1950s. She experienced the same inability to find a job at a law firm because of her gender. Both women ultimately settled for clerical positions, with O'Connor starting out with no salary.

After the 1954 *Brown v. Board of Education* decision, came greater emphasis on civil rights for all citizens of the United States. Things slowly began to change as many Americans sought equality as guaranteed by the Constitution regardless of race or gender.

Some postwar women left the restricted sphere of their daily lives to become involved in education during the 1950s in unexpected ways. In 1957, nine African American students, including six young women, sought to lawfully attend the all-white Central High School in Little Rock, Arkansas.

The state's segregationist governor responded by deploying the Arkansas National Guard to keep them out. He ultimately ordered public schools in the city to be closed rather than admit black students. A group of socially prominent women organized the Women's Emergency Committee to Open Our Schools. More than 1,400 women ultimately joined the group. Despite harassment and death threats, the women spoke publicly in favor of reopening Little Rock's public schools, fully integrating them, and removing segregationists from the Little Rock school board. After their success in Little Rock, they advocated for educational issues as well as advising similar groups in cities such as Atlanta and New Orleans into the 1960s.

The members of the Women's Emergency Committee to Open Our Schools stepped well beyond the assigned roles of their daily lives in postwar society. They served as an example to young women who were being inspired by the civil rights movement.

But for many women in the postwar years, regardless of education, their daily life was confined to the home. According to Brett Harvey (1993), women who were fortunate enough to attend college in the postwar era aspired to "the classic ideal of a college education: opening of the mind, exposure to new challenging ideas, development of the ego and identity necessary to function in the world" (45). But Harvey asks, "What use was all this to someone who would then spend most of her time tending small children, cleaning her house, and entertaining her husband's boss?" (45).

HEALTH AND HEALTHCARE

In many ways, issues involving health and healthcare in the daily lives of American women in the postwar era was an improvement over that of their mothers and grandmothers. Until the passage of the Food, Drug, and Cosmetic Act in 1938, women and children were routinely prescribed such addictive drugs as laudanum, morphine, and opium for minor conditions. An advertisement in the 1890s promised a syrup that would provide inexpensive relief of children's coughs. The syrup was marketed as Bayer Heroin, which is exactly what it was.

Even women's cosmetics could be a minefield in the first half of the 20th century. A brand of mascara called Lash Lure was found to cause blindness from its dangerous chemical composition. Gourauds's Oriental Cream, billed as "Beauty's Master Touch" left women's faces disfigured by the effects of poisoning from the mercury it contained. A product to remove body hair, which women were told was hideous, contained the active ingredient in rat poison, causing side effects in human females including paralysis. With predictably damaging results to women, Lysol advertisements through the early 1950s hinted at its use as an internal feminine hygiene product and contraceptive in addition to its corrosive power in cleaning toilets.

After the federal Food, Drug, and Cosmetic Act was passed in 1938, quality standards were set for many products in what had previously been an unregulated field. Still, even some approved health-related products came with a downside.

In the postwar years, doctor-prescribed hormone replacement therapy (HRT) helped alleviate women's discomfort during menopause, the end of her reproductive capability. However, women on HRT were found to have a higher risk of blood clots, breast cancer, heart attack, and strokes.

Many women in postwar America were screened for cervical cancer by undergoing the Pap test, which could detect precancerous changes in the cells of a woman's cervix. However, some women avoided it, finding the invasive procedure to be painful and humiliating at the hands of their doctors—almost all of whom were male.

Having few options for birth control, each sexual act could easily mean pregnancy for a postwar American woman. Marriage was said to be the societally approved natural state for women, but being married meant submitting to sex on demand. Motherhood often took place nine months after the wedding night. One notable couple, Elvis and Priscilla Presley, were married on May 1, 1967; their daughter Lisa Marie was born exactly nine months later, on February 1, 1968.

Many women of the postwar era describe having multiple children uncomfortably close together. While many certainly enjoyed motherhood, having so many offspring so close together was not an optimal situation either for the women or their children.

One possibility—if the husband gave permission to her doctor—was for a woman to obtain an awkward, unpleasant contraceptive diaphragm that had to be inserted into her body before each sexual encounter.

Finding information on other types of contraception that a female could control was not an option. Through an 1873 act of the U.S.

Congress known as the "Comstock Laws," contraceptives were banned as obscene, making it a federal offense to distribute birth control information. The Comstock Laws were enforced until 1965 when they were found to be unconstitutional by restricting the right to privacy.

The point actually became moot in 1960, when the U.S. Food and Drug Administration (FDA) announced approval of an oral contraceptive tablet for birth control, later simply abbreviated as "the Pill."

Some husbands forbade their wives from using birth control. Doctors usually required the husband's permission before prescribing the Pill for a woman. But for many females, for the first time in human history, millions of American women in the postwar era had a safe, effective means to be part of the decision when or if to become pregnant.

Despite opposition from social conservatives and religious groups, in a 1965 Supreme Court ruling, married couples in the United States received the right to use birth control. It was denied to millions of other women until 1972, three years after men landed on the Moon, when the Supreme Court legalized birth control for all U.S. citizens regardless of marital status.

For those women in postwar America who became pregnant, there were a number of dangers in their daily lives of which many were unaware. One was smoking cigarettes during pregnancy. Along with general health issues for humans, studies found that tobacco use by pregnant women often resulted in miscarriages and health risks to the unborn baby. When a 1952 article appeared in the popular magazine *Reader's Digest* titled "Cancer by the Carton," there was tremendous backlash by the tobacco industry, which sought to discredit the researchers.

Some doctors, almost all of whom were male, encouraged women to smoke during pregnancy to calm their nerves or to keep their weight down, since being thin would help them remain attractive to their husband even during pregnancy. Some physicians warned pregnant women *not* to quit smoking, claiming it would be too stressful on her body to stop. Smoking about four cigarettes per day (almost 1,500 a year) was the usual recommendation for expectant mothers by doctors. Brandt (2007) states this guideline was often based on what were called various "new studies" (160), many of which were funded by the tobacco industry and released periodically to garner confusion.

It was not until 1981, well after the immediate postwar era, that expectant mothers were warned about consuming alcohol during pregnancy. Studies found that fetal alcohol syndrome resulting from the unborn child being exposed to alcohol during the mother's pregnancy could cause birth defects, growth problems, learning disabilities, and irreversible brain damage. According to Golden, "in the early 1950s, doctors discovered new applications for alcohol in their obstetrical practices" (32) for the relief of pain. Among the results, "patients became euphoric, pain was relieved, and [they felt that] alcohol, because it was a food, provided nourishment" (33). Often the baby appeared to be born healthy, although the effects of fetal alcohol syndrome usually cannot be diagnosed in a child until well after it is born.

A nightmarish issue for many women that emerged in the late 1950s was the damage done by the drug thalidomide, which pregnant women took for morning sickness. Taking the drug resulted in severe birth defects, such as babies being born without arms and legs. Hundreds of doctors in the United States received samples of thalidomide during the clinical testing period and provided it to their patients. Thalidomide was withdrawn from the market in 1961, but not before news photos of children with no arms and/or legs gave nightmares to many American mothers-to-be.

As bad as the thalidomide tragedy was, there was one disease that especially produced nightmares in American mothers: polio. For decades, polio, also called infantile paralysis, ravaged healthy children, seemingly overnight. Women were terrified by pictures of youngsters in iron lungs, which victims needed to keep breathing. With no one sure how polio was transmitted, mothers lived in dread that their children would catch the disease. No child was immune. In 1952, there was an especially deadly polio epidemic across the United States. Tens of thousands of American children succumbed. Young patients who survived the disease returned to school in wheelchairs or on leg braces. Many were left with wasted, crippled limbs for the rest of their lives.

However, in 1953 came what many women considered a miracle: the Salk vaccine. Named for Dr. Jonas Salk, the vaccine was administered to millions of children in public schools. In a relatively short time, the scourge of polio was virtually eliminated in the United States.

However, in the Cold War era, politics became a factor. According to Oshinsky (2006), there were opponents to the polio immunization program. The prospect of "vaccinating children *en masse*, free of charge, [led] to a furious debate about the perils of 'socialized medicine'" (7), which was considered Communistic.

Another health hazard for postwar women and their unborn children was the danger of contracting German measles, also called rubella, during pregnancy. An expectant mother becoming inadvertently exposed to rubella could result in miscarriage or stillbirth. The disease could also be responsible for brain damage to the unborn child.

Many postwar scientists who worked in the medical field painstakingly sought solutions to the healthcare issues that affected women of the era. However, one element that impacted the health and healthcare of women in postwar America in a less than desirable way came from an unlikely source: their own doctors. Ehrenreich and English (2010) state that postwar-era women were "subjected to both insensitive and hazardous treatment: unnecessary hysterectomies, over-medicated childbirth, involuntary sterilizations, and the almost universal condescension of male doctors" (8). The authors state that females of that era were not supposed to know anything about their own bodies or participate in their own care. Women who asked too many questions of their doctors—virtually all males—including those about pregnancy (a state that males never experienced) "found themselves labeled, right in their medical records, as uncooperative or neurotic" (8).

At any stage of pregnancy, especially the latter stage, any number of things can go wrong. The woman's energy is drained. Resistance to contagious disease is weakened. Her swollen body is weighed down, and it is hard for her to sleep, with no position being comfortable.

Once in labor, the exhausting process of giving birth to the baby could last for hours or even days. Possible complications for the woman included blood loss, infections such as postpartum sepsis, dangerously high blood pressure, obstructed labor, and organ damage. There were hazards to postwar women from anesthesia, deep sedation, episiotomies, hemorrhaging, and damage to both mother and child from the doctor's use of large metal tongs called forceps to extract the baby from her body.

Midwives who were utilized by poor women in the postwar era were often found to provide healthcare during childbirth that was at least as good if not better than hospitals. But in general, the level of healthcare for women of the postwar era, pregnant or otherwise, often depended on their socioeconomic level and access to health insurance.

Women of the postwar era who survived into the latter stages of life encountered other challenges. Many looked forward to the time when they would no longer suffer from painful monthly menstrual periods or run the risk of becoming pregnant. That late-life transition for women, called menopause, arrived with its own set of problems.

Long the subject of jokes by male comedians, menopause was not funny to the postwar women enduring it. Typical effects of menopause could include anxiety, chills, depression, difficulty concentrating, dry skin, hot flashes, insomnia, irritability, hair loss, memory problems, slowed metabolism, and weight gain. Often a woman's marriage might suffer when she experienced painful intercourse due to vaginal dryness.

In the 1950s, some doctors used radiation on women to deal with menopause. The doctors approached it in terms of how it affected the woman's husband, such as her loss of sex drive or diminishment of her youthful-looking attractiveness to him.

Some aspects of health and healthcare for American women in the late postwar era improved with the increase in the number of females in the medical field, a profession that had traditionally been barred to women. According to the Yale University Library, from 1930 to 1970, a period of 40 years, about 14,000 women graduated from medical school. But from 1970 to 1980, a period of only 10 years, more than 20,000 women graduated from medical school.

Much of this increase could be attributed to the passage of Title IX of the Higher Education Act Amendments in 1972, which prohibited educational institutions who received federal funds, including medical schools, from discrimination based on gender. Within two years of Title IX's passage, the percentage of women entering American medical schools more than doubled.

After Title IX, one area of medical practice that saw an increase in female practitioners was gynecology, which deals with women's healthcare. Many women patients found a female doctor to better understand their health issues, with the doctor having experienced many of them herself.

In the postwar era, there was not much many women could do about health-related issues such as domestic abuse by their husbands. Male authority figures such as the police often expressed the assumption that it was the woman's fault for "provoking" her husband. There were few laws at the time to protect battered women, and "wife beating" was not a subject most people talked about.

Sometimes, in response to the stress of living with domestic abuse or the frustration of spending their life confined at home, many women in postwar America were prescribed psychological drugs such as tranquilizers. The pills, with trade names such as Miltown, were often called "Mother's little helpers," although men took them in equal numbers.

With expensive new medical equipment being developed in the postwar era, a challenge for many women came with sharply rising costs in healthcare. For poor women, widows, the elderly, or others of the postwar era who did not have access to medical insurance through the workplace, paying for healthcare became an obstacle. To help alleviate the situation, Medicare was enacted in 1966 despite the vehement opposition of social conservatives, insurance companies, and the American Medical Association who called it "socialized medicine."

Health and healthcare for women in postwar America was sometimes less than ideal. But starting in 1960, despite religious concerns, they had the option for something no female in thousands of years of human history had dared to dream: a contraceptive pill that was a safe, effective way for a woman to be part of the decision when or if she would bear children.

LITERATURE

In the course of their daily lives, women in postwar America had a number of choices when it came to entertainment and information, including the novelty of television. Even with that electronic marvel, books retained their popularity through the postwar years.

Some aspects of traditional "women's work" had been alleviated by shiny new postwar-era appliances such as washing machines and vacuum cleaners. Therefore, increased leisure time was within reach for many women. In addition, after the poverty of the Great Depression of the 1930s and the austerity of the World War II era in the 1940s, many women in postwar America had access to some degree of disposable income for the first time in their lives. Often, it was part of a household "allowance" that housewives received from their husbands, but if a woman budgeted carefully, it could be hers to spend on items such as books.

Many women of the postwar era, especially those in the newly developed suburbs, were living far from their original hometown and were trying to navigate through the uncertainties of their new lifestyle. There were books on cooking, decorating, entertaining, and fashion. There was even a guide to childcare, such as the best-selling book by Dr. Benjamin Spock, instructing them in how to perform their role as mothers.

Some women spent the majority of their daily lives isolated at home tending small children. They often welcomed the chance to find respite from bickering youngsters by escaping into a book that was less instructional. Some wanted to appear cul-

Lorraine Hansberry (pictured here) was the first African American female playwright to have a show performed on Broadway. Her best-known work, *A Raisin in the Sun*, made its Broadway debut in 1959. The show was a major hit, dramatizing the daily lives of an average African American woman and her family as they experienced racial segregation. (Library of Congress)

tured and sophisticated among friends; one way to do that was through reading. With the advance of postwar technology, publishing companies found economical ways to produce mainstream books, allowing a wider array of works to be marketed. Postwar women proved to be a prime audience.

For those women who were on a budget, inexpensive mass-market paperback editions were increasingly successful in the postwar years. Paperbound books could be conveniently purchased in places that women frequented, such as pharmacies and grocery stores. In addition, many women found the small size of paperback books to fit conveniently in a purse.

Women might hear of the latest bestsellers on radio or television, in newspapers and magazines, or from their friends. There were many to choose from, as the postwar years became a golden age for publishing in the United States. The 1950s produced mainstream bestsellers that became classics, such as *Advise and Consent, Doctor Zhivago, East of Eden, From Here to Eternity, Lord of the Flies,* and *The Man in the Gray Flannel Suit.* [Authors and publication dates for books cited in this section can be found in Appendix A.]

Some books of the postwar era contained content that was considered shocking. Some had main characters who were female. A few had both, such as the shocking females in *Lady Chatterley's Lover, Lolita,* and *Peyton Place.*

There were also voices reflecting the African American experience in the United States. They could be found in works by black authors in the postwar era such as *Another Country, Black Like Me, Invisible Man,* and *Notes of a Native Son.*

Amid the optimism and prosperity of the 1950s, some books of the era took a critical look at postwar American culture, such as *The Affluent Society, The Hidden Persuaders, The Organization Man, and The Other America: Poverty in the United States.*

A postwar novel called *The Catcher in the Rye* was said by some critics to promote youthful rebellion and disrespect of authority, traits that were frowned upon in the 1950s. Some social conservatives pointed the finger of blame at women who sought outlets for themselves in the wider world. The critics maintained that if mothers stayed at home raising their children properly, the future of America's next generation could be saved.

Others looked to a different kind of future. The novel *Atlas Shrugged* promoted a capitalist economy based on individualism in contrast to business owners facing laws and regulations they felt were burdensome. It came as a surprise to many that author Ayn Rand was a woman.

Fahrenheit 451 was a postwar-era novel that portrayed a dystopian world of the future in which books are banned, censored, and destroyed by the government's book-burners, called "firemen." Citizens in *Fahrenheit 451* are discouraged from thinking, instead becoming mindless followers. Although two female characters are significant to the plot, one simply voices her belief that the world was not always that way, while the other is a housewife who does little but stay in the family home. Some observers found it ironic that *Fahrenheit 451* itself became banned in the United States.

A trend that evolved during the postwar era was the number of female authors whose books became bestsellers. They included *Bonjour Tristesse* by Françoise Sagan, *Désirée* by Annemarie Selinko, *The Guns of August* by Barbara Tuchman, *My Cousin Rachel* by Daphne du Maurier, *The Prime of Miss Jean Brodie* by Muriel Spark, *Ship of Fools* by Katherine Anne Porter, *Silent Spring* by Rachel Carson, and *To Kill a Mockingbird* by Harper Lee.

Two popular books heralded the immense changes that would affect the daily lives of women in postwar American society. Betty Friedan's *The Feminine Mystique* and Helen Gurley Brown's *Sex and the Single Girl* were both bestsellers that became cultural touchstones.

Sylvia Plath's novel *The Bell Jar* dealt with issues for postwar-era women including the demands of family versus selfhood, quest for identity, sexual double standards, and female power (or lack of same).

Elizabeth Janeway's postwar novels also focused on the struggles of women in society. She began writing potboilers such as 1945's *Daisy Kenyon* about a woman in a romantic triangle. But by the late postwar era, she was writing more pointedly in works that included *Man's World, Woman's Place: A Study of Social Mythology*.

With works in the 1950s such as *A Shower of Summer Days* and *Faithful Are the Wounds*, May Sarton was noted for her use of erotic female imagery as she addressed themes of gender and sexuality.

In the course of their daily lives, postwar women might also read works from the era that have since become classics, often surprising readers that they were written by female authors. Patricia Highsmith's *Strangers on a Train* took on a dark tone with one of its themes being how an average person can be convinced to commit murder.

Shirley Jackson's novel *The Haunting of Hill House* is said by many critics to have revolutionized the modern ghost story. Jackson's short story "The Lottery" continues to shock readers to this day, with its key theme being the danger of blind conformity. According to Hale (2020), "Jackson's dark aesthetic mined the quiet tensions of wifehood in postwar America and specifically her own tumultuous marriage to create chilling psychological horror" (7).

Those women reflected the writers of the era cited by Van Doren (2008) when he stated that postwar authors had "more than just chronology in common . . . [they] were aware of the great change that was occurring" (434) in American society.

Some postwar women discovered earlier writings such as those by African American author Zora Neale Hurston. Her novel *Their Eyes Were Watching God* explores the journey of a teenage girl pursuing her destiny.

Readers might also peruse Lorraine Hansberry's essays in the postwar African American journal *Freedom*. Hansberry's writings railed against limitations based on gender or race. When her play *A Raisin in the Sun* opened on Broadway in 1959, Hansberry brought the black experience to all types of audiences.

Van Doren (2008) includes Toni Morrison as an important postwar woman of color who was writing throughout the 1950s and 1960s, although her breakthrough came with her novel, *Song of Solomon*, which was not published until the 1970s. He states, "Morrison embodies the African American voice" (495), seeing the reality of life in America from both the inside and the outside.

A group who definitely felt themselves to be outsiders belonged to the emerging movement in postwar society called the Beats. They expressed solid support for African American culture as well as experimental alternative lifestyles that did not conform to the expectations of postwar society. Works by some Beat authors became unlikely bestsellers, such as Allen Ginsberg's *Howl*, Jack Kerouac's *On the Road*, and *Naked Lunch* by William S. Burroughs. What women in postwar America usually did *not* find among the Beats were female authors. Knight (1996) claims that for the most part, the women of the Beat generation "stayed underground" (1).

In the course of the daily lives of average postwar women, one of the main sources of discovering literature of the era came from popular magazines. In addition to *Life* and *Look*, bestsellers were often serialized in top women's magazines of the time such as *Good Housekeeping*, *Ladies' Home Journal*, and *McCall's*.

For those postwar women whose daily lives did not permit a lot of time for books or magazines, whose reading skills might be limited, or who simply enjoyed brief articles, there was a popular monthly magazine called *Reader's Digest*. Its conveniently small size consisted of 30 articles per issue, allowing the reader to look at one per day. Along with funny, uplifting snippets in features such as "Humor in Uniform" and "Life in these United States," there was a vocabulary page aimed at self-improvement. Toward the end of each month's issue, there was a condensation from a current book or a lengthy article that often explored issues of the day. *Reader's Digest* was the publication that printed the 1952 article, "Cancer by the Carton," the first exposé of the health hazards of cigarettes, setting off a national debate.

For those who preferred to have books sent conveniently to their home, several programs gained increased popularity in the postwar era. They were especially popular with women who lived in new suburbs with no nearby public libraries. The Book of the Month Club and the Literary Guild regularly provided new books that they deemed to be of interest to their subscribers.

In 1947, a group of intellectuals formed the Great Books Foundation to promote what they considered to be worthy books beyond the bestseller lists, exposing readers to intellectual ideas. One of the foundation's goals was to guide its readers into forming discussion groups in schools, libraries, and community centers.

Some women in postwar America did not need to be directed into forming groups. They did it themselves through book clubs.

Since before the American Revolution, book clubs in the United States have traditionally been a stronghold of women's ideas as well as a form of socialization. Among male authority figures, women's book clubs have also been suspected of fostering subversive female thoughts.

Benjamin Franklin's book club for men called the Junto, created in 1727, is often credited as the first in the nation. However, in 1634, Anne Hutchinson organized a discussion group for female colonists to examine religious texts, even before their ship landed at the Massachusetts Bay Colony. After arriving, Hutchinson continued to keep a women's reading group organized. However, by 1638, she found herself banished by Governor John Winthrop, quoted in Gunn (1994), for the crime of maintaining "a meeting and an assembly" in her home, something that was "not comely in the sight of God nor fitting for your sex" (159).

The book clubs formed by women in postwar America fared better. Estimates indicate that millions of women belonged to at least one book club in the postwar years. In the suburbs, they were often held in private homes. Some women brought their children with them if they were unable to find a babysitter.

There are several works that were often adopted by book clubs as well as being popular among individual readers. These books are worthy of special note, as they pertain to women of the postwar era.

In 1954 and again in 1961, the film version of *Gone with the Wind* (GWTW) was reissued to movie theaters around the nation after its initial release in 1939. Some women of the postwar era were inspired to read or reread the Civil War–based novel. Even if they had read it as young women, as adults in the postwar era, they focused with more mature eyes on GWTW's strong female character, Scarlett O'Hara. They saw how the fictional Scarlett resisted what was considered a woman's proper place in the 1860s, which in many ways was not too different from their own.

Published during the latter part of World War II, the novel *Forever Amber* was, on the surface, a historical romance set in 17th-century England. It also happened to feature overt female sexuality. Its author, Kathleen Winsor, followed up with the semiautobiographical *Star Money*. The heroines in both of her books sought their own path, living not through husbands and children but forging their own identity.

One book caused as much of a stir in the postwar era for its headstrong female characters as *Gone with the Wind* and *Forever Amber* had done. It was the semiautobiographical *Peyton Place* by Grace Metalious. This 1956 blockbuster novel was condemned by social conservatives for the independence of its women characters as well as its frank depiction of female sexuality. *Marjorie Morningstar*, another bestseller of the postwar era, was written by a man, Herman Wouk. While the aforementioned novels written by women underscore female independence, *Morningstar* does not. Unable to achieve her goal of becoming an actress, Wouk's heroine ultimately finds her niche in life by getting married and becoming a suburban housewife. This novel, written by a man, was serialized in women's magazines, edited almost exclusively by men.

Although Rona Jaffe's *The Best of Everything*, a novel about "career girls" in New York, was written in 1958 by a woman, it was purchased for a film adaptation before the manuscript was edited. Some observers wondered if its story line may have been influenced by the men who controlled production of the 1959 movie based on the book. Much of the plot concerns single girls having love affairs with married men. Other young women, in their office, work as secretaries while waiting for marriage, their "real job." In what some saw as a cautionary tale, their female boss is still single, having become a lonely, bitter "career woman."

Even in literature, the Cold War was never far from the mainstream of women's daily lives in postwar America. Lara Prescott, author of *The Secrets We Kept* (2019), claims that America's Central Intelligence Agency (CIA) secretly helped publish Boris Pasternak's 1957 novel *Dr. Zhivago*, a popular book that was known to most average American women. *Dr. Zhivago* was banned in the

Soviet Union for alleged criticism of the Russian Revolution and the Soviet system. Books by banned Russian authors that were secretly smuggled into the USSR could show Soviet citizens the freedoms and lack of censorship enjoyed in America while also underscoring the repression under Communism.

As part of their daily lives, many women in postwar America enjoyed reading the era's current literature for entertainment, enlightenment, and escape. Few were aware of what were, in some cases, the true stories behind the books, often more dramatic than fiction.

MEDICAL ADVANCES

A number of medical advances that impacted the daily lives of women in postwar America could be categorized with the letter *P*: polio, pharmaceuticals, pregnancy, and the Pill.

A tremendous relief for postwar mothers came with the 1953 announcement that an anti-polio vaccine developed by Dr. Jonas Salk had been proven safe and effective. This announcement followed an especially deadly nationwide polio epidemic in 1952. Prior to the announcement of the Salk vaccine, postwar-era polls showed that the only thing American women feared in their daily lives more than polio was nuclear war.

The daily lives of women, especially those with children, were greatly improved by the steady medical advances taking place in pharmaceuticals. During the postwar era, childhood diseases including chicken pox, measles, mumps, and rubella (German measles) were common. Most children survived unscathed. Yet even in the post–World War II era, hundreds of American children were killed by measles, just as soldiers had died of the disease during the Civil War a century before.

During the postwar era, there was one medical condition that people simply did not talk about: cancer. Several types of the disease that affected women were especially kept under wraps, such as breast cancer or cancer of the reproductive organs such as the cervix or uterus. In 1943, just prior to the postwar era, a test developed by Dr. George Papanicolaou enabled small tissue samples to be scraped from the female reproductive system as a smear for analysis of abnormal cells that could indicate cancer. The "Pap" test was offered routinely for postwar-era women throughout their lives, reducing the number of deaths due to cervical and uterine cancer.

Since the dawn of time, pregnancy and childbirth could be risky for women. The postwar era was no different. Studies indicate that prior to World War II, a great number of American women gave birth at home, often with the assistance of midwives. However, during the postwar era, hospital births with modern equipment became more of the norm.

At the hospital, most women underwent general anesthesia during childbirth, rendering them unconscious. With mothers therefore unable to push the baby out, the doctor used large steel tongs called forceps to extract the baby, occasionally injuring the mother and/or infant in the process.

In the postwar years, there was increased interest by women in having greater control of their own childbirth process. Many learned about more pain-free "natural childbirth" based on techniques introduced in 1951 by French obstetrician Fernand Lamaze. Soon, many women in postwar America and their male partners took "Lamaze classes" that were growing in popularity.

Some women who wished to conceive but were unable to do so found themselves involved in controversy. A practice called artificial insemination became more widely available in the United States during the postwar era. However, social conservatives demanded that the procedure be banned, with some calling it a form of adultery.

For women who wanted control over when or if to become pregnant, a revolutionary medical advance was approved by the FDA in 1960. It was an oral contraceptive tablet that was soon popularly abbreviated simply as the Pill. Despite opposition by social conservatives and some religious groups, for the first time in history, women had a safe, effective means to avoid becoming pregnant.

Another advance in contraception for women during the postwar era was the intrauterine device (IUD). A doctor placed an IUD, usually made of nylon, plastic, or stainless steel, inside a woman's uterus. Tens of thousands of women in postwar America used it for birth control. The nonhormonal device could be left in place for years before being withdrawn by a doctor when so desired. However, the IUD occasionally caused heavy bleeding in women as well as severe infections. As with birth control pills, which were linked to breast and uterine cancer, more IUD testing through the postwar era brought improvements to female contraception, making it safer for most women.

At the end of women's reproductive life, hormone replacement therapy (HRT) became popular during the postwar years to reduce the discomforts of menopause. Doctors prescribed HRT drugs to replace lost estrogen, although some forms of hormone replacement therapy were later said to have harmful side effects including blood clots, heart attacks, and strokes.

Starting in the 1960s, a grassroots women's health movement emerged. The goal was to spotlight health issues and improve healthcare for all women. Informal self-help groups focusing on women's health sprang up around the country, with most sources indicating there were more than 1,000 such groups by the end of the 1960s.

There were other major medical advances that impacted the daily lives of women in the postwar years, reflecting the atomic age in which they lived. These involved the use of radiation. Most women had heard about radiation in connection with the specter of nuclear weapons that hung over their heads in the Cold War era. But radiation was also used in many medical situations. Unfortunately for many women, they were told there was no danger in this type of radiation.

Mammogram technology involved X-rays, a type of radiation that "sees" beneath the skin to produce a black-and-white picture of the inside of the body. Because different tissues absorb different amounts of radiation, X-ray images show parts of the body in varying shades. Mammograms were used to check for abnormalities in the breast tissue and breast cancer in women who had no outward signs of the disease as well as those who discovered lumps or other problems. Critics claimed that studies found mammography itself could cause cancer in both the patient and the X-ray machine operator, often a woman. Therefore, as the postwar era wore on, medical advances produced safer mammography techniques.

During the postwar era, radiation-based X-rays were frequently used in a number of women's health-related situations. In the 1950s, they often involved a high dose of radiation. X-rays were used to scan the abdomens of pregnant women to observe the status of their unborn babies, such as the position in which the fetus was carried in the womb. By the end of the 1950s, ultrasound emerged as the safer alternative to X-rays for prenatal scans. But well into the mid-1970s, statistics show that almost a third of pregnant women were still being subjected to X-rays.

It was not only pregnant women on whom radiation was commonly being used in the postwar era. In the 1950s, X-rays and radium were used on women to "treat" everything from heavy menstrual periods to asthma.

One use of X-ray technology in the postwar years was strictly for profit. In 1957, medical journals began describing conditions in which average women and children were experiencing severe pain and damaged skin in their legs and feet. The cause was ultimately linked to the use of an X-ray device called the fluoroscope.

Marketed under trade names such as the Pedoscope, women customers at some shoe stores were told that using this X-ray machine would illustrate whether they were buying shoes for their children or themselves that were the wrong size. It was implied—or stated directly—that if a woman bought shoes for her children that were too small, she was damaging her offspring for life by deforming their sensitive bones and joints. If women demurred, the salesperson implied that they were hopelessly out of fashion, behind the times, and bad mothers. With women's shoes, especially high heels, often uncomfortable anyway, female customers were told they too could find the best fit by having their own feet X-rayed to locate "pressure points," using the machines, which were designed to look like an attractive wooden cabinet.

It was not only women customers and children who were injured by this unnecessary X-raying. Frequently, it was a woman employee in the shoe store who operated the fluoroscope machine, often up to 15–20 times a day. The radiation produced by the machine itself, along with radioactive leakage due to lack of maintenance, commonly added up to a hazardous situation for those women.

Hundreds of these machines were used in shoe stores nationwide in the postwar era. Ultimately, in 1957, Pennsylvania became the first state to ban their use, with other states soon following.

Another medical advance for women in postwar America came in the area of drug testing. Although women have traditionally made up 51 percent of the population in the United States, for the most part, they were not included as subjects in clinical trials or medical research during the postwar era.

That meant that the dosage for drugs and various aspects of newly developed treatments were designed for men. Doing so did not take into account women's smaller body mass or the fluctuations in their systems due to breastfeeding, hormonal issues, menstruation, menopause, or pregnancy. It was considered less complicated—and therefore less expensive—to work with males.

During the postwar era, some pharmaceutical companies claimed that they did not test on women due to their desire to "protect" females from the rigors of drug testing. However, as in the case of a cholesterol drug marketed in 1959, the product was found to cause baldness, a condition that could arguably be said to produce a more traumatic loss for a woman than a man.

With the postwar rise of the women's health movement, there were accusations by women that men's health issues were receiving more research attention and funding than women's. Many alleged that drug companies were not addressing the separate health issues of the female half of the population.

It was not until 1993, well past what is generally considered the postwar era, that data began being analyzed for gender differences. That year, a federal law required women to be included in clinical trials. Results were to be sorted by gender, with information cited accordingly.

There was even less research being conducted on nonwhite people, such as that for sickle cell anemia, the most common genetic disorder among African Americans. Although sickle cell's genetic transmission was determined in 1949, it was not until the mid-1970s that significant progress was made in therapeutic advances for the ailment.

One medical advance in the postwar years involved an area that was often not considered in terms of health. As the postwar population generally grew fatter, chemical substitutes were developed for Americans, especially women, who wanted to cut down on their sugar intake. Saccharin and cyclamates became extremely popular after being marketed by themselves as sweeteners for coffee or tea as well as also being included by manufactures in soft drinks, salad dressings, and other postwar products often billed as "diet" or "lite."

During the latter part of the postwar era, the Food and Drug Administration determined that saccharin and cyclamates posed health hazards including cancer and birth defects. The manufacturers disputed the findings, but by 1970, products containing cyclamates were removed from grocery shelves. Later, food containing saccharin was required to carry a warning label under the Saccharin Study and Labeling Act of 1977, although after subsequent research, the warning was later removed.

Both men and women of the postwar era consumed the artificial sweeteners. But there were those who claimed that women were more at risk from possible health-related side effects from those chemical substances due to women's smaller body mass. And in the postwar years as always, women were under pressure to keep themselves thin, youthful looking, and attractive to men, even to the detriment of their health.

NEWS MEDIA

In the course of their daily lives, women in postwar America had a number of options available to them in order to keep up with current events. Some were traditional, while another—television—was excitingly new.

The postwar era was a golden age for American newspapers, with many cities having both morning and evening editions. A number of small towns had their own weekly newspapers that covered local doings. But due to the impact of radio and television, competition among newspapers in the postwar era grew fierce. Many merged or simply went out of business.

Except for some small-town weeklies, stories by female reporters were rare throughout the 1950s. Most postwar women had only ever heard of one woman reporter who wrote for a "big city" paper: Nellie Bly, the pen name of Elizabeth Cochran Seaman. Around the turn of the century, Bly had attained fame for her reporting in the *New York World* newspaper about her solo trip around the world in 72 days, setting a record for such a feat and outdoing Jules Verne's fictional tale, *Around the World in Eighty Days*. Also for Joseph Pulitzer's *World*, she wrote a sensational story about going undercover in a horrific mental asylum. Covering the Woman Suffrage Parade of 1913, Bly correctly predicted that it would be 1920 before female American citizens would be given the right to vote.

After Bly, women usually did not come to the forefront of newspaper reporting until World War II. Some women courageously covered combat zones, including reporters and photographers such as Margaret Bourke-White, Martha Gellhorn, and Marguerite Higgins, who often battled military officials as well as the enemy. Other female journalists were temporarily allowed to do traditionally male jobs as editors until the men returned from the war.

Photojournalist Mary Marvin Breckinridge used her middle name, Marvin, to evade the prejudice against women in journalism at the time. However, the award-winning Flora Lewis was a foreign affairs columnist and correspondent who wrote under her own name for several prestigious publications, including the *New York Times* and *Washington Post*. Her name would have been familiar to women throughout the postwar era as they lived their daily lives.

Many women journalists who wanted to continue their newspaper careers in the postwar years found themselves relegated to what were called the women's pages. This section of a newspaper covered items assumed by male editors to be of interest to women and was generally known as the 4-F's: family, fashion, food, and furnishings.

Some, such as Dorothy Jurney, were told by their employers that they were not candidates for any editorial positions apart from the women's pages because they were female. At the *Miami Herald*, Jurney subtly began shifting the women's section to include more hard news of interest to the female population—a move that proved successful and went on to influence women's page editors at other postwar newspapers.

One American woman of the postwar era who controlled the women's section for a major newspaper did not need Jurney's influence or that of anyone else. Nor did anyone tend to argue with the direction in which she took the women's pages. The family of Dorothy Buffum "Buff" Chandler owned the *Los Angeles Times* and *Los Angeles Mirror*. During the postwar era, she moved the women's pages away from being the traditional kind of women's section dedicated to society doings and "fluff" into more substantive reporting. According to Halberstam, "she was always in there pushing and demanding, fighting for early air-pollution studies and legislation, fighting for better conditions and pay for women, molding the women's sections of the two papers to her own causes and visions" (272).

Sometimes even men found items of interest in the women's sections. "Ann Landers" was the pen name adopted by Esther Lederer when she began writing a nationally syndicated advice column in 1955. The following year, in 1956, a competing advice column was launched nationally. Called "Dear Abby," the writer went by the pen name of Abigail Van Buren. In real life, she was Pauline Phillips—none other than the sister of Esther "Ann Landers" Lederer. Both advice columns became a beloved part of many women's daily lives.

Besides newspapers, there were other print media that carried the news to postwar women. Weekly news magazines such as *Time* and *Newsweek* differentiated themselves from daily newspapers in the marketplace by stressing their ability to offer more in-depth reporting as well as analysis of complex issues. A feature that became popular after its inception in 1952 was the "News You Can Use" column in another publication, the weekly *U.S. News & World Report*.

Many African American women of the postwar era received their news from magazines aimed at black readers such as *Ebony*, *Jet*, and

Hue. John H. Johnson founded *Ebony* just after the end of World War II. According to Carroll (2017), *Ebony* was inspired by *Life* magazine, adding that *Ebony's* "monthly circulation reached 250,000 within a half year and rose to 315,000 by 1950" (121). However, Carroll states that after the flashpoint of the school integration crisis at Little Rock, Arkansas, in 1957, some black commentators were critical of *Ebony*, "the nation's most popular black publication, which [they felt] was a lifestyle magazine more than a protest publication" (151).

Beyond print, women in postwar America also utilized electronic news media. Radio, while somewhat in a state of decline during the 1950s from its peak in the 1930s and 1940s, prided itself on the ability of offer "breaking news flashes" as events happened, which newspapers could not. Radio was greatly assisted in maintaining its listenership by having car radios installed as a standard feature in the flashy new postwar automobiles that were sweeping the country. It was also a medium of choice for housewives of the era who could listen to radio while performing their daily chores.

Regardless of where they tuned in to radio, whether at home or in the car, what female listeners heard was the sound of male voices. Women who sought a place as radio newscasters were told that female voices did not carry authority.

However, there was one familiar female voice who brought news and commentary to her listeners on CBS Radio, someone who had been a mainstay of patriotism through the World War II years: singer Kate Smith. Known for her wartime rendition of "God Bless America," Smith hosted a daytime radio broadcast until 1958. On her show, *Kate Smith Speaks*, she was one of the first to publicly denounce racism in 1945, when she called for racial and religious tolerance in order to achieve true peace in the postwar years.

Another rare female voice that postwar women might have heard on the radio as they lived their daily lives was commentator Dorothy Thompson, who was called the first lady of American journalism at the time. According to Edwards (2019), Katharine Hepburn's character in the 1942 movie *Woman of the Year* was modeled after Thompson. In addition, Edwards says that *Time* magazine carried a cover story about Dorothy Thompson, with the magazine stating, "[Thompson] and Eleanor Roosevelt are undoubtedly the most influential women in the U.S." (185). During the 1950s, Thompson urged women to stand up for their rights, also being one of the first to voice concerns about the dangerous influence of television.

Radio's Thompson may have been accurate in her concerns about television. Few saw its ultimate impact not only on postwar news media but in all facets of American life.

Many of the men who were newscasters on radio made the move to television news in the early 1950s, becoming popular with female viewers. While the television industry was more concerned with entertainment, short newscasts were wedged into the schedule as a public service. Some of the men who switched from radio to television in the postwar years included Edward R. Murrow and Walter Cronkite, who is credited with popularizing the word "anchorman." Indeed, they were virtually all *men*.

During the 1940s, female journalist Pauline Frederick had served as a war correspondent, providing both print and radio reporting. But she was one of those women who were told that a female voice in broadcasting did not carry authority. During the postwar years, however, Frederick won a position with the fledgling ABC television network, covering the 1952 political conventions. Never before had the conventions been televised, and Pauline Frederick soon earned recognition as the first woman to work on air for an American television network. When she was hired by NBC to cover the United Nations, the novelty of seeing a woman correspondent on a major network made her a household name.

There was another of the handful of women who broke the mold in television news during the postwar era. Charles L. Ponce de Leon (2015) notes that the NBC television program *Meet the Press* had journalist Martha Rountree serving as moderator beginning in 1947. He states that the show "attracted attention among politicians, journalists, and viewers who enjoyed its regular diet of political inside dope" (17). Serving until 1953, Rountree is the only female moderator in the history of the long-running show.

Although important news stories, scientific advances, thought-provoking issues, and a nascent movement toward women's rights all took place during the postwar era, there was an underlying reality: the role of women at the time. Ogden (1986) claims that significant topics were often overlooked by the news media aimed at women. Instead, "the image makers in the magazines, on the radio, and on television guided girls toward their wedding days and their tidy houses in the suburbs" (174).

POPULAR CULTURE

The overall taste of average people, rather than that of the sophisticated elite, is generally what is considered to be the realm of popular culture. Also called "pop culture," it might encompass the art, fashion, ideas, music, writing, and mass media favored by average people in a particular society at a given time.

In 1953, many American women acquired their first television set in order to watch the coronation of England's Queen Elizabeth II (pictured here). Soon, the queen and her family were well known in the daily lives of American women as the royals became considered to be a kind of aristocratic soap opera. (Library of Congress)

High culture might consist of classical music by symphony orchestras, great artworks, literary classics, thought-provoking drama, and intellectual concepts. Popular culture, on the other hand, is said to have more mass accessibility and wide appeal. Some define it as the public taste of the moment, often something fun, transitory, and unlikely to stand the test of time.

Generally, popular culture is driven by the cultural tastemakers of the age. These are individuals, industries, and institutions that have the power to shape the common taste, often with an underlying profit motive.

Popular culture has prevailed throughout human history. Excavations reveal that in the days of the ancient Roman Empire, arenas for theatrical events and athletic competitions such as blood sports were built not only in Rome itself but also at her widespread colonial outposts. Along with temples and government buildings, such venues for popular culture were often among the first be to be constructed in Roman colonies as a way to keep the citizenry diverted.

Although Shakespearean plays today are considered high culture, it must be remembered that in the Elizabethan England of his time, William Shakespeare wrote for the masses. Hoping to attract audiences to the theater in which he was part owner, it is unlikely he felt he was writing for the ages.

Never before were tastemakers for America's popular culture more prevalent than in the postwar era. Before World War II, newspapers, magazines, and radio had traditionally shaped popular tastes. But the revolutionary change during the postwar era for transmitting popular culture was the coming of television.

When the 1950s began, a television set was an expensive investment. Since it was usually affordable only by wealthy people who were used to high art forms, many early television programs often were produced to appeal to the cultural elite. In the early 1950s, these included thought-provoking anthology dramas in what is today considered the original golden age of television. Programs such as *Kraft Television Theater, Playhouse 90,* and *The United States Steel Hour* presented serious topics meant to appeal to the wealthy elite. That group would have been most likely to own a television set and comprised people who presumably were more interested in intellectual diversions than the masses would have been. With early television shows being produced in New York City, those programs often starred Broadway actors in presentations created by top writers.

But by the latter part of the 1950s, about 90 percent of American families could afford to buy a TV set. Watching television was a common leisure activity that figured prominently in the daily lives of women in postwar America.

Production studios moved to Southern California, where they could film exterior shots in temperate weather year-round. Domestic situation comedies, usually with women in the role of housewife and mother, became the vogue.

Networks wanted to keep sponsors happy by appealing to the greatest number of people as inoffensively as possible. Some were guided by the term "lowest common denominator" as the target to aim for. They also recognized that American women greatly influenced what the family watched on television as part of their daily lives. Often the programs that were most appealing to women came in the form of situation comedies that were based in the fictional home of the main characters.

This type of domestic "sitcom" programming proved to hold a significant place in the popular culture of the postwar era and therefore in the daily lives of women. Some top shows included those that centered on female characters such as *The Donna Reed Show, I Married Joan, My Little Margie, Our Miss Brooks,* and *Private Secretary.* Women were featured prominently as wives and mothers on programs such as *Leave It to Beaver* and *Ozzie and Harriet.* The television sitcom that held a leading spot in the popular culture of the postwar era, as well as into the future, was *I Love Lucy.*

The influence of television on the popular culture of postwar America and in the daily lives of women cannot be overstated. Women from coast to coast saw the same thing on the three national television networks, from fashions and hairstyles to expectations about their role in the postwar era as wives and mothers. Even those fictional sitcom women who were employed in the workforce, such as those on *Our Miss Brooks* and *Private Secretary*, were actively—some might say desperately—seeking a husband.

One woman who had a job as well as a family became an unlikely popular culture icon in the postwar era. England's new queen, Elizabeth II, succeeded to the throne in 1952 upon the death of her father King George VI. She was the first female reigning monarch (as opposed to being the wife of a king) since Queen Victoria who died in 1901. Of greater note to many American women was the fact that the coronation of Queen Elizabeth in June 1953 was televised. It was the first time the general public could watch the thousand-year-old ceremony. Many American families bought their first television set in order to watch the glamorous, historic occasion.

Although they resided across the Atlantic, televising the queen and her family in the postwar era led to the royals becoming part of America's pop culture as essentially an aristocratic soap opera. In the 1950s, for example, many American women followed the romantic tribulations of Queen Elizabeth's younger sister, Princess Margaret, as if she was a beloved character on a soap opera.

In 1958 there was a watershed occurrence in England that was scarcely noticed in the United States. That year, the queen announced that debutantes would no longer be presented at the English court. But in America, Heymann (1989) states, "One of the few enduring traditions that [American] high society retained after World War II was the Coming Out party" (67).

"Coming out" at a debutante ball was a way to introduce an upper-class young woman into high society and present her to potential husbands. It was also a way to show off her family's wealth and social status. This tradition became even more ingrained in America's postwar popular culture with the 1953 publication of a book by socialite Consuelo Vanderbilt Balsan called *The Glitter and the Gold* in which the author described the arcane world of life as a debutante.

Throughout the 1950s, American debutantes became part of the nation's popular culture. Their activities were followed by many women with great interest. It was a postwar demonstration of the concept of being "famous for being famous," which was aided significantly by the popular media.

Richardson (2019) notes that one name would have been known to most women of the era: Brenda Frazier. She was "the most famous debutante of the twentieth century, whose face sold cars and perfumes. . . . [She] claimed in a 1963 *Life* magazine article, 'I was a fad, the way midget golf was once a fad, and flagpole sitting.' " (4).

Major postwar American magazines such as *Life*, *Newsweek*, and *Time* covered debutante balls as well as the young women who were annually dubbed by columnists to be "Debutante of the Year." In 1947, soon after the end of World War II, popular newspaper columnist Cholly Knickerbocker (real name: Igor Cassini) proclaimed the "Queen Deb of the Year" to be Jacqueline Lee Bouvier, who went on in the 1960s to become Jacqueline Kennedy Onassis.

The postwar era also saw the rise of African American debutante balls in the United States. Although racially segregated, they served many of the same purposes as the debutante balls did among whites: seeking a suitable husband for daughters and allowing affluent black families to connect with other successful African Americans. Among Hispanic Americans, the "quinceañera" party for a teenage daughter was often a similar type of event.

In America's postwar society, there was another kind of pop culture royalty: film stars, especially movie actresses, who were of great interest to many average women. When the Academy Awards began to be televised in 1953, many women in postwar America tuned in to watch their favorite stars, see the elegant fashions, and cheer for their preferred Oscar nominees. Sometimes male stars arrived at the Oscars not with a starlet on their arm but a new kind of pop culture figure: high-fashion models.

Through the mass media that they perused in the course of their daily lives, most women in postwar America knew the names and faces of top models such as Anita Colby, Dorian Leigh, and Dovima. But the model who was the brightest star in the pop culture galaxy of the 1950s was Suzy Parker. In their daily lives, many average women tried to emulate the face that earned Parker the distinction of being the first model to earn $100,000 a year. She was also able to parlay her fame in the 1950s as a model into a movie career.

Another part of the popular culture that influenced many postwar women in the course of their daily lives was the annual Miss America pageant. After the pageant began being televised in 1954, average women could note what was considered the epitome of ideal American beauty in the postwar era. The Miss America pageant was an annual high point of popular culture during the postwar years, becoming the highest rated program on television. Most average women were familiar with each year's reigning Miss America, especially those who later attained show business careers such as Lee Meriwether (Miss America 1955), Marilyn Van Derbur (1958), and Mary Ann Mobley (1959).

For the most part, the daily lives of average American women during the postwar era were centered on home, husband, and children. However, there were some stirrings in the sphere of pop culture that pointed to new directions for women. Some were rooted in the "funny pages" that were read by many impressionable young girls as well as their mothers.

Probably, the most famous female comic strip character of the postwar era was Brenda Starr, created by Dale Messick. At the peak of its popularity in the 1950s, the series about a female newspaper reporter with flaming-red hair ran in 250 newspapers. She was named for pop culture icon, debutante Brenda Frazier, and for being a "star." The comic's creator, Dalia Messick, adopted the pen name "Dale," which sounded less feminine, due to prejudice against women cartoonists in the industry. But the fictional Brenda Starr's exotic romantic adventures knew no bounds. As a role model, this female cartoon character combined glamour, strength, and intelligence. Brenda Starr is said by many cultural observers to have inspired many young women of the postwar era and beyond.

Apart from the printed page, the entertainment technology of the postwar era created pop culture opportunities for women beyond their role in daily life as housewives. Television brought several pioneering women to the mainstream across America.

During the postwar era, female comedians such as Phyllis Diller, Totie Fields, and Joan Rivers went from performing in small local nightspots to national exposure on television shows such as those hosted by Jack Paar and Ed Sullivan. These women broke new ground for female comedians by writing their own material, although in much of it, they made harsh fun of themselves through self-deprecating humor. An outlier was Elaine May whose comedy routines in the 1950s foreshadowed the satiric, sophisticated humor of the 1960s without disparaging herself.

Moms Mabley, born in 1894 as Loretta Mary Aiken, was a veteran of what was called the Chitlin' Circuit of African American vaudeville shows. Despite her popularity, her wages as a black woman were low. However, she persisted as a stand-up comedian for six decades, finally achieving mainstream success on popular postwar television shows such as Ed Sullivan's. Appearing as a toothless old woman in a shabby housedress and floppy hat, she was able to tackle subjects such as racism as well as the double standards among men and women. Her raunchy humor on record albums was even further removed from what was expected as "proper" for a woman.

Another female comedian who presented herself in a less-than-attractive onstage persona was Minnie Pearl. The real-life Sarah Ophelia Cannon appealed to mainstream audiences as well as fans of the burgeoning postwar country music scene. She starred at Nashville's legendary Grand Ole Opry throughout the postwar years as well as regularly appearing on television's *Ozark Jubilee* in the late 1950s and *Hee Haw* beginning in the 1960s.

Television allowed some female pop culture figures to find mainstream audiences. Postwar advances in the recording industry allowed them and other female entertainers to present material that was not permissible on TV, especially for women.

Americans could buy off-color comedy record albums to play in the privacy of their homes or among friends at parties. Some of the most popular among such albums of the postwar era were by a raunchy female comic who called herself "Lusty" Rusty Warren. She enjoyed enormous success with albums that had titles such as *Sin-Sational* and *Songs for Sinners*. After graduating from the New England Conservatory of Music, she found steadier work in the 1950s and 1960s by creating a different kind of act built around the topic of sex from a female perspective. Warren has sometimes been called the Mother of the Sexual Revolution, with a career that was timed perfectly to intersect with the coming of the birth control pill in 1959.

There was one notable American woman of the postwar era who encapsulated the height of mainstream pop culture: Grace Kelly. Average women knew that she was not only a glamorous Academy Award–winning movie star but that she also became a real-life princess by marrying Monaco's Prince Rainier. Her blonde beauty was, for many American women, the postwar feminine ideal. The news media erupted into an unprecedented frenzy surrounding Kelly's 1956 wedding, bringing every detail into the daily lives of American women. With that event, a new standard of feverish popular culture was set for the postwar era and for decades to come.

SCIENCE

In the course of living her daily life, an average postwar American woman probably made dinner for the family as usual on October 4, 1957. It was a day like any other. Like many other American women, she looked forward to a high point of the evening, relaxing together as a family while watching the premiere of a new television situation comedy about middle-class suburban life called *Leave It to Beaver*.

Suddenly, for women in postwar America and their families, the world changed in an instant.

There was a news flash that the Soviet Union had launched Sputnik, the world's first space satellite, into orbit over the earth. As if that were not bad enough, U.S. military forces with their much-vaunted, taxpayer-funded distant early warning radar system (the "DEW Line") knew nothing about it, nor did any other agencies responsible for America's defense. According to Dickson, the Russian satellite "passed twice in easy detection range of the United States before anyone in authority knew of its existence" (11). To many Americans, it meant that their Communist enemies in Russia had had at least two chances to blow up the United States from outer space.

Science suddenly took center stage. It was a topic that had not generally concerned average women in postwar America in the course of their daily lives. However, in the new age of Sputnik that was thrust upon them, science now took on a new urgency.

Most average postwar women understood the implications of nuclear science, the field that had developed atomic weapons. With the constant threat of cataclysmic nuclear war, some women feared for their lives and those of their children.

To others, the march of science in the postwar era was something that brought forth wonderful new consumer goods such as television. As the science of broadcasting progressed throughout the 1950s, television sets grew larger than their original tiny screens. By the latter part of the decade, television went from black-and-white to color, scientific feats that may not have been understood but were appreciated by many.

Scientific discoveries were bringing forth new enhancements for television as early as 1950, a time when relatively few Americans had a television set of their own. "Lazy Bones" tuning allowed viewers to change channels from the comfort of their favorite chair by using a handheld device that plugged into the television set.

It was the first successful attempt at a television remote control device.

Also in 1950, a prototype of the telephone answering machine was developed, even though many American women across the country still had to use the multifamily "party line" until a private phone could be installed in their home.

During the 1950s, automobiles could be equipped with power steering, marketed as a plus for women drivers in order to easily control the huge American cars of the postwar era.

The first patent for barcode scanning technology came in 1952. This promised a shorter time in the grocery checkout line for women shoppers.

In 1953, science brought forth Saran Wrap, a plastic wrapping material to seal and preserve food. It became a valued kitchen helper for many women. In 1954, the first nonstick pan was produced, promising ease of cleanup for housewives, as they washed the dishes. Marketed as "Teflon," it was an offshoot of nuclear science, where the substance was used to coat valves in containers of radioactive uranium. The wife of an engineer suggested using the material to coat her pots and pans in order to keep food from sticking.

For women in postwar America who worked in clerical jobs outside the home, a scientific miracle created by an average woman was introduced in 1956. Invented by a secretary named Bette Nesmith, "Mistake Out," later renamed "Liquid Paper," covered mistakes in typewriting, eliminating the need to retype an entire page or risk facing an irate boss who did not tolerate typographical errors.

Bette Nesmith was one of the postwar-era women who found themselves raising a small child alone after a divorce. Her story combined science with desperation. After she created the formula for the correction fluid at her kitchen table, other secretaries saw her using it to fix mistakes and asked for some. Her young son Michael helped by filling tiny bottles with the creamy substance.

Bette applied for a patent, founded a booming business, and became a wealthy woman who created several charitable foundations to help other women. Her son, Michael, who had helped fill the tiny bottles of Liquid Paper, achieved renown in his own right as part of the 1960s singing group the Monkees.

Most average women of the postwar era did not know the name of Bette Nesmith nor the names of other women who stepped out from their assigned role in the home to make scientific discoveries during the postwar years. Along with being unknown in women's daily lives, there was often a reason why their names were also lost to history.

After graduating high school, a postwar-era girl named Margaret Rossiter went on to Yale University where she took a course in the history of science. One day she asked if there had ever been any women scientists. According to Dominus, "the answer was absolute. No. Never. None" (44). Although someone brought up Marie Curie, two-time winner of the Nobel Prize, "even Curie was dismissed as merely the helper to her husband" (44).

Researching the subject of female scientists, Rossiter discovered women from her own lifetime in the postwar years whose contributions were unknown to most people. Some women in postwar America sought to expand the limits of their prescribed daily lives. One, Grace Murray Hopper was a computer scientist who led a team in the 1950s that created the first computer language compiler as well as developing COBOL, a high-level programming language that is still used today.

Marie Maynard Daly was the first African American woman awarded a doctorate in chemistry upon her graduation from Columbia University in 1947. During the 1950s, she pioneered research into the effects of cigarette smoking on the lungs as well as work on the linkage between cholesterol and heart disease.

Cancer researcher Jewel Plummer Cobb was the granddaughter of a slave. She was an advocate for increasing the presence of women and people of color like herself in science. During the 1950s, she worked with the National Cancer Institute at Harlem Hospital in New York City, making gains in the use of chemotherapy to combat cancer.

Two women scientists of the postwar era were denied Nobel Prizes while their male colleagues received the prestigious award for the same work. One was astrophysicist Jocelyn Bell Burnell for her work in the discovery of pulsars. Chemist Rosalind Franklin's work was minimized when her male teammates received the Nobel Prize for unraveling DNA.

Katherine Coleman Johnson's hometown in rural West Virginia did not have a school for African American children past the eighth grade. Nonetheless, in 1953, with superior math skills, she was employed by the National Aeronautics and Space Administration (NASA), which at the time consisted almost exclusively of white males. There, she became known as a "computer in skirts." Astronaut John Glenn specifically asked for Johnson to verify the spaceflight calculations that had been done by electronic computers when they were installed at NASA, refusing to fly his historic 1962 orbital mission until she did so. The behind-the-scenes work of Johnson and other postwar African American women at NASA was recognized in the 2016 movie *Hidden Figures*.

In 1958, chemists Ethaline Cortelyou and Betty Lou Raskin began speaking out about the widespread practice of hiring women scientists only for lower-level support positions despite their proven skills being equivalent to male scientists on staff. Cortelyou and Raskin blamed the prevalent postwar-era dogma that women's daily lives should be spent in the home. Raskin's 1959 essay in the *New York Times* was titled, "Women's Place Is in the Lab, Too."

There were some bright spots for women in the sciences during the postwar era. One was a competition for students known as the Westinghouse Science Talent Search that began in 1942 and accepted girls as contestants. Among thousands of competitors in the postwar years, only one young woman made it into the Top Ten, Joanna Russ in 1953. One generation later, in 1980, Lisa Randall, a theoretical physicist working in cosmology who was born in 1962, became the first woman to earn first place.

Westinghouse finalists have collectively received millions of dollars in scholarships, going on to earn honors including Nobel Prizes and MacArthur Fellowships (often called "Genius Grants"). However, Puaca (2014) notes that preference for awarding scholarships to male students persisted, "as did the assumption that women scientists were bad investments because they might leave the workforce after marriage" (55).

While most women in postwar America lived their daily lives without a great deal of knowledge about women in the sciences, some slow progress was being made in at least acknowledging the paradigm. Margaret Rossiter coined a phrase to describe the banishment of women scientists from the historical record. She called it "The Matilda Effect." Rossiter named the phenomenon for Matilda Gage who, in the 1800s, was a pioneer in writing about women scientists erased from history although they worked alongside the men who received the credit.

Matilda Gage had a daughter who married a man named L. Frank Baum. Matilda spent half of every year living with the couple. Her son-in-law Frank Baum went on to write a book called *The Wonderful Wizard of Oz*, which has since become a classic. In a famous line from the 1939 movie, *The Wizard of Oz*, Baum's characters in the Land of Oz were told to "pay no attention to that man behind the curtain."

In much the same way, his mother-in-law Matilda is the namesake of "The Matilda Effect," describing those women in postwar America who spent their daily lives making significant contributions to science but whose gender kept *them* "behind the curtain."

FURTHER READING

Ackmann, Martha. *The Mercury 13: The True Story of Thirteen Women and the Dream of Space Flight*. New York: Random House, 2004.

Balsan, Consuelo Vanderbilt. *The Glitter and the Gold: The American Duchess—in Her Own Words*. New York: St. Martin's Press, 1953.

Brandt, Allan M. *The Cigarette Century: The Rise, Fall, and Deadly Persistence of the Product That Defined America*. New York: Basic Books, 2007.

Carroll, Fred. *Race News: Black Journalists and the Fight for Racial Justice in the Twentieth Century*. Chicago: University of Illinois Press, 2017.

Cassidy, Marsha. *What Women Watched: Daytime Television in the 1950s*. Austin: University of Texas Press, 2005.

Coe, Lewis. *The Telegraph: A History of Morse's Invention and Its Predecessors in the United States*. Jefferson, NC: McFarland, 2003.

Dickson, Paul. *Sputnik: The Shock of the Century*. New York: Walker & Company, 2007.

Dominus, Susan. "Sidelined." *Smithsonian*, October 2019, pp. 41–53, 80.

DuBois, Ellen, and Lynn Dumenil. *Through Women's Eyes: An American History with Documents*. Boston: Bedford/St. Martin's, 2008.

Edwards, Anne. *Katharine Hepburn: A Remarkable Woman*. Lanham, MD: Rowman and Littlefield, 2019.

Ehrenreich, Barbara, and Deirdre English. *Witches, Midwives, and Nurses: A History of Women Healers*. New York: The Feminist Press of the City University of New York, 2010.

Gallagher, Winifred. *How the Post Office Created America: A History*. New York: Penguin, 2017.

Gilbert, Lynn, and Gaylen Moore. *Particular Passions: Talks with Women Who Have Shaped Our Times*. New York: Clarkson Potter, 1981.

Golden, Janet. *Message in a Bottle: The Making of Fetal Alcohol Syndrome*. Cambridge, MA: Harvard University Press, 2005.

Gunn, Giles. *Early American Writing*. New York: Penguin, 1994.

Halberstam, David. *The Powers That Be*. New York: Knopf, 1979.

Hale, Julie. "Living between the Lines." *BookPage*, March, 2020.

Harvey, Brett. *The Fifties: A Women's Oral History*. New York: HarperCollins, 1993.

Hendricks, Nancy. *Senator Hattie Caraway: An Arkansas Legacy*. Charleston, SC: The History Press, 2013.

Heymann, C. David. *A Woman Named Jackie*. New York: Carol Communications, 1989.

Hope, Judith Richards. *Pinstripes & Pearls: The Women of the Harvard Law Class of '64 Who Forged an Old Girl Network and Paved the Way for Future Generations*. New York: Scribner, 2003.

Kanfer, Stefan. *Ball of Fire: The Tumultuous Life and Comic Art of Lucille Ball*. New York: Knopf, 2003.

Knight, Brenda. *Women of the Beat Generation: The Writers, Artists and Muses at the Heart of a Revolution*. Berkeley, CA: Conari Press, 1996.

Ogden, Annegret. *The Great American Housewife: From Helpmate to Wage Earner, 1776–1986*. Westport, CT: Greenwood, 1986.

Oshinsky, David. *Polio: An American Story*. New York: Oxford University Press, 2006.

Ponce de Leon, Charles L. *That's the Way It Is: A History of Television News in America*. Chicago: University of Chicago Press, 2015.

Prescott, Lara. *The Secrets We Kept*. New York: Knopf, 2019.

Puaca, Laura Micheletti. *Searching for Scientific Womanpower: Technocratic Feminism and the Politics of National Security, 1940–1980*. Chapel Hill: University of North Carolina Press, 2014.

Rader, Peter. *Mike Wallace: A Life*. New York: Thomas Dunne Books, 2012.

Ramsburg, Jim. *Network Radio Ratings, 1932–1953: A History of Prime Time Programs through the Ratings of Nielsen, Crossley and Hooper*. Jefferson, NC: McFarland, 2012.

Raskin, Betty Lou. "Woman's Place Is in the Lab, Too." *New York Times*, April 19, 1959. https://www.nytimes.com/1959/04/19/archives/womans-place-is-in-the-lab-too-how-can-we-fill-our-need-for-more.html.

Richardson, Kristen. *The Season: A Social History of the Debutante*. New York: Norton, 2019.

Van Doren, Charles. *The Joy of Reading*. Naperville, IL: Sourcebooks, 2008.

"Women Medical Graduates in the 1940s and 1950s." *Yale University Library*. http://exhibits.library.yale.edu/exhibits/show/100-years-women-ysm/women-medical-graduates-in-the.

4

MATERIAL LIFE

As a concept, materialism is closely related to the kind of rampant consumerism that was a significant factor in the daily lives of many American women in the confident, optimistic 1950s. Consumerism in the postwar United States was an attitude in which people enthusiastically embraced the idea of buying things. Materialism, therefore, might be expressed as the acquisition of the items they sought.

All human civilizations have had their share of possessions as part of their material life. Tombs of ancient Egyptian nobles were packed with items that they were convinced would be needed in the afterlife, just as they had needed them before death. Dripping in gold, few of the items, either large or small, would today be classified as necessities.

In 1954, psychologist Abraham Maslow published a book called *A Theory of Human Motivation* describing a hierarchy of needs that have been common to humans through the ages. With a coincidental nod to the ancient Egyptians, Maslow's hierarchy is usually represented in the shape of a pyramid.

The base of Maslow's theoretical pyramid is formed by necessities such as food, water, shelter, and clothing. Once those requirements are met to ensure survival, other categories appear further up on the triangle. These are associated with self-esteem and social belonging. By the 1950s, those needs would become intertwined.

Postwar consumers, especially women who had few other outlets in their daily lives, inferred from the messages all around them that basic needs now included items that were once luxuries. That conclusion expanded into the notion that their self-worth—and that of their family—came from acquiring them.

As part of a woman's domestic mission in the postwar era, it was impressed upon her that part of her obligation to her family was making sure they were firmly "keeping up with the Joneses." That meant buying more things, better things, newer things— a mission that was doomed to failure. The moment a woman brought the items home, they were condemned by planned obsolescence. As soon as a neighbor bought something better, items that had once been a source of pride began to look outdated and outmoded and therefore unwanted. For a woman who did not want to fall behind or be seen as a social misfit, the cycle of consumerism began again.

The common perception, fostered by manufacturers and the advertising industry, was that buying their product was the way to increase happiness and/or reduce feelings of loneliness. This was an appealing prospect to many suburban women who were isolated in their daily life and unsure of themselves amid the new lifestyle of postwar suburbia. However, studies later found that when material objects were pursued as a way to gain happiness, the opposite took place, contributing to feelings of *un*happiness. It never quite seemed to be enough. For many women, the quest to stay on top of postwar materialism took a psychic toll.

Materialism was nothing new. Even before the Industrial Revolution of the late 19th and early 20th centuries, William Wordsworth wrote a poem in the relatively bucolic age of 1806 called "The World Is Too Much With Us," stating:

> The world is too much with us; late and soon,
> Getting and spending, we lay waste our powers;
> Little we see in Nature that is ours;
> We have given our hearts away, a sordid boon! (144)

Why, then was the postwar era so strikingly different, "a sordid boon," especially for women? First, most women of the postwar era remembered the Great Depression of the 1930s and World War II in the 1940s. During those two decades, the ability to purchase consumer goods was limited by the economic hardship of the Depression and the rationing of wartime.

Even if rationing had not been in place during World War II, industrial firms that manufactured wartime goods often found themselves enjoying lucrative defense contracts from the government. It was not as profitable to manufacture consumer goods even if the businesses could obtain the necessary raw materials. Generally, they could not, since most such resources, including aluminum, coal, iron ore, petroleum, and tin were being reserved for the war effort.

A by-product of the war was that with the men gone for military service, women were hired to do jobs that traditionally were limited to males. Many women found, for the first time in their lives, the exhilaration of having their own "pocket money" to spend on whatever they wanted. No longer was every penny needed to help support the family during the economic downturn of the Depression. In addition, with men being deployed during the war, there were no longer husbands, fathers, or other male authority figures controlling what women could and could not do with money they earned. Although women found there were not a lot of consumer goods to buy during the war, they could save their money and dream about what would be available when peacetime arrived.

Manufacturers who received infusions of government financing during wartime found they had the cash reserves to quickly retool from weapons to domestic goods after the war. Material items rolled off the assembly lines into the hands of eager postwar consumers who had been denied them for two decades.

At the same time, returning veterans received educational benefits from the GI Bill. Many studied new, exciting subjects such as advertising, marketing, and psychology. Ad agencies snapped up college graduates who were both mature employees and ready to put their knowledge to work. Their mandate was to create strategies that encouraged people, especially women, to buy whatever products they were selling. While women were not usually hired in the "man's world" of advertising, entire divisions of male marketers were devoted to determining what women would want to buy and how to persuade them to do so.

At the same time, there was a stunning technological development that made the material life of the postwar era different from any other in human history. This marvel was an electronic box that sat in people's living rooms every day, manipulating their buying choices in a high-stakes game of show and tell. It was called television, and it revolutionized the material life of postwar Americans.

No longer could consumers simply see pictures of the product, as with print ads. Nor were they limited by merely hearing about the goods, as with radio. With television, they could both see and hear about the products on display, often enhanced with animated characters, brief playlets, or celebrity endorsements as well as repetitive messages that reverberated in people's minds, urging them to make the purchase.

Finally, there was one other factor influencing the material life of women in postwar America. When GOP vice presidential candidate Richard Nixon made his televised "Checkers Speech" in 1952, he made a point of saying his wife Pat wore not mink but a "respectable Republican cloth coat." According to Marling (1996), after he and Dwight Eisenhower won the election, Republican first lady Mamie Eisenhower appeared on the steps of the White House in a luxurious full-length fur coat. When asked what it was made of, she shot back "Mink, of course," adding "a broad smile and a winning tinkle of her charm bracelet" (31). After years of sacrifice, this was a new attitude for American women to absorb, coming right from the top. Thrift was out; luxury was in.

Although the phrase would not be popularized until the 1960s, in the material life of the postwar years, "the times were a'changin."

AUTOMOBILES

The automobile revolutionized the daily lives of women in postwar America as having a private vehicle went from being a luxury to a necessity.

Cars, in one form or another, had existed since around the turn of the 20th century, although in the early years, these "horseless carriages" were the toys of the wealthy. Mass-market vehicles such as Ford's Model T burst on the scene for the middle class during the 1920s. Car sales were buoyed by the opportunity for men to buy an automobile on credit, a financial option not open to females.

Women of the 1920s were often disparaged by males as being unfit to drive a car. There were attempts at restricting females to driving only small battery-powered cars that were slower, only went about 50 miles without recharging, and could not handle steep hills. In addition, most American roadways of that time were unpaved, causing cars to get mired on impassable surfaces in anything but ideal weather. A woman driver could face a risky situation if her car got stuck on a lonely road.

Among the millions of cars being sold in America during the postwar era, women were often behind the wheel, at least in advertisements. Marketers made assumptions about what a female would want in a vehicle. Women could not receive credit to buy a car in their own name, but they could often influence their husband's choice. (Walter Arce/Dreamstime.com)

The stock market crash in 1929 brought economic disaster. In the Great Depression of the 1930s, few average Americans could afford either to buy a new car or operate an existing model. Some vehicles were repossessed by finance companies when people who had bought them on credit could not afford to keep up their payments. Often, drivers kept an old Model T going as long as they could, but they still needed to buy gas, oil, tires, and replacement parts, which could be costly.

In 1941, America entered World War II. Throughout much of the 1940s, gasoline, oil, tires, and parts were not available due to wartime rationing and restrictions on items needed for the war effort.

However, by the end of the war, the idea of a woman driver was much more ingrained in people's minds. Women had performed admirably as wartime ambulance drivers, couriers, mechanics, and truck drivers. A role model for many was England's teenage Princess Elizabeth. The future monarch, known as today's Queen Elizabeth II, was widely seen in photos performing her work as a truck driver and mechanic after enlisting in the Women's Auxiliary Territorial Service, a female branch of the British army.

When the war ended, the idea of average women behind the wheel was no longer a novelty. Cars started rolling off American assembly lines. Postwar prosperity made automobiles into a symbol of something far more than a basic means of transportation. Buying from the American automakers was the patriotic thing to do in the postwar era, helping to bolster the nation's economy by purchasing a car and showing pride in the booming industry of the United States. In the Cold War era, the flashy, fabulous cars made in the USA were also an international symbol of the nation's superiority over the Soviet Union, whose shoddy little autos were fodder for stand-up comics.

While a new postwar-era vehicle often had to be purchased on credit, the specter of the 1930s was long forgotten by most Americans. In the prosperity of the 1950s, most people in the United States were confident in the promise of full employment and secure jobs.

Amid the heady postwar atmosphere of consumerism, there was no better symbol of material wealth than a shiny new car sitting in the driveway. Cars of the 1950s literally did shine. Appealing to both men and women, they were emblazoned with sparkling chrome. Tail fins gave automobiles the sleek futuristic look of jet airplanes and rocket ships. Marketing experts were assured that women loved them.

With the auto industry changing designs almost annually, no newly prosperous American wanted to be stuck with an outdated car. Men and women were thrilled to bring home a gleaming new car every few years, an exquisitely visible symbol of their ability to keep up with the Joneses.

The glitzy, roomy automobiles of the 1950s were perfect for the times. With the passage of the Interstate Highway Act in 1956, new coast-to-coast freeways made driving safe and easy, two factors that appealed to women. According to Girard (2009), when World War II ended in 1945, Americans bought fewer than 70,000 cars. Ten years later, by 1955, new car sales approached 8 million (90). Among the millions of cars being sold in postwar America, women were often behind the wheel.

Historian Alistair Cooke (1977) referred to the automobile of America's postwar era as an "easy escape hatch" (374). For females, it was also quite a bit more. Its impact on the daily lives of most women in postwar America was incalculable.

The rise of the automobile in the postwar era created the America of today. It was because of the car that much of our nation's landscape looks the way it does. It spawned industries such as fast food franchises, huge supermarkets, motel chains, and sprawling shopping malls. For American women, these new enhancements greatly freed them from living their daily lives within the confines of the home.

During World War II, American women were asked to do their part by taking jobs, doing everything from working in factories to ferrying aircraft. After the war, they were asked to do their part by staying home. Most women understood that returning veterans had earned the right to preferred positions in the workplace. Many were happy to spend their daily lives as housewives and mothers, especially as it was being instilled in them throughout the postwar era that the domestic sphere was a woman's highest and best calling.

Other women wanted to work in addition to their duties at home. Some *had* to work to support their families. Educated women could generally find a place in a few jobs that were approved for females such as teachers or nurses. Many others could only find positions in the low-paid "pink collar" workforce as clerical staff, domestic help, or waitresses. Whatever their reasons and whatever type of job these women found, they somehow had to get to work.

Women who lived in urban centers often had access to public transportation such as city buses or subways. But in the postwar era, many lived in the expanding suburbs where there was little if any public transportation.

In the early postwar years, most suburban families only had one car. As the usual breadwinners, males needed it to get to their jobs. If they lived in suburbia, they often drove themselves to the workplace on the new parkways that were being constructed. This left women isolated and frequently frustrated within the boundaries of the home, with little in the way of available transportation in the new suburbs.

But if a woman had a driver's license, she might use the car to drive her husband to the local railway station where he could catch a commuter train. In that way, she could have an escape hatch of her own during the day until she picked him up again at night.

Obtaining a license meant learning to drive, and as Marling (1996) states, "Life in the 1950s imitated art—as seen on TV" (6). Inevitably, the situation comedies of the postwar era depended on the cliché of a woman learning to drive. Writers predictably turned out scripts based on what was considered the hilarious premise of a woman behind the wheel: confused by the gearshift, unable to use turn signals, even forgetting to look where she's going while using the rearview mirror to apply lipstick. Sitcom viewers could expect her to slink home with a dent, crumpled fender, or worse, offering an improbable story of how a tree jumped out at her.

The pattern was set with the "Lucy Learns to Drive" episode of the hit comedy *I Love Lucy*, airing in 1955. In it, the Lucy character insists on learning to drive the new family car. After one discouraging lesson from her husband, Lucy decides she knows enough to teach her friend Ethel. However, in the course of that lesson between the female friends, Lucy confuses the gearshift, clutch, and brake as if they were interchangeable. The women proceed to wreck the car before it is insured. Most sitcoms offered a similar variation on this theme.

But for women who surmounted the perception that they would wreak havoc by sitting in the driver's seat, having their own mobility was a revelation. In the course of her daily life, many a postwar woman found that it became the mobile equivalent of a room of her own.

At first, most women used the car to go shopping. In the early days of postwar suburbia, there were few conveniently located grocery stores and retail establishments. When the idea of one-stop-shopping for women caught on, commercial centers mushroomed across the land. With female shoppers in mind, malls sprouted up, paving over former potato fields and acreage that had recently only been populated by cows.

Most sources put the number of shopping centers at fewer than 10 at the end of World War II in 1945. Ten years later, there were thousands. Soon the malls became enclosed to counteract inclement weather. After that, many became veritable indoor theme parks. They were all designed to please women shoppers and accommodate the automobile.

Suburban supermarkets also sprang up, with relatively inexpensive land in the suburbs providing acres of paved parking. Rather than exclusively stocking staples that a woman might need in the course of her daily life such as milk, eggs, and fresh produce, supermarkets began carrying more in the way of prepackaged foods.

These products were presumably catering to the mobile housewife's lack of time and her need for convenience. In the midst of the postwar baby boom, food industry executives reasoned that if a woman had a car, she would use it for her children. A mother might take the kids to school, transport them to scout meetings, and be the chauffeur for Little League games. She would take her children to music and dance lessons as well as dental appointments and visits to the doctor. A woman's access to a car meant adding to the domestic chores in her daily life. More mobility meant more responsibility, and marketers reasoned that this would cut into her meal-preparation time.

As the postwar era progressed, automobile manufacturers and advertising executives sensed a new target market for cars: the female half of the population. At first, car ads were basically aimed at men, emphasizing automotive power and styling. If a woman was pictured, she was usually draped over the chassis sporting a bikini, or perched primly in the front seat, with kids in back, dressed as if for church. But as more women began to buy cars, or at least influence the husband's purchasing decision, admen responded by making assumptions as to what women would want in a vehicle that was part of their daily lives.

Some emphasized ease of handling, safety, and reliability with women in mind. Others went in other directions such as fashion. Ford's "Motor Mates" campaign of the early 1950s was meant to appeal to the perceived female fixation on frivolities with a line of coats and purses that matched certain Ford vehicles. In 1955, Chrysler introduced the Dodge "La Femme," an automobile with a pink-toned exterior as well as matching interior touches such as rosebud upholstery. The car came with matching handbag, raincoat, and umbrella. Its advertising campaign featured the tagline, "designed for Your Majesty, the modern American Woman," but it was a royal flop. The vehicle was discontinued in 1957.

While some automakers at least attempted to appeal to women, albeit in a somewhat condescending way, there was a significant stumbling block. At many dealerships, women could not receive credit in their own names to make the purchase. Equal credit opportunity regardless of gender would not arrive until 1974.

Nonetheless, it was the automobile that made postwar life in suburbia much more pleasant for its female residents. Many suburban women had moved from urban areas where they were used to taking public transit or simply walking wherever they needed to go. For them, having a car as part of their daily lives was a lifeline, a welcome step away from the confinement of the isolated suburban home.

For rural women, the car was a godsend. Suburban women might feel isolated in their home, but they usually had neighbors within walking distance whom they could visit or at least chat with over the backyard clothesline. In the 1950s, rural areas still constituted more than a third of the American landscape. With the amount of acreage needed to grow crops profitably, farms were physically located a great distance away from each other. Perhaps more importantly, they were far from towns with shopping, activities, and entertainment. They were also far from marketplaces at which women could sell farm products such as fresh eggs or crafts like quilts that were often ways for a farmwife to earn a little "pin money."

Rural women were not daunted by the big automobiles of the 1950s. They were used to hitching up wagons in order to travel—a mode of transportation equally familiar to their great-grandmothers in the 1800s. Having a car was a huge step-up. It insulated them from the elements and made it possible to attend educational presentations as part of their daily lives such as agricultural extension programs, join a church group, or become part of a book club. In a car, they could make it back home much more quickly than by horse and wagon, usually in time to make dinner.

The postwar rise of the automobile coincided with the demise of other forms of transportation. Cross-country trains and buses went into a decline from which they never entirely recovered. But there was another form of transportation on the horizon that cars could not diminish: air travel.

For most women in postwar America, having the mobility of an automobile was more than enough. But others looked to the skies. Many cited 1930's aviator Amelia Earhart as a role model, later managing to break through the clouds themselves. In 1953, Jacqueline Cochran was the first woman flyer to break the sound barrier, which she did with legendary pilot Chuck Yeager following behind.

Automobiles of the postwar era brought life-changing mobility to the daily lives of many American women. After mastering the automobile, some women were inspired to set their goals even higher.

CLOTHING

Regarding fashion in the daily lives of average women in the postwar era, the essential story starts with the glamorous "New Look." It was heralded as just that—something fresh and exciting after years of austere clothing during the Depression and World War II. While the flowing skirts and cinched-in waistlines of dresses in the postwar era made a fashion statement that looked forward, that same fashion statement had its roots in the past.

In 1899, economist Thorstein Veblen published *The Theory of the Leisure Class* in which he addressed what would become known as conspicuous consumption. Like consumers in the 1950s, many Americans at the turn of the 20th century were enjoying the fruits of the Industrial Revolution. They were emerging from the centuries-old pattern of subsistence when people apart from the wealthy were forced to make their own necessities of life. In those times, many had aimed for simple survival at best.

By the turn of the 20th century, Veblen observed that there was more behind the act of purchasing goods rather than

In the postwar era, tailored suits with tight waistlines and straight "pencil" skirts generally had to be worn with long girdles. Combined with high-heeled shoes, even walking could be a challenge. In the Cold War era, fashions carried a patriotic message about U.S. prosperity, which was that under the capitalist system, average American women were ladies of leisure. (Auckland Memorial War Museum)

making them at home as part of their daily lives. Average people relished showing off their purchases in front of others in an attempt to demonstrate their status.

Veblen saw women's fashion in 1899, with yards of voluminous skirts and the tight, constricting corsets that created an "hourglass figure," as a walking display of conspicuous consumption meant to impress others. A woman wearing such impractical clothing obviously did not need to perform manual labor to survive.

By the midcentury years following World War II, much of the world struggled to survive after the devastation of the war.

America, emerging unscathed, soon began fighting the Cold War against Communism. As part of that ideological clash, the United States presented its way of life for average people as vastly superior to the Soviet system. This extended to the realm of female fashion. As part of their daily lives, American women had to strive to look better than Soviet women, displaying their patriotism as well as their healthy good looks.

Therefore, the women's clothing of the postwar era emerged like a radiant butterfly after the grim days of the Depression and the austerity of World War II. Christian Dior's "New Look," introduced in 1947, hit the fashion scene like a bombshell. Huge, billowing calf-length skirts in lush materials swelled above multiple layers of crinolines beneath. Nipped-in waistlines were constricted by tight girdles. The bustline was boosted by attention-getting pointed "bullet" brassieres. All in all, it was feminine, it was opulent, and it was wildly impractical, making the bold statement that American females had the wealth and leisure to drape themselves in such lavish garments. The clear implication was that under America's capitalist system, females did not have to labor in factories as part of their daily lives the way Soviet women did.

The exact opposite of the New Look, also symbolic of women's fashion in the 1950s, was equally impractical in its own way. Tailored suits with tight jackets and calf-length straight "pencil" skirts were confining, with the skirt kept in line by girdles that extended down the lower body. Combined with high-heeled shoes, even the act of walking was no simple thing. Like the New Look, tight, straight pencil skirts made a patriotic statement for the world to see: with the prosperity inherent in the capitalist system, the wearer was an average American woman of leisure.

After the dreary, understated colors of the Depression and wartime, multicolored prints such as bold florals and festive polka dots burst forth in the postwar years. They sent a message around the globe that even in fashion, the daily lives of women in the United States was lived in a way that was simply more fun than the drab Communist system.

Under it all, the ever-present girdle usually came with garters on which to attach nylon stockings. Even under long calf-length skirts, women rarely went bare-legged.

Television was never far from any aspect of women's daily life the 1950s, and fashion was no exception. Especially on TV sitcoms, housewives wore attractive shirtwaist dresses during the course of their fictional daily lives, even while cleaning. On television, these day dresses were often worn with high-heeled shoes, plus pearl necklaces that were either real or of the faux "costume" variety. In their own daily lives, many average women in postwar America sported similar kinds of day dresses, if not heels and pearls.

Several factors spurred the tremendous growth in the women's fashion industry during the postwar years. Even amid the nation's burgeoning prosperity, attire that was attractive but was also reasonably priced proved to be a plus for many women. One element contributing to the affordable cost factor was the ever-increasing capability of clothing manufactures to mass-produce garments. The other was synthetic fabrics.

The catchphrase "Better Living through Chemistry" was originally popularized amid the rise of postwar-era synthetic materials such as nylon, polyester, and acrylics. They were called "miracle fibers," and to many women, they were. "Drip-dry" garments simplified laundry day. No-wrinkle fabrics such as Dacron® minimized the need for ironing. Stretch materials made of synthetic blends offered figure control.

With all the inexpensive synthetic materials readily available, New York artist Vera Neumann came across parachute silk on sale at an army surplus store. Painting directly on the lush natural silk, she signed her creations, launching the first "signature scarf" in fashion history. Known as "Vera Scarves," they were immediately popular, drawing fans not only among average women but also postwar fashion icons such as Grace Kelly and Marilyn Monroe.

Postwar women's hairstyles complemented their attire. It was usually short with soft curls for what was called a "natural" look. The fact that the average woman had to sleep on painful, unforgiving curlers at night to achieve the natural look was an open secret. Some women emulated first lady Mamie Eisenhower by sporting her signature look of short, girlish bangs on her forehead.

Television, newspapers, and women's magazines provided a virtual at-home showroom for the latest postwar female fashions. In the course of their daily lives, average American women could keep up with fashion trends while they were keeping up with the Joneses.

They outfitted their daughters for school much like themselves, in skirts and dresses. In the Cold War years, conformity was key. For girls, that was reinforced by the era's most popular television program for young people, *The Mickey Mouse Club*. Mankowski states that like adult postwar women, girls of that era "were defined by their bodies and had to strive to meet strict standards of beauty" (n.p.). Even the youngest *Mickey Mouse Club* "Mouseketeers" had to conform to the standard, with perfectly curled hair and well-pressed below-the-knee skirts of their Mouseketeer uniforms, conforming to female beauty ideals in the postwar era.

Teenage girls, even at their most rebellious stage, usually conformed by wearing what was arguably the most symbolic piece of clothing of the 1950s: poodle skirts. The wide skirts might vary by being decorated with birds, cars, or flowers in addition to the eponymous poodle, but combined with the teen "uniform" of cinch belt, neckerchief, and white blouse, teens were still conforming to the standard in their own daily lives.

Some women of the postwar era who had worked in factories during World War II had discovered the comfort and freedom of pants. Certainly on most occasions in the 1950s, skirts or dresses were the norm. But informal events such as backyard barbeques allowed the opportunity for tailored slacks as well as the shorter Capri pants or pedal pushers, generally with a constricting girdle underneath.

Some women of the postwar era did transgress from the norm by becoming identified with the Beat movement. These women wore their hair long and natural, often also rejecting makeup except for accoutrements such as white lipstick. Black turtlenecks and black slacks constituted their own "uniform."

Other than rebellious female Beats, most women in postwar America wore gloves and hats complemented by attractive handbags whenever they were in public.

African American women of the postwar era generally made the kind of fashion choices that white women did. With a wide range of fabrics and styles, there was usually something for everyone on the socioeconomic scale. Like whites, some black women were slowly entering the workplace in jobs that were not limited to being domestic servants as in the past. Those in the clerical field wore smart, attractive dresses and business suits like their white counterparts.

Other black women, especially in urban areas, adopted the Beat look, signifying alternative lifestyle choices.

On the front pages of newspapers, usually far removed from the "women's section," a headline across the country in 1954 reported the landmark Supreme Court decision, *Brown v. Board of Education*. That ruling signaled the end of racial segregation in American public schools. Many young black women would be attending public schools among white peers for the first time.

Often, like most teenage girls, they simply wanted to fit in. But there was also a hidden statement in their fashion: by emulating white clothing, they hoped to do so in a way that sent the unspoken message that they were just teenagers like their white classmates. Sometimes it was wishful thinking. Hendricks (2016) notes the experience of 14-year-old Carlotta Walls, one of the African American girls who tried to integrate Central High School in Little Rock, Arkansas, in 1957 as part of a group that was called the Little Rock Nine in the news media. For Walls, "like the other girls of the Little Rock Nine, one of her biggest concerns was what to wear" (93).

As it turned out, worrying about their school clothes was not the biggest concern. Regardless of what they wore, surviving hate-spewing mobs and suffering daily torments by white classmates and even some teachers took precedence. The dress that Carlotta Walls wore that first day was special to her because it was store-bought for the occasion, not homemade as the rest of her clothes were. That dress now resides at the Smithsonian Institution in Washington, DC.

Other black women of the postwar era were determined to resist Eurocentric attempts at "whiteness" in fashion. Reclaiming their Africa-based heritage, some black women began sporting African prints and styles. Others rejected the arduous hair straightening process that they endured to look more like white women. Especially in urban centers, some began wearing their hair in the short, natural style that would later grow to dramatic size, becoming known as "Afros."

One group of postwar black women cared less about their hair than what they wore over it, especially on Sunday. Church hats known as "crowns" were said to be both a cherished African American custom and a passion for the wearers. Both the women and those observing them claimed that the "crowns" were a silent source of pride, making them stand a little taller, even during the Jim Crow era of the postwar years.

African American women followed fashion trends in magazines aimed at the black community such as *Ebony*. They observed the styles worn by African American entertainers such as Lena Horne and Eartha Kitt. Actress Dorothy Dandridge was a special favorite fashion role model, being the first black woman to be nominated for the Academy Award for Best Actress following her performance in the 1954 film *Carmen Jones*.

In white society, fashion icons of the postwar era also came from the movies. Doris Day combined an All-American wholesome sort of beauty and charm with an upbeat perkiness. With a slim figure that was different from the general "womanly" standard for postwar females, Audrey Hepburn exuded grace. The icon whose very name symbolized that trait was Grace Kelly, whose classic upscale fashion style as an actress was only eclipsed when she became a real-life princess.

Fashion designers became icons for average American women. Often, their designs were copied and sold for cut-rate prices at nationwide chain stores. At the top of the list was Christian Dior who had been widely publicized for his revolutionary "New Look" after World War II. French fashion star Coco Chanel bounced back after the war with sophisticated looks that were often sported by upper-class American "ladies who lunch." In 1955, Chanel introduced her signature quilted handbag with its gilt chain strap and interlocking C initials, decades before other designers emblazoned their trademark on apparel as walking advertisements.

American designer Clare McCardell popularized a "country" look for leisure wear using materials such as gingham. Cristóbal Balenciaga incurred the wrath of many American men in 1957 with the introduction of his "sack" dress that came without a waistline.

Loosely sacked or tightly cinched, women in postwar America liked to look nice in the course of their daily lives and also believed it was their patriotic duty to do so. More than at any time in the past, most could afford to do so. They even had the money and desire to incorporate perfume, once a luxury item, into their daily fashion. Along with what women wore, fragrance was part of their image. Top brands of the postwar era included Arpège, Chanel No. 5, Chantilly, Evening in Paris, My Sin, Shalimar, and Tabu.

Women's clothing in the postwar era was a mix of glamour and wholesomeness, of sophistication and conservatism. The average American woman had to look stylish and young, in marked contrast to the media image of Soviet women who were worn down, old before their time, and haggard—all under the yoke of the socialist system.

American women wore clothes to present themselves in ways that helped promote the superiority of life in the United States. Even in fashion, it was important to send the message worldwide that the American way was the best way. As they had done in World War II, women in postwar America did their part.

FOOD AND DRINK

In the course of her daily life, the average postwar American woman developed a somewhat ambivalent relationship with her kitchen. On the one hand, most embraced the societal message of the 1950s that an important part of her assigned role as a housewife meant that the kitchen was her special domain. On the other hand, advancing technology, food manufacturers, and the advertising industry worked together to reduce the amount of time she needed to spend there.

For the most part, many rural women of the postwar era carried on as farmwives had done for generations. Well into the postwar years, rural women generally grew their own vegetables and nurtured fruit trees as well as raising poultry and livestock to provide their families with food.

The average postwar American woman understood that a major part of her assigned role as a housewife was to be a cook. New "convenience foods" like frozen dinners, processed food, and items in cans and boxes were marketed to women as a way for her family to have more time together, which was generally meant to be spent in front of their television. (Stokkete/Dreamstime.com)

Women in urban centers could follow their own decades-old tradition of walking to a nearby butcher, fish market, fruit stand, and greengrocer on a daily basis. Having easy access to fresh food helped streamline meal planning for many urban women.

But it was in the new suburban communities where a food-related revolution was taking place. In the early 1950s, many suburbs did not yet have supermarkets or grocery stores of any kind. Houses were situated on small plots that did not lend themselves to enough vegetable gardening to feed a family. In addition, with many young families having only one car, it was difficult for women to shop for groceries on a frequent basis.

Technology joined hand in hand with the food industry to meet the need. Freezer compartments in refrigerators led to an upsurge in frozen foods. "Convenience foods" provided ease of preparation and cleanup. Advances in canning permitted food items of all sorts to be sealed in handy, affordable tins. Other food items, especially snack foods, were sold in bags and boxes that stayed reasonably fresh on shelves.

The growing number of processed foods carved out an increasing presence at grocery stores. These are food items that have been modified or preserved through chemical and mechanical operations by the manufacturer. At mealtime, women could prepare processed foods quickly and easily, especially when partnered with the new electric appliances that were popping up in the average postwar woman's kitchen.

Many women found they did indeed enjoy convenience rather than being tied to the kitchen for the preparation and cleanup of three meals day. Postwar housewives bought more convenience foods, and as they did, food manufacturers continually introduced hundreds more new products that kept rolling off their conveyor belts and onto grocery shelves.

Women found that their families enjoyed the taste of processed foods as well as—or sometimes better than—homemade. There was a reason for that. Processed foods were manufactured to appeal to the taste buds, and some, critics said, left people who consumed them craving more. Critics asserted that processed foods had little nutritional value and contained ingredients such as preservatives that were empty calories at best, if not potentially harmful. However, food companies assured housewives that their products were good, wholesome fare. In an age when people tended to trust what they were told by authorities, most women accepted those claims.

In the event that there were leftovers, new products flowed from the burgeoning plastics industries of the postwar age. Women loved merchandise such as plastic wrap and resealable plastic containers as much as they enjoyed major appliances.

Advances in refrigerated trucks allowed foodstuffs to be transported from across the country to nationwide markets. In addition to spacious new refrigerators that came with their own freezer compartment, affordable freestanding freezers for the home also became more commonplace. Food could be kept fresh for longer periods of time in the home.

Fresh fruits and vegetables were grown in warm-weather states before being shipped all across the country. Bountiful harvests in mid-America yielded wheat, corn, and other grains. Fish, poultry, pork, and beef were plentiful. Most women in postwar America had access to nutritious food year-round.

But to be truly "modern," the average postwar American housewife was sold on the concept of convenience. Canned, boxed, and frozen foods were in style. Cookbooks rolled off the presses emphasizing that less time in the kitchen meant more time for women to be with their families. Children could be taken to music lessons or sports programs. There could be more quality "togetherness" time with her husband.

In addition, the average woman could contribute to the family's standing in the community, as well as her husband's chances for advancement at work, by transforming herself from a dull housewife to a sparkling hostess. Many new cookbooks placed the emphasis on entertaining.

One of the most popular cookbooks of the era was published in 1951 by food authority Poppy Cannon who wrote for the top women's magazines. Her bestseller, *The Can Opener Cookbook*, promised that it would reveal how to turn the simplest materials into a chef's delight. Its cover stated that it was "a guide for gourmet cooking with canned or frozen foods or mixes."

Using convenience items that were probably already on hand, women were assured of impressing guests, from the suburban neighborhood set to those times when her husband unexpectedly brought the boss home for dinner.

Recipes in women's magazines overwhelmingly promoted products being marketed by their advertisers, from convenience foods to labor-saving appliances.

For those times when even opening a can was too time consuming, a housewife could look to her freezer. The first official

"TV Dinner"-brand frozen meal was introduced by C. A. Swanson & Sons in 1953. The meat and vegetable components of these prepackaged frozen meals were nestled into individual compartments on a shiny aluminum tray. Low-cost TV dinners maintained consistent portion control, removing the daily decision about what meat and vegetables to serve away from the lady of the house. In addition, there was ease of cleanup—no dishwashing required.

The cardboard box that the frozen meal came in was designed to suggest a television set, complete with picture screen, knobs, and dials. With that subliminal suggestion, marketers hoped American women and their families would spend more time eating off trays in front of the television, which many did. At mealtime, people could consume prominently placed commercials along with their dinner.

However, there were still women who preferred to choose their own ingredients, cook their own meals, and serve them at the dinner table with their own family gathered around. It required planning and frequent trips to the grocery for fresh food, but many women felt it was worth it to prepare home-cooked meals for the family.

Chicken, fish, beef, and pork were popular main dishes for dinner. Vegetarians were often considered "health nuts." Meats were usually accompanied by some form of potatoes, which kept well at home for a week or two, giving rise to the "meat and potatoes" standard that could be found throughout the land.

The meal was completed by some sort of vegetable on the side, plus perhaps a salad. Some type of bread was almost always on the table. Then dessert was served. Leftovers, especially items such as meat loaf, could be made into sandwiches and packed in a brown bag for Dad and the kids to have for lunch at school or work the next day.

Many women in postwar America took pride not only in hearty dinners but also in preparing a hot breakfast to fortify their families as they started their day. A scene in the 1998 movie *Pleasantville*, set in 1958, shows a groaning table full of food, with one character's breakfast serving consisting of pancakes, eggs, sausage, bacon, and ham steak. Biscuits, waffles, and an array of other breakfast items were also available choices. *Pleasantville* may have been fiction but was not too far off the mark.

Yet sometimes even the most dedicated postwar housewife enjoyed a break from cooking three meals every day or even choosing convenience items. Eating out was a treat that was usually saved for special occasions. In the early 1950s, a sit-down restaurant might have been the venue of choice, but as the decade wore on, more and more Americans were able to combine their love of automobiles with eating at fast food stands.

At drive-in establishments such as McDonalds', families could wear casual clothes, pile the kids in the back seat, and enjoy consistently delicious items such as hamburgers, fries, and milkshakes without leaving the cozy confines of their car.

As in the case of processed convenience foods, fast food was criticized for having little nutritional value as well as for its sameness. But the sameness was the point. A housewife might burn the roast or undercook the potatoes, but fast food was consistent. Most people liked it.

With all these dining choices, postwar housewives also had to be responsible for what their family drank as a beverage to accompany their meal. Traditionally, Americans consumed water, coffee, tea, milk, or fruit-based drinks with their meals. Women and children were advised to drink two large glasses of milk each day, made possible by refrigerated trucks that could bring fresh dairy products from the farm to the supermarket.

Carbonated beverages had been available to American customers at soda fountains since the late 1800s. In the 1920s, soft drink vending machines and "home packs" with six bottles in a cardboard carrier were introduced. But it was with the confluence of factors in the postwar era that the consumption of soft drinks skyrocketed. Improved trucking transport, manufacturing innovations, mass production, and inexpensive packaging such as aluminum cans joined forces with the advertising and fast food industries. Although drinks such as milk or water were available at fast food restaurants, there were often "combo" deals that included soda as part of the price.

If women felt concerned that their children were drinking less milk and more soda, they were reassured by the soft drink industry as well as marketers. Advertisements featured children, some as young as babies, enjoying carbonated beverages. Many showed happy family groups at the dinner table or at leisure enjoying bottles of "pop," with the clear implication that mothers could help create happy families by bringing family members together over their choice of soda.

Along with soft drinks, there were also "hard" drinks in the postwar era, some of which played a part in the daily lives of women in postwar America. The 1950s, according to Cheever (2016), were "awash in alcohol" (2).

An ironic consequence of the Prohibition in the 1920s led to more alcohol consumption among women. Speakeasies and nightclubs of the 1920s attracted a female clientele by offering mixed drinks aimed at women customers. By the 1950s, women enjoyed having the money and social acceptance to buy liquor, drink at bars, host alcohol-fueled parties, and show their sophistication by mixing cocktails that had exotic names such as the Mai Tai, Pina Colada, Pink Squirrel, Singapore Sling, and Sloe Gin Fizz.

An entire culture emerged, built around the consumption of alcohol by postwar women. There were fashionable cocktail dresses and cocktail hats, meant to be sported at cocktail parties during cocktail hour. Women could serve cocktail food and mix their drinks in an array of cocktail glasses.

That was the "fun" side of women and alcohol during the 1950s. The other side was the one that most outsiders didn't see: the bored, frustrated, and sometimes abused women feeling trapped in unhappy lives that were not the picture-perfect ideal as seen on television. Women enjoyed the social acceptance to purchase alcohol themselves and could usually afford to do so. Many had the chance to drink it as part of their daily lives when their families were at work or school. Rising female alcoholism was one of the downsides of the bountiful array of food and drink in the postwar era.

There were also innumerable women in what was called the "Other America," often minorities, who lived outside the general prosperity. Some of these women went hungry, often so that their children could have what little food was available.

Others were tantalized by the images in food commercials on television, purchasing inexpensive processed items and "junk food." Ironically, instead of looking malnourished, they began gaining weight due to the additives and preservatives that were often found in such products. With the processed foods and sugary drinks all around them, many American women of the middle and lower classes became heavier.

In an era where a woman's looks were paramount, it was frowned upon for her to be fat. Upper-class women had access to the types of exercise and dietary programs that could keep them slim. Marketers set their sights on all the others.

For many women of the postwar era, there were such popular weight-loss regimens as grapefruit diets, cabbage soup diets, and liquid diet products that were meant to be consumed instead of eating a meal. Diet cookies and diet candies were intended for snack time. In 1952, the first carbonated diet soft drink, a quasi ginger ale called "No-Cal" was introduced. It was soon followed by diet colas and food items usually termed "lite."

Some advertisements for weight-loss products of the 1950s came with taglines promising that women could lose 10 pounds in a month "without dieting or exercise." Movie star endorsements and ways for women to "slim the way the stars slim" were always popular marketing themes.

A dark side effect of food and drink in the postwar era was the proliferation of diet pills. Some advertisements aimed at women promoted addictive methamphetamine products to curb appetite as well as to treat depression. At the time, there was not much of a connection between junk food and weight gain that was being publicized. If a woman got fat, she was considered to be at fault for lacking self-control and eating too much. Many turned to diet pills. It is unknown how many women of the postwar era spent their daily lives hungry and addicted.

Although many women kept their weight down by exercising and doing housework, according to a 2010 report by the Center for Disease Control and Prevention on overweight and obesity, poundage increased throughout the postwar era. Experts concluded that contributing factors were those that constituted large portions of the daily lives of average American women during that time. Those elements included consuming processed foods, hours of sitting in front of the television, and regular meals at fast food restaurants—all of which grew in popularity during the postwar years.

HOUSING

Much of the attention on housing for women in postwar America centers around those who lived in suburbia. Indeed, the new suburban communities that sprang up in the postwar era revolutionized daily life in the United States, especially for women. Many moved to suburbia with husbands, fathers, or other males who were able to receive credit from banks for the mortgage or who qualified for low-cost loans through the GI Bill. But beyond suburbia, there were two other groups of women in postwar America who lived their daily lives in quite different environments.

In many ways, rural women of the postwar era lived the kind of lives that had been traditional for decades. After World War II, those who remained on the farm or ranch or in an isolated mining community often lived in a home that had been in the same family for years. Some were large and comfortable while others were small and ramshackle. Most rural women did not think of their home as a material item in the same way as something like a television or automobile. Instead, it was often considered to be a continuation of family tradition.

Along with daily chores such as cooking, childcare, and cleaning that took place inside the home, most rural women also helped work their family's farm or ranch. They joined in in cultivating the crops and tending the livestock. Some women owned and/or operated their own farms or ranches.

With the extensive mechanized agricultural operations that were becoming the norm in America's heartland as the postwar years progressed, distances between rural homes could be enormous. More physically isolated than their urban or suburban counterparts, rural women often depended on each other to assist with childbirth and caring for children, sharing heavy workloads, and trading goods such as quilts or other crafts with each other. In order to do that, they needed transportation to carry them miles between homes on rural roads.

Traditionally, rural transportation meant a horse and wagon. Even with the greater availability of automobiles after World War II, many rural women lived in homes that were located far from paved roads. Sometimes there were roads that were covered with gravel or shale. But they often ended in a rutted, unimproved dirt track that could be bogged down in mud after a rainstorm or by melting snow, making them impassable.

Isolated rural women often spent the bulk of their time at home, unable to go to club meetings, attend extension classes, or socialize on a regular basis. But most were able to attain some of the fruits of postwar prosperity by equipping their houses with as many modern conveniences as the family could afford. A new radio or television could be a woman's lifeline to the world. It all depended on whether her home had access to electricity.

The availability of rural electrification varied from state to state. Through not-for-profit electric cooperatives, more rural citizens gained access to electrical power. But the availability of electricity varied from state to state in the heartland. For example, in the postwar era, about 90 percent of Iowa farms had access to electricity. However, well into the 1950s, no power lines were available to some rural areas of Arkansas, home to a third of its farm families.

Those rural women who were not initially terrified by electricity found it to be almost miraculous. Soon they were able to purchase electric stoves, refrigerators, washing machines, and other labor-saving devices, many on credit. They could install a telephone for communication and electric pumps to make indoor plumbing possible. In the postwar era of the 1950s, the modernization of the homes of many rural women allowed them to join the 20th century.

After World War II, the Housing Act of 1949 created the Rural Development program under the direction of the U.S. Department of Agriculture to help keep Americans on their family farms and ranches. Despite such assistance, there were still pockets of poverty in places such as the rural mining communities of Appalachia and among tenant farmers in the South. As the postwar era wore on, many unmarried women left what they felt were limited opportunities in rural areas to try their luck in towns and cities.

Author Betsy Israel (2002) follows the trajectory of those young women who went to live in urban areas, often being called "bachelor girls." The postwar era was a time when marriage was considered by most Americans to be the only life for a woman, yet "there were thousands who, setting aside domestic destiny, graduated or just left home with something else in mind besides a wedding" (186).

Certainly, there were reports of assault, crime, dirt, murder, noise, robberies, and various other hazards associated with "the big city." But along with those, many young American women of the postwar years also found urban living to be everything a metropolitan Chamber of Commerce said it was. They discovered improved career prospects, diversity, educational options, entertainment galore, excitement, inspiration, medical facilities, plentiful culture, public transportation, recreation, restaurants, stunning views of city skylines, even professional sports teams. All a young postwar American woman had to do was afford it.

With few exceptions, rentals were the norm for housing in urban centers. With the postwar housing crunch, rents in cities were high. Some young women had family support or personal savings; some had roommates to cut costs. Most had career opportunities to help pay the rent—at least until they got married and lost their jobs.

For African American or Hispanic women in the de facto segregation of postwar urban culture, there were color lines on housing. In predominantly black neighborhoods such as Harlem in uptown Manhattan, conditions were often overcrowded and difficult. But the African American women who lived there did not have the option of moving to the newly developed suburbs. Nonwhite women and their families were excluded from suburbia by what were called "protective covenants" as well as by unspoken agreement among white residents or developers. Often nonwhites were denied credit by banks to buy a suburban house. Black veterans found it difficult to utilize the benefits of the GI Bill, including low-interest home loans. The plight of postwar-era blacks seeking better housing in Chicago is dramatized in the 1959 play (and 1961 movie) *A Raisin in the Sun* by Lorraine Hansberry.

Therefore, women from minority and immigrant groups did not tend to find housing in suburbia. This was especially true of African Americans who fled rural life in the South by coming to northern cities. While minority women may have experienced the downside of urban living with its substandard housing, they found that segregated neighborhoods were often the only choice for many.

For those who were not classified as nonwhites, there were different types of housing across the economic spectrum available to postwar women in urban areas. Many who could not afford their own apartment or who preferred company found traditional boardinghouses to their liking. Most postwar-era boardinghouses offered meals and companionship. Some were for women only, while others were co-ed.

For those women who could afford it, there was the option of a small apartment, often in a less-expensive Bohemian area of the city that attracted artists and writers. One typical path was followed by author Betty Freidan. After college, she moved to a then affordable area of New York City known as Greenwich Village. She had a career as a magazine writer, but after marrying, she lost her job. Moving with her husband and starting a family in the suburbs, Friedan found she missed the excitement of living in the city. Her observations about women's lives in postwar suburbia led to writing *The Feminine Mystique,* her landmark book published in 1963.

Apart from boardinghouses and private apartments, there was another type of housing for postwar women that was available in larger cities. In New York, there were "women only" apartment/ hotel residences. The best known of the postwar era was Manhattan's women-only Barbizon Hotel. Among the thousands of "career girls" who found housing there, residents of the Barbizon included future stars such as Grace Kelly.

For single young women who migrated westward, a similar type of housing emerged in Los Angeles. The Hollywood Studio Club (HSC) catered to would-be movie stars of the postwar era.

According to Beauchamp (2019), the women-only residence provided a home for postwar-era starlets such as Kim Novak and Marilyn Monroe before their later fame. Beauchamp states that "of the thousands of women who lived at the HSC over the decades, only a small percentage found stardom" (131). However, in the urban environment of Los Angeles, they often did find opportunities for work as support staff at movie studios or in other types of businesses.

Whether they were unmarried women in the expanses of rural America or living amid city lights, for most postwar women, there was usually one goal: marriage. It was not just a pleasant dream; there was a real urgency to escape from living the solitary life. Single young women often found that by a certain age, usually their mid-20s, the world saw them as pathetic "spinsters" or "old maids." Betsy Israel (2002) states that in the 1950s, "single life stood out more than ever as a social aberration" (184).

Therefore, young women had an eye out for an eligible man with whom to walk down the aisle. The next step for many was going with their husband to the suburbs.

The postwar era saw tremendous growth in housing that was built in areas that were neither rural nor urban. It was called suburbia, a place that would strongly impact the daily lives of many women in postwar America.

The average suburban development was generally located near a city, allowing a relatively easy commute. With more postwar Americans able to buy their own car, the booming automobile market made suburbs possible. Suburbs, in turn, fueled the automobile industry with a steady demand for cars.

Although suburban communities eventually sprang up across the country, today the most well known of the postwar suburbs was the vast development called Levittown, near New York City. For better or worse, Levittown came to exemplify the American suburbs of the postwar era.

Much of the criticism of Levittown came from its sameness. Just as in the auto industry, construction of the homes was based on the assembly-line process. Buyers could choose some basic variations in design, such as homes called the "Ranch" or "Cape Cod." Although there was room for later expansion, what women found was that their new homes were essentially four rooms on a concrete slab.

The general floor plan of Levittown homes consisted of two bedrooms, a living room, and a kitchen/dining area. The four rooms covered a space of 750 square feet. On the outside, the homes were placed on identical plots of land that measured 60 × 100 feet.

In the face of criticism about their "cookie cutter" developments, most women didn't care, at least at first. They loved that their homes had more space and more privacy than apartment living. Suburban homes were clean and new. If they paid their mortgage as agreed, homeowners could not be evicted by landlords or have their rent raised without notice. They were not forced to live with family members while they tried to save money. In Levittown, the sparkling new homes already came equipped with appliances, so women did not need to spend time and money shopping for items such as a stove, refrigerator, and washing machine. With their husbands' financing through the GI Bill, they could move right in.

Critics never seemed to understand how much suburban house-wives appreciated their homes, at least in the beginning. Many felt the same way as the young postwar-era wife who was quoted by Ferrer and Navarra (1997) as saying: "We were living in a two-room apartment in Queens with my mother. When [developer Bill] Levitt called to say he had a home for us . . . we jumped at the opportunity and bought it sight unseen" (42).

With women's prime roles revolving around being wives and mothers, Levitt perceived their needs in the design of the houses and the development at large, influencing future home construc-tion across America. As a woman's perceived domain, the kitchen was centrally located, in many ways, the "hub" of the home. A large picture window allowed women to easily watch their chil-dren playing in the yard. Sidewalks made it safe and convenient to stroll with baby carriages.

A yard allowed women to plant gardens for flowers or a few veg-etables. They could also plant trees, watching them grow along with their children. Even though many women certainly felt isolated in the suburbs, there was at least the physical proximity of neighbors who were usually women similar to themselves. In the course of their daily lives, even when hanging out the laundry, there was the potential for contact between a woman and her neighbors.

Women in the rising middle class of postwar America found a number of housing options for themselves and their families. Amid the general prosperity of the 1950s, along with housing benefits from the GI Bill, many American women could live their daily lives in their own home, which to many was the greatest material pos-session of all.

POSSESSIONS

The vast array of possessions in the homes of average American women in the postwar era did not happen by accident. Rather, it was due to a unique set of circumstances in a particular place and time.

Following World War II, much of the world struggled to survive and rebuild after the devastation of the war. America, emerging unscathed, looked to a bright future as the primary global superpower.

During the 1940s, many manufacturers received government financing to produce arms and material for the war effort. When the conflict ended, they had cash reserves on hand that enabled them to quickly retool assembly lines from wartime weaponry to postwar consumer goods.

Manufacturers also had new technologies that evolved from wartime commodities into fun items for the average American woman's home. These ranged from ballpoint pens to transistor radios, from Super Glue to spray cans—all of which an average woman might use in the course of her daily life. Manufacturers did not have to try selling tired old products that had gathered dust since the 1930s. Holding tremendous appeal for female consumers, everything was shiny and new, the perfect complement to the postwar era's brave new world.

Moreover, manufactures had an eager customer base. Between the Great Depression of the 1930s and the austerity of the war years, American women were more than ready for new things after two decades of deprivation.

To keep the postwar American economy strong, the government worked with business and industry to stave off a recession. For white males, there was virtually full employment in the postwar years. That security gave them the money to buy whatever they wanted for their families through cash or easy credit.

Some women had savings put away from their war work, but they were encouraged to spend it, not keep saving it. Through the mass media messages of the Cold War era, American women believed that buying as many possessions at they could was the patriotic thing to do. It was a way not only to bolster the economy of the United States but also to show the benefits of the capitalistic way of life as opposed to the deprivations of the Communist system in the Soviet Union.

Certainly, women who lived in the poverty-stricken regions of "The Other America" wanted to be part of the national buying spree, but they did not always succeed. Yet, while many postwar women living their daily lives below the poverty line in depressed regions such as Appalachia or the Cotton Belt of the Deep South may not have had indoor plumbing, they often had a washing machine.

Housing and automobiles were generally a middle-class family's most significant monetary investment. For women, possessing those items was a source of security and freedom as well as pride. They felt confident in those purchases because the messages they received from their government and the mass media reinforced the notion that they needed to buy and keep buying.

That concept was clearly demonstrated by representatives of the highest level of government. As widely broadcast by the news media, U.S. vice president Richard Nixon sparred with Soviet premier Nikita Khrushchev during the famed "kitchen debate" in 1959. At an international trade fair in Russia that both leaders attended, Nixon asserted that the upper-middle-class model home on display was attainable by any average American worker.

Of particular interest was the model kitchen, the domain of the postwar American woman. Nixon claimed that through their modern appliances, even middle-class American women were able to lead carefree lives as ladies of leisure. Khrushchev countered that Soviet women could take pride in their role as workers who were equal to men in rebuilding their devastated country.

The American kitchen items on display during the trade fair had been provided free of charge by their manufacturers. The sheer number of such products, said to be used by average women in the typical American home, was overwhelming. There were large appliances such as dishwashers, electric ranges and ovens, refrigerators with ice makers and automatic defrosters, vacuum cleaners, washing machines, and gas or electric dryers.

As they did in many American homes, large appliances took center stage in the model display, while scores of small appliances vied for room on the kitchen counters. Smaller devices included items such as blenders, electric skillets, floor waxers, handheld mixers, ice crushers, pressure cookers, steam irons, toaster ovens, and even milkshake makers. Khrushchev claimed not to be impressed.

Just as the placement of a picture window in suburban homes allowed women to keep an eye on their children, the picture window could also allow neighbors to keep an eye on each other.

A family's possessions could be in full view of the world, suggesting they were fulfilling the national directive to stock the house with possessions. Not only did many American women feel the need to "keep up with the Joneses" but also the era of McCarthyism was not the time to go against the national grain by being seen as nonconformists. In order to conform, American homes continued filling up with possessions.

However, there were costs to some women that were effects from the allegorical law of unintended consequences. All those labor-saving possessions did indeed free a housewife from backbreaking chores such as doing the family's laundry by hand. But many women soon began to feel that their usefulness was being diminished. After the husband went off to work and children to school, time often weighed heavily.

It was especially true of suburban women who felt isolated, having few outlets for their frustration. This unexpected development would constitute a significant factor cited by Friedan (2013). She found that the problem was attributed by some male pundits to women having too much education or being granted the right to vote. According to Friedan, some dissatisfied women living amid all their possessions felt like a "two-headed schizophrenic" (67), or at the very least, ungrateful.

For all the consumer products flooding the marketplace in the postwar era, there were three possessions that rose to an iconography apart from simply being material goods. It would not be overstating the case to say that they revolutionized the lives of millions of women in postwar America.

The first was ownership of an automobile by African Americans. With a personal car, black women were freed from the incessant humiliations of bus and train travel in the South where African Americans were forced to sit in the back of buses on seats that were often broken. Traveling by train saw them compelled to use "colored" waiting rooms before being shunted into segregated railcars. There, the "colored"' restroom facilities lacked the amenities of the bathrooms for whites. Black travelers had to cram suitcases under their feet, as there were no luggage racks on the segregated railcars. Even on interstate bus lines, it was not until 1955 that the Interstate Commerce Commission ruled they could not be segregated by race.

Therefore, owning a car meant that a black woman was not forced to watch her family denigrated into inferior status while simply trying to travel from place to place. Additionally, in some postwar situations, a car became a lifeline as well as a tool in the civil rights struggle. For example, during the Montgomery, Alabama, bus boy-cott of 1955, fleets of personal autos were used to take black women to their jobs as maids in the white part of town, so the women could continue to earn a living while protesting unfair treatment in pub-lic transportation. More cars also meant the ability to ferry more and more activists, including young women, to nonviolent sit-ins, marches, and other forms of protest in the postwar era.

However, even in personal cars, African Americans still had to use caution while motoring, especially in the South. The term "Driving While Black" (DWB) was not yet in vogue during the postwar era, but the risk was always there. DWB is a play on the words "Driving While Intoxicated" (DWI), which is unlawful in most jurisdictions. For literally no reason, African Americans could be stopped and harassed by white law enforcement officials, simply by virtue of their race. Black women were especially vulnerable to harassment by whites, more so if their car broke down on a deserted road.

Throughout the postwar era, many hotels and restaurants refused to serve blacks. Some communities proclaimed themselves "sundown towns," meaning that African Americans had to be gone by 6:00 p.m. To help find places where they were not unwelcome, African American travelers of the postwar era had *The Negro Motor-ist Green Book*, abbreviated as the *Green Book*, a series of guidebooks that identified safe havens for black travelers. Published between 1936 and 1966 by Victor Hugo Green, an African American mail-man in New York City, the *Green Book* helped African American motorists avoid danger and inconvenience while traveling in their cars.

Avoiding public transportation by having a personal car was con-sidered by many black women to a least be a step forward, where their children were not imprinted with the mark of discrimination at best, or at worst, put in danger.

The second possession that grew into something much bigger than itself was an air conditioner. For northern women, the abil-ity to keep their home cool in summer was a pleasant relief. In the South, it was revolutionary. Affordable air conditioning allowed an entire region that was still devastated by the Civil War of the 1860s to enter the 20th century.

In the early postwar era, air conditioners could be purchased as window units that cooled one room. But before long, real estate developers saw the potential in a central cooling unit that con-trolled the temperature in the entire house. Utility companies also saw the potential in more consumption of electricity. Houses were designed with the electric cooling system in mind and could be built more cheaply, with thinner walls and fewer windows. Thus, residential housing became less expensive.

But the truly revolutionary aspect was how air conditioning launched the development of a vast, virtually untapped region of the nation. The oppressively hot South and Southwest were now open for business. With air conditioning, office buildings could be constructed to provide new kinds of jobs beyond farming. In the postwar era, suburbs mushroomed as rural women and their families could leave the farm for a new kind of life in affordable suburban homes. The population of states in the "Sunbelt" such as Arizona, Florida, Georgia, Texas, and the Carolinas exploded. Businesses relocated from northern cities to the less-expensive South. Women could seek jobs in the clerical field rather than the cotton field.

Finally, there was a third possession that burst forth from being a simple kitchen utensil to a radical new way of life for some women in postwar America. Introduced in 1946, it was a small plastic household item called Tupperware. Under the marketing expertise of a woman named Brownie Wise, the resealable storage containers were sold not in stores but in the comfort of a woman's home.

"Tupperware Parties" provided part-time work that was often extremely lucrative for tis female sales representatives. Women could plan a gathering around their household schedule and still meet the needs of their husbands and children.

Even those men who forbade their wives to seek a job outside the home could be mollified. On the surface, Tupperware gatherings appeared to simply be a house party for neighborhood women where they could socialize and even bring the children. But in a larger sense, the Tupperware party concept gave millions of women in postwar America a sense of purpose. It allowed them to use their talents, develop confidence, refine their sales techniques, and bring in a substantial income. This simple plastic possession allowed women to follow the postwar ethos of staying in the home but also to expand beyond its confines.

From small appliances to big cars, from air conditioning to washing machines, and from toaster ovens to Tupperware, the possessions of American women in the postwar era often became more than simply being store-bought material goods. In fact, millions of postwar women in the United States did not even have to make a trip to the store to obtain the possessions they desired. Mail-order catalogs were regularly published by companies such as JC

Penney, Montgomery Ward, and especially Sears Roebuck with its famed "Wish Book." Catalogs provided women in postwar America, especially those in rural areas, with the world's biggest store right in their mailbox.

The list of merchandise available in postwar mail-order catalogs was almost endless: appliances; baby carriages; bicycles; electric blankets; jewelry; musical instruments; saddles; sewing machines; sporting goods; toys; and a vast selection of children's, men's, and women's clothing. Throughout huge isolated regions of the nation, farmwives and ranchers' daughters could be as stylish as women in the big cities.

In addition, mail-order catalogs provided a lifeline for African Americans in the Jim Crow South. Most businesses catering to white shoppers did not allow blacks to try on clothing. Many storekeepers did not even welcome having blacks in the store, requiring them to stand outside and look in the window. Mail-order catalogs provided a much wider window on the world of consumer items, possessions that black people could attain just as easily as whites.

There was another element in the cornucopia of possessions among most American women in the Cold War era: exposing foreigners to the American way of life and the material wealth generated by capitalism. According to historian Alistair Cooke (1977), postwar advertising executive Bruce Barton proposed combatting Communism by stating, "What we ought to do is send up a flight of B-29s and drop a million Sears Roebuck catalogs all over Russia" (317).

FURTHER READING

Beauchamp, Cari. "Sorority of Stars." *Vanity Fair*, Holiday Issue 2019/2020, pp. 120–125, 131.

Callahan, Michael. "Ladies in Waiting: Sorority on E. 63rd St." *Vanity Fair*, March 16, 2010. https://www.vanityfair.com/culture/2010/04 /barbizon-hotel-201004.

Cannon, Poppy. *The Can-Opener Cookbook*. New York: Thomas Crowell, 1955.

Cheever, Susan. *Drinking in America: Our Secret History*. New York: Twelve Books, 2016.

Cooke, Alistair. *Alistair Cooke's America*. New York: Knopf, 1977.

"Fast Stats." Data and Statistics, Overweight and Obesity, *Centers for Disease Control and Prevention*. https://www.cdc.gov/obesity/data /index.html.

Ferrer, Margaret, and Tova Navarra. *Levittown: The First 50 Years*. Charleston, SC: Arcadia Publishing, 1997.

Friedan, Betty. *The Feminine Mystique*. New York: Norton, 50th anniversary edition, 2013.

Girard, Jolyon, ed. "Daily Life in the United States, 1940–1959." *The Greenwood Encyclopedia of Daily Life in America*. Westport, CT: Greenwood, 2009.

Hansberry, Lorraine. *A Raisin in the Sun*. New York: Vintage, reprint edition, 2004.

Hendricks, Nancy. *Notable Arkansas Women: From Hattie to Hillary, 100 Names to Know*. Little Rock, AR: Butler Center Books, 2016.

Israel, Betsy. *Bachelor Girl: The Secret History of Single Women in the Twentieth Century*. New York: William Morrow, 2002.

Mankowski, Diana. "Pretty Girls and Strong Boys: Mouseketeers and the Cold War." *The Ultimate History Project*. http://ultimatehistoryproject.com/mouseketeers-and-cold-war.html.

Marling, Karal Ann. *As Seen on TV: The Visual Culture of Everyday Life in the 1950s*. Cambridge, MA: Harvard University Press, 1996.

Maslow, Abraham H. *A Theory of Human Motivation*. Eastford, CT: Martino Fine Books, reprint edition, 2013.

"Nixon-Khrushchev Kitchen Debate, July 24, 1959." *C-SPAN.com*. https://www.c-span.org/video/?110721-1/nixon-khrushchev-kitchen-debate.

Olian, JoAnne, ed. *Everyday Fashions of the Fifties as Pictured in Sears Catalogs*. Mineola, NY: Dover Publications, 2002.

"Pleasantville Breakfast Scene." https://www.youtube.com/watch?v=FovNFJIaEy8.

"Quick Facts." *Iowa Association of Electric Cooperatives*. https://www.iowarec.org/media-center/quick-facts.

Veblen, Thorstein. *The Theory of the Leisure Class: An Economic Study of Institutions*. Mineola, NY: Dover, Thrift Editions, 1994.

Wordsworth, William, with introduction by Stephen Gill. *William Wordsworth: Selected Poems*. New York: Penguin, 2004.

5

POLITICAL LIFE

As quoted in Maza (2019), "Women [are] barred from civil and public functions and therefore cannot be judges or hold a magistracy" (50). Maza adds that women, being "considered weaker [are] ignorant of legal matters, and lacking in judgment" (51).

Although those statements were written about the status of females in ancient Rome, they were not too far removed from the lives of women in postwar America in the 1950s, who lived 2,000 years later.

In the decades since America became a sovereign nation in 1789, it took until after World War II, 160 years later, for the first female to be appointed to a judgeship in a federal district court. That happened in 1949, when President Harry Truman appointed Burnita Shelton Matthews to the U.S. District Court for the District of Columbia.

After receiving her law degree, Matthews had been rejected by professional lawyers' associations, which were all male. When her nomination for the district court underwent the confirmation process in Congress, she heard the allegation that women were unfit to be judges.

Matthews went on to serve as a senior judge until her death in 1988. She was able to see the first woman, Sandra Day O'Connor, appointed to the U.S. Supreme Court in 1981, almost two centuries after the court's founding.

Most postwar women were steered into their assigned place, as housewives confined to the home. Still, a few women sought a different kind of house: the House of Representatives.

Women comprised 51 percent of the nation's population in 1950. However, out of 435 seats in the U.S. House of Representatives that year, only 9 were occupied by females.

In the U.S. Senate during 1950, only one seat was held by a woman, Margaret Chase Smith of Maine. By the end of the decade in 1959, Smith was joined by another woman, Maurine Neuberger from Oregon. This doubled the number of women elected to the Senate, although it still amounted to only 2 out of 100.

The number of females elected to the U.S. House of Representatives rose to 17 in 1959. But comprising less than 4 percent of Congress, it was hardly near the 51 percent of the population that were women.

In the postwar era, few aspects of life did not feel the icy hand of the Cold War. That was especially true in government. Many Americans seemed to feel it was a time for swagger instead of subtlety and for confrontation rather than cooperation. Women, they felt, were not fit for that kind of arena.

One woman did come forward to enter the fray. According to Dolan et al. (2018), Senator Margaret Chase Smith was "the first Republican to come out against the Communist witch hunt conducted by Senator Joe McCarthy" (207). Smith delivered her "Declaration of Conscience" speech on June 1, 1950. Three weeks later, the United States sent troops to Korea to fight the North Koreans who were backed by the Communist Chinese. Kalb (2018) notes that this action in the "intensity of the Cold War had the ironic effect of sidelining Smith and elevating McCarthy" (73).

Apart from a few female trailblazers such as Smith, the spheres of government and politics in the postwar era were the domain of males. Because of the laws and policies in place under that arrangement, women were affected in their daily lives in a number of detrimental ways, although those situations were usually attributed to being "just the way it is."

For example, women could not get credit in their own names. This was a significant disadvantage for females who were single, divorced, or widowed. If divorced, the husband took the credit standing with him when he left. With no credit rating of her own, a woman was considered to be a poor risk by lenders just at the time many women needed as much financial security as they could get for themselves and their children.

In the postwar era, there were millions of women living in the United States who were still able to remember firsthand the time before 1920, the year when America's female citizens gained the right to vote. At least women could vote during the 1950s. In that respect, some political aspects of postwar society in the United States were an improvement. In other ways, there are those who might state that the nation's government and its political realm still had a long way to go.

GOVERNMENT AND LAW

Government is generally defined as the system by which public policy is administered. It represents the authority that holds power over the men and women it oversees.

In the 1950s, a time that appeared to be a serene era for many Americans, the avuncular Dwight Eisenhower seemed the ideal

Sarah Hughes (back to camera) was only the third woman in American history to serve as a federal judge. In 1963, she gave the oath of office to Lyndon Johnson on Air Force One after President Kennedy's assassination and is the only woman ever to have sworn in a U.S. president. This picture of Hughes administering the oath is considered the most famous photo ever taken aboard Air Force One. (Cecil Stoughton/Lyndon B. Johnson Library)

president. However, with the rise of McCarthyism, the advent of the Cold War, the specter of nuclear weapons, and the restrictions placed on average American women, there were dark currents just beneath the surface. Adding to the volatility of the era was the coming of television, arguably the social media of its day. Aided by the burgeoning advertising industry, political and governmental messages could be televised quickly to Americans from coast to coast. Many of its messages were aimed quite intentionally at females.

In the course of their daily lives, most postwar women could hardly be unaware of the governmental investigations on Communism. Hearings were held in the House of Representatives by the House Un-American Activities Committee (HUAC) as well as those that were spearheaded in the Senate by Wisconsin Senator Joseph McCarthy. A form of his name, "McCarthyism," became a household term. Many men and women lived in fear that their past actions, associations, or even innuendo might come back to haunt them.

As part of the government's investigations in the 1950s, a blacklist was put into effect, in which individuals suspected of left-wing leanings, including civil rights activism, were denied employment. The entertainment industry was the most highly publicized.

Women were not immune to being blacklisted. They included actresses Barbara Bel Geddes, Ruby Dee, Ruth Gordon, Lee Grant, and Judy Holliday along with singers Lena Horne and Hazel Scott. Even "exotic dancer" Gypsy Rose Lee found her name on the blacklist.

When the nation was born, the framers of the Constitution formed the U.S. government so that no one element could assume an overabundance of power. In the postwar era as well as today, three branches comprise the federal government. The executive branch centers around the president. The legislative branch consists of the houses of Congress, which are the Senate and the House of Representatives.

When many people think of government, their first thought might be the executive and legislative branches, since the individuals who serve there are elected every few years, making them highly visible to the general public.

Some people do not always remember the third branch of government: the Supreme Court. The nine judges on the Supreme Court, called "justices," are appointed for life. The high court's day-to-day operations are rarely noted by the general public until there is a controversial landmark decision.

Such was the case in 1954 when the Supreme Court issued its ruling on *Brown v. Board of Education.* That decision determined racially segregated schools to be unconstitutional since they violate the equal protection clause of the Constitution's Fourteenth Amendment. With the *Brown* decision, Trachtman states that the court overruled "more than a half century of precedent" (69) that had allowed local governments, especially in the Jim Crow South, to enforce a mandate of "separate but equal" in public facilities such as schools. The facilities for blacks were said to always be separate but never equal.

With the *Brown* ruling, some cities and towns erupted in violence. Mobs threatened African American students who lawfully tried to attend classes, as was the case in 1957 at Central High School in Little Rock, Arkansas. Also, as in Little Rock, some locales closed the public schools rather than integrate. While the wealthy could send their children to private schools, many average women were concerned about their children's education and therefore that child's future.

During the 1950s, there were laws on the books that affected women even though few people called attention to them or were even aware they existed. Apart from those issued by the federal government, there were laws in individual states that were still on the books during the postwar era, though rarely enforced. Those include one in Michigan, still in effect as of 2019, in which a wife must obtain her husband's permission before she can cut her hair. It is not known to be stringently pursued by law enforcement.

However, during the postwar era, there were laws on the books that certainly were enforced, affecting women in significant ways. For example, regardless of financial status, a woman could not get a credit card in her own name until well into the 1970s.

A woman standing trial during the postwar era did not do so before a jury of her peers. The legal concept does not mean that she has to be tried by an all-female jury, but in the postwar era, it generally meant she *would* be tried entirely by men. The custom of all-male juries was questioned in cases such as the conviction of Gwendolyn Hoyt in 1957. Her defense claimed that she had suffered long-term abuse by her husband, but the all-male jury deliberated for less than a half hour before finding her guilty, sentencing Hoyt to 30 years of hard labor. Observers pointed out that none of the members of the male jury had probably ever suffered spousal abuse.

In their policy regarding the lack of female jurors, most states relied on the idea that a woman could not stand up to the ordeal of hearing gory details in criminal cases. There was also a mindset that women might be too sympathetic to criminals. States could choose to exclude women jurors from their courtrooms until a Supreme Court decision in 1975.

Women of the postwar era who worked outside the home found that sharing the happy news of expecting a baby soon led to the unhappy news of losing their job. Future Supreme Court justice Ruth Bader Ginsburg, among untold numbers of other women, encountered that kind of job loss while working as a clerk in a Social Security office in 1955. It was not until 1978 that a law was passed to alleviate that situation.

There was also not much that women of the postwar era could do to avoid the condition—pregnancy—that cost them their jobs. Taking birth control or even receiving information about it was unlawful until a Supreme Court ruling in 1965 in which married women won the right to safe, effective oral birth control (if the husband approved). It was not until 1972 that the Supreme Court granted America's unmarried women the right to utilize contraception.

A 1971 Supreme Court decision turned out to be a landmark for women across the nation. The case of *Reed v. Reed* was based on an Idaho statute from 1864 that required a father to be preferred over a mother in administering the estate of a deceased child. In *Reed*, the parents were divorced. The husband's argument was that his ex-wife was "too dumb" to administer their son's small estate, which the wife herself had built as a college fund for the child. With the Supreme Court's decision to also consider the mother as precedent, *Reed v. Reed* was the first major case to address outright discrimination based on gender.

While there were very few women who served as judges in the postwar era—and none on the Supreme Court—the situation slowly began changing. In 1962, Sarah Hughes was nominated for a Texas federal judgeship by longtime friend Lyndon Johnson when Johnson was vice president under John F. Kennedy. Hughes was the sole female judge appointed by Kennedy, the first female federal judge in Texas, and only the third woman in the nation's history to serve as a federal judge. A year after her appointment, Judge Hughes was called to administer the oath of office to Lyndon Johnson on Air Force One after Kennedy's assassination. With the presidential oath usually being administered by the chief justice of the Supreme Court, Sarah Hughes is the only woman in American history to have sworn in the president of the United States. The photograph of Hughes administering the oath to Johnson is often cited as the most famous photo ever taken aboard Air Force One.

According to Milligan (2017), "women have made great strides—and suffered some setbacks—throughout history, but many of their gains were made" in the postwar era (n.p.). However, housing discrimination on the basis of gender and credit discrimination against women were not rendered unlawful by Congress until 1974.

As more women were appointed to judgeships and elected to Congress, the structure of government and law slowly began to shift. Still, it was rarely noticeable in the daily lives of postwar women until they experienced it directly, such as attempting to get credit or housing in their own name. Because of messages all around them regarding the role of women in postwar America, many simply assumed "that's just the way it is."

As noted on the House of Representatives website, women elected between 1955 and 1976 tended to legislate regarding issues that affected women's lives, more so than under the male-dominated Congress of the past. During the late postwar years, women in government often addressed traditional gender-based inequities in areas such as access to education, childcare, hiring, relief for single parents, and workplace compensation.

When Sandra Day O'Connor was appointed to be the first woman justice on the Supreme Court in 1981, she remained the only woman to serve on the high court bench for a dozen years even though there were several other openings during that time frame.

When Ruth Bader Ginsburg was appointed in 1993 to be the second woman in American history to serve on the Supreme Court, there was an interesting phenomenon. Except for their gender, Justice O'Connor and Justice Ginsburg could not have been more different. Carmon and Knizhnik (2015) state that "the white-bobbed Arizonan [the conservative O'Connor] and the dark-haired bespectacled Brooklynite [the liberal Ginsburg] didn't look or sound anything alike . . . and yet, people constantly confused the two justices" (112). Their dissimilarities apparently were not enough to differentiate them to males since they were both women.

Both O'Connor and Ginsburg had graduated at the top of their respective law school classes in the 1950s. During that era, it was highly unusual for either of them to have been in law school in the first place. They were both among a handful of women in the midst of hundreds of male students. In Ginsburg's case, she was one of nine women out of more than 500 men at Harvard Law. After graduation, neither O'Connor nor Ginsburg could find work as an attorney in the 1950s, being told quite openly that law firms did not hire women.

Despite their shared experiences, Justice Ginsburg expressed her pleasure that they also had vast differences. Neither woman represented *all* women.

While the role of women in government and their influence on the laws of the nation seemed to be at a standstill during the postwar era of the 1950s, there was still cause for cheer. Women in the United States could actually vote. However, McKnight (2018) claims that when the U.S. House of Representatives passed the Nineteenth Amendment in 1918, the state of Mississippi opposed it. According to McKnight, "Mississippi did not ratify the Nineteenth Amendment until 1984" (n.p.).

It was not until the all-male Mississippi Senate voted to ratify the Nineteenth Amendment in 1984 that women officially became enfranchised citizens of that state. Fifteen years after men walked on the moon, women in Mississippi were formally granted the right to vote.

POLITICS

Government differs from politics in the sense that government holds the power to create the laws of the land. Politics is the way to attain that power and keep it. In the United States, that means politicians must get elected to a public office. In the case of judicial appointees, it involves determining how to be appointed. Essentially, politics is the means that are used to gain and hold power. Under the American system, that is usually synonymous with elections.

The laws pertaining to elections date back to 1788 when the Constitution, our nation's founding document, was officially ratified. It left the determination of voter eligibility to the individual states, most of whom granted voting rights only to white male property owners. This left a wide swath of people in the United States who could not vote, including African Americans, Native Americans, poor whites, and women.

Abigail Adams was married to Founding Father John Adams and was the first wife of a U.S. president to live in the White House. As quoted by Holton (2009), on March 31, 1776, she penned a letter to her husband who was at Philadelphia serving in the Continental Congress arguing the case for American independence. In her letter, she wrote, "In the new Code of Laws which I suppose it will be necessary for you to make I desire you would Remember the Ladies. . . .

Remember all Men would be tyrants if they could" (99).

According to Holton, John Adams's response made reference to groups including enslaved African American people and Native Americans. Adams wrote to Abigail, "I cannot but laugh. . . . Your letter was the first intimation that another tribe, more numerous and powerful than all the rest, were grown discontented" (102).

In 1870, the Fifteenth Amendment gave African American men the right to vote, at least officially, if not in practice everywhere. Fifty years later, the Nineteenth Amendment was enacted in 1920, giving American women the

Slowly, some women in postwar America entered the political arena. One of the most successful was Margaret Chase Smith (pictured here). In 1950, she moved from the U.S. House of Representatives to the Senate where she was the only woman serving there until 1960 when Maurine Neuberger was elected. (National Archives)

right to vote. Many women living in the postwar years recalled the time before they were allowed to vote as citizens of the United States, a right denied to them based solely on gender.

The postwar era brought something new to America's political process. Advertising, which was becoming a big business in the 1950s, extended its power into politics. Along with the traditional means of spreading political messages—magazines, newspapers, public speaking engagements, parades, rallies, and radio—advertisers found a godsend in the unsurpassed power of television. Thus television, the most powerful mass medium of the day, joined forces with the advertising industry and professional political operatives to great effect.

The utilization of basic advertising principles in postwar politics was something new. Republican Dwight Eisenhower ran twice,

Dwight Eisenhower, nicknamed "Ike," ran for U.S. president in 1952 and 1956, winning both elections. His campaign team came up with the slogan "I Like Ike," a catchphrase that appeared on thousands of mass-produced campaign buttons that were worn by many women in postwar America. (Dwight D. Eisenhower Library)

in 1952 and 1956. His campaign team produced brief snippets for television ads showing their candidate, nicknamed "Ike," being acclaimed by adoring crowds but not saying much. His admen also came up with the snappy slogan "I Like Ike," which appeared on thousands of mass-produced campaign buttons that were worn by many women. The slogan was also short enough to appear on bumper stickers, with the election of 1952 being the first documented presidential campaign to utilize adhesive political bumper stickers on cars.

The Democratic candidate, Adlai Stevenson, refused to do the new kind of political advertising, especially quick, catchy television ads. According to Halberstam (1993), Stevenson stated that it was the worst thing he'd ever heard of, adding, "Selling the presidency like cereal. How can you talk seriously about issues in one-minute spots?" (232).

Stevenson's team came up with a slogan of their own, "I Love Adlai Madly," which was spotted on some women but was less popular than Ike's, especially among men. Stevenson ran against Eisenhower twice, both in 1952 and again in 1956, losing by a landslide both times.

As political advertising techniques became more specialized, the postwar era was a line of demarcation from the past. Packard (1957) stated that "the days of whistle-stops and torchlight parades were over" (164).

Since that time, according to Carroll and Fox (2018), "pollsters and campaign consultants routinely try to figure out what issues or themes will appeal specifically to women" (6) along with those aimed at men. But Dolan et al. (2018) point out that "beyond party affiliations, women also differ from one another by race, ethnicity, and social class" (221). Therefore, political messages directed at females had to be subdivided.

Some postwar women experienced the restlessness and lack of fulfillment that was described by Betty Friedan in her book, *The Feminine Mystique*, which she had researched in the late 1950s. The vast majority of women in postwar America remained in the home, but some looked elsewhere, going against the grain.

Some began locally, running for seats in their state legislature or town council. If they won, they discovered that those legislative bodies served as valuable training grounds for learning basic lawmaking and political procedures. One, Millicent Fenwick, was elected to her local town council in 1957, later moving to the New Jersey state legislature and eventually the U.S. House of Representatives where she became known as "The Conscience of Congress." She memorably stated that as a woman, her early posts enabled her to learn where the currents were, "like a fish," and how to move with them to get things done.

Slowly, more women of the postwar era entered the political process and were successful at it. In 1950, Margaret Chase Smith of Maine moved from the U.S. House of Representatives to the nation's Senate where she was the only woman serving in the upper chamber at the time. In the 435-member House that year, there were nine women from all over the country.

When the decade ended in 1960, there were 17 women in the House and two women, Maurine Neuberger and Smith, in the Senate. Some pundits joked that the two women "cancelled each other out," with Neuberger a Democrat and Smith a Republican. Apart from both of their home states (Oregon and Maine, respectively) coincidentally having their major city named Portland, Neuberger and Smith appeared on the surface to have little in common.

But they saw things from a female perspective, especially in areas such as equal pay for equal work regardless of gender. Another perspective, one brought by a woman outside the white upper middle class, was added in 1964 when Representative Patsy Mink of Hawaii became the first woman of color to serve in Congress.

During the postwar years of the 1950s, however, the sense that women belonged at home was ingrained in the minds of many Americans. Anyone who doubted it had a cautionary tale in Coya Knutson. A Democrat from Minnesota, Knutson financed her quest for the U.S. House of Representatives by selling land she had inherited from her father. Her exhausting campaign in 1954 included hiking into fields to talk to farmers individually. In an upset, she won that year's male-dominated general election for Congress.

As one of the few women serving in Congress at that time, Knutson was by all accounts an effective legislator, advocating for federal student loans, funding for school lunches, and agricultural programs to aid the rural constituents of her state. She won reelection to Congress in 1956 and was well regarded both in her home district and on Capitol Hill in Washington.

But when she again ran for reelection in 1958, the opposition teamed up with her estranged alcoholic husband who had battered Coya before she left him, taking their adopted adult son with her. A letter was released to newspapers by the opposition, said to be from the husband, under the heading "Coya, Come Home." Her constituents, feeling she was not sufficiently devoted to her husband, voted her out of office. Despite her effectiveness as a legislator, Coya Knutson's political career ended abruptly. Minnesota later elected a professional wrestler as its governor, but another woman would not be sent to Congress from that state until the year 2000, four years after Coya Knutson's death.

In the article "Postwar Gender Roles and Women in American Politics" on the House of Representatives website, it is stated that during the postwar era, the societal expectations for what constituted a woman's proper role outside the home also constrained women who were members of Congress. Senator Maurine Neuberger, who took office in 1959, is quoted as saying that women were handicapped in the rough-and-tumble struggle of political campaigns because society held them to different standards than men.

Neuberger noted the mindset of "a woman's place is in the home," also stating that a female running for office has to walk a fine line during her campaign. Women candidates cannot appear indecisive or weak but also cannot come across as pushy or arrogant. Especially in the postwar era, when women were still a novelty in politics, a male might be perceived in a positive light as "assertive" at the same time a woman was considered "aggressive" when both spoke and acted the same way.

Gracie Pfost served as a member of Congress from Idaho from 1953 to 1963. On the House of Representatives website, Pfost is quoted as saying a woman in politics "must be willing to have her every motive challenged, her every move criticized," adding that she must also "submit to having her private life scrutinized under a microscope" as well as being "the subject of devastating rumors every day."

Postwar women in the political arena hoping to find an exemplar from the previous generation of female politicians found little help. Just like in the postwar era two decades later, Hattie Caraway of Arkansas was criticized when she ran for the U.S. Senate in 1932. She often heard that "a woman's place is in the home" and that she should be staying home to care for her children. At the time Caraway ran for office, her three grown sons were West Pointers and army officers who presumably did not need much of a mother's care.

Caraway won the 1932 election, becoming the first woman elected—and later reelected—to the U.S. Senate. She served her state well until 1945 and was one of the sponsors of the GI Bill, which was so vital to America's postwar prosperity. According to Hendricks (2013), in 1945, on her last day in the Senate, her all-male colleagues gave her a remarkable standing ovation, adding that "she also received from a colleague what was no doubt intended as a compliment: 'Mrs. Caraway is the kind of woman Senator that men Senators prefer'" (116). He stated it without apparent irony, since Caraway was known throughout her Senate career as "Silent Hattie."

Besides elected public offices, there are other positions in the service of the nation that most postwar women probably did not consider to be political. It was not often something that impacted their daily lives. Yet Article II of the U.S. Constitution states that the president, as an elected official, "shall nominate, and by and with the Advice and Consent of the Senate, shall appoint Ambassadors, . . . Judges of the Supreme Court, and all other Officers of the United States."

Therefore, some seemingly nonpolitical offices such as ambassadorships were extremely political in nature. Ambassadors to foreign lands are often assigned on the basis of political favors. If in their daily lives, women in postwar America did not concern themselves a great deal with female ambassadors, it was because there weren't many. According to the Pew Research Center, as of the year 2016, only about 9 percent out of almost 5,000 ambassadors who served in foreign countries since the founding of the nation were women.

Eugenie Anderson broke through the diplomatic glass ceiling as America's first female ambassador in 1949 when she was appointed by President Harry Truman to the U.S. Embassy in Denmark. As such, in 1950 she became the first American woman to sign a treaty. After being appointed by President John Kennedy as ambassador to Bulgaria in 1962, Anderson became the first American woman to represent the United States in a Soviet-bloc country.

Many more average American women may have been aware of an ambassadorial appointment that took place in 1953 due to the publicity surrounding the selection. Clare Boothe Luce, who had written a popular play called *The Women*, was rewarded by President Eisenhower to be the American ambassador to Italy, a posting that was considered very desirable. The story was covered by most postwar news media, including *Time* and *Life* magazines, which were owned by Ambassador Luce's husband.

Women in postwar America also did not have much of a chance to see female politicians portrayed in movies or on television. A low-budget 1953 science fiction film called *Project Moonbase* contains the small role of "Madame President." Set in the futuristic world of 1970, it accurately predicts the real-life moon landing in 1969. However, it was premature in its forecast of a time when the United States might have a female president.

Two postwar-era books were published in 1959 and later turned into popular movies. In the first, *Advise and Consent*, women were peripheral characters who basically existed only to support their politician husbands. In the second, *The Manchurian Candidate*, there is one of the most iconic female characters in fiction, portrayed chillingly by Angela Lansbury as a woman who first appears to be a stereotypical supportive political wife but emerges as something quite different.

In the latter postwar era, *Kisses for My President* (1964) presents a fictional tale of the first woman elected to be the chief executive. However, it actually centers around how her unenthusiastic husband copes with being the nation's first male "first lady." The fictitious female president is accused of being soft on Communism and ultimately resigns the presidency she had fought so hard for in order to devote herself to her family after discovering she is pregnant.

For the most part, women who made gains in postwar politics appreciated the public offices they held, on whatever level. They also recognized the reality of a woman running for president. In the postwar era, only three women are documented as seeking the presidency, all in 1952. They were Ellen Linea Jensen (representing the Washington Peace Party), Mary Kennery (American Party), and Agnes Waters (American Woman's Party). They barely registered at the polls.

During the postwar years, women in public office generally worked hard at the jobs they held without keeping a covetous eye out for the chance to become president. Myers (2008) claims that Senator Margaret Chase Smith, one of the most successful of the postwar women in politics, was once asked what she would do if she woke up in the White House. Smith responded, "I'd go straight to Mrs. Truman and apologize. Then I'd go home" (185).

FURTHER READING

Carmon, Irin, and Shana Knizhnik. *Notorious RBG: The Life and Times of Ruth Bader Ginsburg*. New York: Dey Street Books, 2015.

Carroll, Susan, and Richard L. Fox, eds. *Gender and Elections: Shaping the Future of American Politics*. New York: Cambridge University Press, 4th edition, 2018.

Dolan, Julie, Melissa Deckman, and Michele Swers. *Women and Politics: Paths to Power and Political Influence*. Lanham, MD: Rowman & Littlefield, 3rd edition, 2018.

Halberstam, David. *The Fifties*. New York: Villard, 1993.

Hendricks, Nancy. *Senator Hattie Caraway: An Arkansas Legacy*. Charleston, SC: The History Press, 2013.

Holton, Woody. *Abigail Adams: A Life*. New York: Atria 2009.

Kalb, Marvin. *Enemy of the People: Trump's War on the Press, the New McCarthyism, and the Threat to American Democracy*. Washington, DC: Brookings Institution Press, 2018.

Maza, Clelia Martinez. "Roman Citizenship: Prize to the Ancient World." *National Geographic History*, November/December 2019, pp. 50–51.

McKnight, Stephanie. "Woman Suffrage." *The Mississippi Encyclopedia*, 2018. https://mississippiencyclopedia.org/entries/woman-suffrage.

Milligan, Susan. "Stepping through History: A Timeline of Women's Rights from 1769 to the 2017 Women's March on Washington."

US News and World Report, January 20, 2017. https://www.usnews
.com/news/the-report/articles/2017-01-20/timeline-the-womens
-rights-movement-in-the-us.

Myers, Dee Dee. *Why Women Should Rule the World*. New York: Harper-
Collins, 2008.

Packard, Vance. *The Hidden Persuaders*. New York: Pocket Books, 1957.

"Postwar Gender Roles and Women in American Politics." History, Art
and Archives, *United States House of Representatives*. https://history
.house.gov/Exhibitions-and-Publications/WIC/Historical-Essays
/Changing-Guard/Identity.

Trachtman, Michael. *The Supremes' Greatest Hits: The 44 Supreme Court
Cases That Most Directly Affect Your Life*. New York: Sterling, 2016.

U.S. House of Representatives Office of History and Preservation. *Women
in Congress 1917–2006*. Washington, DC: U.S. Government Printing
Office, 2006.

Zainulbhai, Hani. "Few American Women Have Broken the Glass Ceiling of Diplomacy." *Pew Research Center*, July 22, 2016. https://www
.pewresearch.org/fact-tank/2016/07/22/few-american-women
-have-broken-the-glass-ceiling-of-diplomacy/.

6

RECREATIONAL LIFE

For most women in postwar America, having even a moderate amount leisure time for recreation was itself something of a new phenomenon. In the urban industrial centers of the late 1800s and early 1900s, women had worked long hours for little pay in places such as garment factories or textile mills. In rural areas, farmwives and women who lived on ranches found their work to be never-ending, just as it had been for centuries.

Even amid the general prosperity of the years following World War II, women in poverty-stricken regions such as Appalachia or the Cotton Belt of the South struggled to keep their families afloat as they had traditionally done for generations. Their workload did not leave a lot of time for leisure.

But it was the average middle-class white woman living in postwar suburbia who was able to enjoy the fruits of newfound leisure. At times, some felt they actually had too much leisure, as noted by observers such as Betty Freidan (2013), author of the ground-breaking book *The Feminine Mystique*. According to Friedan, with postwar women confined to the home and with all the labor-saving devices aimed toward the housewife in the age of consumerism, some felt "lazy, neglectful [and] haunted by guilt feelings because she doesn't have enough work to do" (307).

However, for those who found a happy medium between house-work and leisure time, the options for recreation in postwar America increased considerably from those in the past.

Many average women in postwar America had both the time and the prosperity to enjoy recreation as a regular part of their daily lives. With the emphasis on "togetherness" as promoted by women's magazines, recreational activities were the ideal time for women to solidify the family unit. Many might have paraphrased an old adage: "The family that plays together stays together."

Many women were able to take regular vacations with their family in the big, comfortable automobiles of the 1950s. With baby boom children being the focus of many women's lives, activities such as the kind of road trips that could be considered educational were desirable choices for recreational leisure. Destinations often included historic sites such as Mount Rushmore or the Statue of Liberty as well as national parks such as Yellowstone and Yosemite.

As postwar women traveled for recreation with their families, they were often frustrated with the kinds of lodgings they found along the way. Accommodations varied wildly in cost and quality. Based on experiences with his own wife and children while travel-ing on vacation, businessman Kemmons Wilson understood what women wanted. Creating the Holiday Inn motel chain in 1952, Wil-son revolutionized travel by providing accommodations nation-wide that were consistently affordable, clean, comfortable, and safe. With the well-being of their families while traveling at stake, women strongly supported his vision.

Some women, either due to desire or budgetary concerns, decided to "rough it" by camping out. Even though the average woman was usually still tasked with doing the cooking and dishwashing at the campsite, it was a step up from the migrant encampments of displaced farmers heading westward during the Depression in the 1930s.

Many postwar families could afford trailers or large station wag-ons where they could stow their camping gear. At the same time, a number of family-friendly campground franchises such as Kamp-grounds of America (KOA) opened up across the country in the postwar years. For many American women of that era, the "great outdoors" became a recreational option. It at least allowed women in-depth quality time with their families plus a rustic change of pace that might in some cases have improved their view of their suburban tract homes when they returned.

The rise of the automobile in the postwar era led to the decline of two forms of recreational transportation that had been market leaders for decades. Railroads were on a downward trend, although many female American travelers still enjoyed recreational travel on cross-country luxury trains with glamorous names such as the *Sunset Limited* and *Super Chief*. Being served their meals on white linen in the dining cars was a plus for many women.

The postwar era also saw the demise of the great passenger ocean liners, many of which had captured the imagination of women from the time they were girls in the 1930s and 1940s. Although luxurious passenger liners were already beginning to yield to airplanes for recreational travel, American shippers launched the SS *Constitution* and SS *Independence* in 1951 as well as the SS *United States* in 1952.

When American actress Grace Kelly sailed to Europe aboard the *Constitution* in 1956 for her wedding to Monaco's Prince Rainier, postwar women were captivated. During the 1950s, the *Constitution* itself appeared in several episodes of the television comedy *I Love Lucy* and in the romantic 1957 movie, *An Affair to Remember*.

But beyond nostalgia and glamour, many women were willing to sacrifice luxury for speed, especially when trying to pack a lot into a one- or two-week annual vacation. Traveling by air, destinations such as Florida, Las Vegas, and even Europe were within reach along with the postwar family favorite, Disneyland in Southern California.

When not traveling, many women took up sports such as golf and tennis as recreational activities. Once reserved only for the wealthy, even middle-class women of the 1950s could enjoy these pastimes at suburban country clubs or public facilities.

The ultimate public facility took on a remarkable new life as shopping became a recreational activity for women of the postwar era. With the accepted societal concept of consumerism after World War II and widespread postwar prosperity, women could indulge in shopping as "retail therapy" where once it had simply been an additional task on their domestic "to-do" list.

It was the coming of shopping mall that took much of the drudgery out of purchasing necessities for the family. There had traditionally been downtown shopping districts frequented by women in cities and even in most small towns. But the shopping malls of the 1950s reflected the age by evolving into a recreational activity beyond basic necessity. Malls combined the postwar upsurge in automobiles, leisure, materialism, suburban life, and technology with the relatively inexpensive land that was available outside urban areas. Developers could plant a shopping center where potato fields had once been.

The general concept of a shopping center was not new. But it was only after financial laws were eased in the prosperous 1950s that real estate developers could safely speculate on bringing the act of shopping to where middle-class American women were moving: suburbia.

Enclosed shopping malls removed the nuisance of inclement weather. One of the earliest such enclosed retail destinations of the postwar era, Valley Fair Shopping Center in Appleton, Wisconsin, opened in 1955. With a vast sea of parking spaces, Valley Fair's big brand-name stores and smaller specialty shops attracted its female customers with a variety of merchandise. With the ease of walking from store to store, women were fascinated by the array of goods they didn't know they wanted until they saw them. Comfortable eateries allowed women to refresh and recharge. Valley Fair set the stage for the recreational element of shopping centers that followed. Women could even feel they were getting exercise by "mall walking."

In 1956, Southdale Center in Edina, Minnesota, perfected the concept. With about 75 stores on three levels, the controlled temperature kept shoppers comfortable year-round. Its 5,000-space parking lot rivalled the population of some of the small towns where women of the postwar era had grown up. Other shopping malls sprang up around the country, encouraging "destination shopping" and bringing a recreational aspect to what had been just another domestic chore for women.

In addition to recreational shopping, there was a vast array of leisure activities from which a postwar woman could choose: movies, music, sports, television, and theater. The unparalleled prosperity and bounty of leisure time in the postwar era allowed more types of recreational options in the daily lives of average middle-class females than at any time in history. Across the nation, American women made the most of it.

EXERCISE AND SPORTS

Throughout human history, there was not much need for women to exercise. Apart from the wealthy, average women stayed active enough in their daily lives just trying to survive. In ancient times, women had to forage to gather foods that would supplement animal meat that the hunters might or might not bring home.

Althea Gibson (at left) was the first African American tennis player to participate in the U.S. National Championships, going on to win five Grand Slam titles in the postwar era. After her triumph at Wimbledon in 1957, she was presented her trophy by England's Queen Elizabeth II. In this picture, Gibson speaks to a group of young women about the game. (Library of Congress)

In agrarian societies such as the United States, in the years prior to the Industrial Revolution, women had physical chores on the family farm to perform along with their usually strenuous household duties like carrying water and washing the family's clothing by hand.

During the first half of the 20th century, the Great Depression of the 1930s often limited the availability of food. So did rationing during World War II in the 1940s—a time when many women engaged in physical activity, working in factories. During those eras, many women were generally able to keep slim by default.

But amid the prosperity of the 1950s and what Elaine Tyler May (2008) called "domestic containment" (16), for women of the postwar era, everything changed. The middle class was growing, literally as well as figuratively. A less-active lifestyle produced larger bodies. Average women started gaining weight as well as inches around the waistline.

Women of the postwar era who were not among those in the prosperous white middle class started gaining weight too, but not due to a sedentary lifestyle. A number of minority women worked as low-paid domestics, which in many cases was the only kind of job they could find. While there was certainly physical labor involved for the women who cleaned other people's houses, that activity was frequently offset at home by consuming inexpensive processed foods and "junk food" that contained large amounts of additives and preservatives.

By the mid-1950s, processed items were readily available in inner cities, had a long shelf life, and tasted good. Processed food was often the only thing that was affordable to women who did not earn enough to buy a steady diet of fresh meat, fruit, and vegetables. In addition, there was little information at the time on the undesirable effects that "junk food" had on health and in weight gain.

Even though middle-class suburban women may have had more money and a greater degree of choices in the food items they consumed, they too started to gain weight. Labor-saving devices did exactly that: they saved labor. Those machines eliminated much of the physical activity for women that was prevalent in previous decades, such as sweeping the house, doing the family laundry by hand, or chopping wood to heat the stove.

The rise of processed foods also affected women who simply enjoyed the flavor and convenience of these modern-age products. Instead of laboring in the kitchen, they might join their families in eating commercially prepared "TV dinners" in front of the television set or go out for fast food, neither of which was conducive to avoiding weight gain.

Television itself was part of the general expansion of American waistlines. More hours spent in front of the TV set meant less time for physical activity, even just taking an evening stroll in the neighborhood. Between postwar labor-saving devices, the rise of processed food, and sedentary time in front of the television, it became a challenge for many American women to squeeze into the tight, straight "pencil" skirts of the era and "New Look" fashions of the 1950s that were designed with snug, nipped-in waists.

One of the most pervasive factors in weight gain among women in postwar America was the discouragement of physical activity for women based on the societal standard for what was "feminine." As stated by Smith (1999), "the 1950s rewarded conformity . . . and stigmatized female athleticism" (64).

Many postwar women recalled the slurs that had been aimed at female athlete Mildred "Babe" Didrikson after she set four world records in track and field at the 1932 Olympics. Didrikson remains the only male or female athlete to win individual Olympic medals in jumping, running, and throwing events. Yet, according to Smith (1999), "with all her success came notoriety for her 'unfeminine behavior'" (3).

The unsubtle sexual innuendo about her "unfeminine behavior" continued until Didrikson married professional wrestler George Zaharias, wore her hair in a long curly style, and made sure to pose for photos wearing dresses instead of athletic attire. Turning her attention to golf in the postwar years, Didrikson also excelled in that sport until her death in 1956.

There was a stigma attached to females pursuing athletics that women in postwar America understood. In the age of McCarthyism, it was dangerous to stand out from the pack as well as to attract inferences of being sexually questionable. The Cold War era of the early 1950s was not a good time for women to seem to enjoy physical activity too much.

Ironically, then, it was also the Cold War that spurred a trend in the late 1950s toward more exercise in the daily lives of American girls. National leaders grew concerned that the young people of America were less fit than their Communist enemies in Russia. In 1956, U.S. president Dwight Eisenhower authorized the President's Council on Youth Fitness. Along with their male schoolmates, girls were expected to perform a series of standard physical activities. Even though the program was meant to be an anti-Communist effort, some critics objected to the activities being required in the public schools as "socialism."

In the case of many schoolgirls, critics did not need to worry. Young women did not want to appear unfeminine by trying too hard or appearing too skilled athletically. Instead of being timed running around a track, many girls strolled leisurely so they would not sweat, which would be the ultimate unfeminine infraction.

However, the mindset slowly began to change as the 1950s wore on. Although most gymnasiums of the postwar era were "men only," there were facilities such as the YWCA that provided a sanctioned space for female exercise.

Some women exercised by themselves or with friends in the privacy of their home. Eventually, they were able to do their jumping jacks and sit-ups with an electronic companion who could be summoned up via the television set that sat in their living room: Jack LaLanne.

Television star LaLanne was considered by some to be a "health nut," but he saw the potential in a televised fitness broadcast aimed primarily at women. Broadcast between 1953 and 1985, *The Jack LaLanne Show* became the longest-running exercise program on American television. His syndicated program was aired during the day, appealing to housewives. LaLanne encouraged women viewers to use common household items that were part of their daily lives such as chairs and broomsticks to perform their exercises along with him. With his good looks and conversational style, LaLanne's popularity grew during the postwar era, making him one of the top fitness celebrities of all time.

Some women didn't bother using chairs and broomsticks when 1950s-era technology was readily available. In the late postwar era, women-only "figure salons" began springing up across the country. There, females used such electronic equipment as wooden stomach rollers and vibrating belts that were meant to jostle away the fat while the passive woman stood still.

With passivity being considered a positive female trait in the postwar years, the Royal Canadian Air Force exercise program became popular with women. Taking no more than 12 minutes out of their daily lives, the plan consisted of simple arm circles, leg lifts, sit-ups, and stretches along with the recommendation of walking or running in place. Women fearful of appearing "unfeminine" by exercising could perform the routine in a short time within the privacy of their home as part of their daily routine.

Two significant forms of women's physical activity took center stage during the postwar years that did not seek privacy. To the contrary, they were quite public.

Both were organized sports teams in which women played prominent roles. In the first, women constituted the entire franchise. The All-American Girls Professional Baseball League (AAGPBL) was in existence from the time it was founded in 1943, when male baseball players went to war, until 1954 when the men's teams were back at full strength. More than 600 women would eventually play in the AAGPBL, which was honored in the 1992 movie *A League of Their Own*.

AAGPBL was at a disadvantage due to the lack of television coverage in the 1940s and early 1950s, but even without that kind of promotion, league attendance reached more than 900,000 spectators at its peak. Some of that appeal had to do not with athletic ability but with a typical standard for women: their attractiveness to men.

Each woman who played in the AAGPBL was required by team owners to wear a short skirt; in that way, the women's legs and backside were on display. Johnson (1994) states, "Whatever the skirt did for management and fans, it failed to protect the players in one of baseball's most fundamental plays, the slide" (80). Johnson adds that after executing the painful play, some players described having legs that were "raw all the time" (96). Some retained life-long scars. Still, the AAGPBL sanctioned the kind of female athleti-cism that prompts many sources to call it the forerunner of today's professional sports for women in the United States.

What the AAGPBL lacked was television coverage. In the post-war era, sports and television grew to become a natural combina-tion. Sports were inexpensive to broadcast, attracted male-oriented sponsors, inspired a loyal fan base of viewers, and could be broad-cast across a wide swath of the nation. Generally, male baseball and football teams took center stage. But there was one notable excep-tion that was co-ed: the roller derby.

Roller derby is a full-body contact sport played by two teams of about a dozen players, each of whom roller-skates at high speeds around an indoor track. Team members race to try getting ahead of players on the other team. Players on the other team try to avoid being passed by blocking rivals or otherwise obstructing their opponents. As with criticism of professional wrestling, sometimes theatrics were used to orchestrate elaborate clashes among indi-viduals as well as crashes in multiplayer pileups. On-site specta-tors as well as television viewers at home, including many average women, loved the rousing spectacle of bodies colliding.

Although it had been around for years, the postwar success of roller derby began in 1948 when it debuted on a nationwide tele-vision broadcast from New York. There were men's roller derby squads, but according to Puglisi (2020), the women's teams were much more popular. Similar to the AAGPBL, the uniforms of roller derby girls were short shorts, which were not designed to provide protection even though the women played by the same rules as the males. However, Puglisi states, "the yearly salaries of men eclipsed those of women by as much as $10,000 to $15,000" (n.p.).

Roller derby held the same allure that women's prison movies had in the 1950s: girls behaving badly. The name of the first wom-en's roller derby superstar of the postwar era said it all: "Toughie" Brasuhn.

Known by her first name, Toughie was able to parlay her roller derby fame into a leading role in the 1949 movie *Roller Derby Girl*.

But the most significant wedding of postwar-era sports and entertainment was not the movies but television. As the number of television sets in American homes grew dramatically, average postwar women were exposed to an increased opportunity to see their gender represented in the world of athletics.

Every four years, the Olympic Games became a huge draw for television. Being an international competition with patriotic pride at stake, the Olympics of the postwar years became more than just a sporting event.

Women influenced something intriguing that happened to the Olympics as more American homes acquired a television set. As noted by Billings (2018), "More women watch[ed] the Games than men, and for the women, they are less interested in the results and more interested in the journey" (42). Based on the interest of average women, American television producers began to adopt more of a "storytelling" formula for the Olympic Games rather than purely win-or-lose competitive sports.

Average women could also enjoy the Olympics as a kind of worldwide travelogue. During the postwar years, the games were held in such picturesque spots as Oslo, Norway; Helsinki, Finland; Cortina d'Ampezzo, Italy; and Melbourne, Australia.

As the postwar years progressed, average women could see more Olympic athletes like themselves. In addition to traditional female Olympic events such as archery, figure skating, and swimming, new women's events were added in the postwar era, including canoeing and speed skating.

Along with white women who were seeing more Olympic athletes like themselves, the color line was broken in 1948 when high jumper Alice Coachman became the first African American woman to win Olympic gold. From a childhood in the segregated South where she was barred from training facilities, she leapt over obstacles of race and gender to set a new Olympic high-jump record. She was presented with her gold medal by England's King George VI. In 1952, Alice Coachman soared over another barrier by becoming the first black woman to earn an international endorsement deal, which she did with Coca-Cola.

With the rise of television in the postwar era, there came more opportunities for average women to see athletes of their gender. After its debut in 1961, ABC's *Wide World of Sports* was a popular weekly program spotlighting athletics from around the globe, including many sports that included women. With its well-known introductory tagline ("The thrill of victory and the agony of defeat"),

American women could see female athletes in such sports as badminton, slow pitch softball, and surfing. More women's sports were added as the series progressed.

With greater opportunities to watch more televised sports as part of their daily lives, some average American women were inspired to move from being viewers of athletic events to becoming participants.

As players, African American women of the postwar era faced more hurdles than white female athletes did, related to both race and gender. Marcenia "Toni" Stone was the first woman to play professional baseball on a traditional men's team, which she did in the postwar Negro League. In 1953, she played for the Indianapolis Clowns, signing with the Kansas City Monarchs in 1954. Despite having superior athletic skills that sometimes outshone her male teammates, she experienced some of the prejudice faced by pioneering male African American ballplayer Jackie Robinson. However, Ackmann (2010) states that in the Negro Leagues, Toni Stone's experience was based not on race but on gender: "Like Robinson, she felt what it was like to be the odd one out, to sit alone in the dugout, to be excluded from the game's camaraderie" (68). Toni Stone retired at the end of the 1954 season due to lack of playing time and to care for her sick husband.

Although the early postwar era was still a dangerous time for female athletes to be seen as "unfeminine," there were a few societally acceptable sports they could play. It helped if the standard outfits were short skirts that male onlookers could enjoy.

Two such sports became enormously popular with women in postwar America: golf and tennis. Not only were their legs exposed in short golf skirts and tennis outfits, but in many cases average women could incorporate the concept of "togetherness" by playing with their husbands, as promoted in women's magazines.

Well-known female American tennis champs of the 1950s included Louise Brough, Maureen Connolly, and Shirley Fry. In 1953, Connolly became the first woman to score a Grand Slam title by winning all four major world tennis matches (Australian Open, French Open, U.S. Open, and Wimbledon) in a single season.

A major barrier in a previously whites-only field was overcome by Althea Gibson, an African American woman who was born in South Carolina during the Jim Crow era. After moving to Harlem in New York City, she learned to play tennis on city streets.

Effectively barred from entering tournaments because they were held at whites-only clubs, other women players lobbied on Gibson's behalf. Althea Gibson became the first black tennis player to participate in the U.S. National Championships. She went on to win major competitions throughout the postwar era, being singles champ, winning five Grand Slam titles, and triumphing at Wimbledon in 1957, where she was presented her trophy by England's Queen Elizabeth II.

Still, Althea Gibson found little success in acquiring endorsement deals or other professional opportunities. As quoted by Molly Schiot (2018), Gibson, who "reigned over an empty bank account" (12), put it succinctly: "The landlord and grocer and tax collector like cold cash, [and] you can't eat a crown" (12).

Another sport available to average women in the postwar era also involved short skirts and short earnings. Women's golf had been popularized in the mid-1500s by Mary, Queen of Scots. She is credited with the term "caddie" (from the French word "cadet") for the young men who carried her clubs.

Affluent women in postwar America could often play golf with their husband and friends at country clubs, while some public facilities also admitted female golfers.

In 1950, the Ladies Professional Golf Association (LPGA) was founded by Babe Didrikson Zaharias along with a dozen other professional female golfers of the postwar era including Alice Bauer, Helen Hicks, Opal Hill, and Sally Sessions.

During its first season in 1950, there were fourteen LPGA tournaments with a total of $50,000 in prize money, a tiny percentage of men's earnings on the professional golf circuit. The disparity between men's and women's earnings in athletics across the board continued well beyond the postwar era.

In any case, many average women in postwar America had more opportunities to enjoy professional or amateur sports as part of their daily lives, either as spectators or as participants. They also had more chances to incorporate exercise into their daily routine.

However, on playgrounds across America, schoolgirls of the postwar era were not usually encouraged to develop athletic skills as part of their daily lives. Instead, they were guided to stay with schoolyard activities such as jumping rope that would not be considered "unfeminine." It would take another generation for that mindset to be altered.

MOVIES

Prior to the postwar era, in the 1930s and 1940s, many average American women made going to the movies a regular part of their lives. It was a way to escape from the grim reality of the Great

Depression of the 1930s that was followed by the anxiety of a nation at war in the 1940s. During those years, for $0.25 (about $3.00 in 2019 dollars), a woman could enjoy a feature film starring glamorous celebrities from Hollywood's golden age.

The emotional power of the movies enabled many women to have a few hours of respite from their daily lives, both physically and mentally. Often, they attended a so-called woman's film, a genre in which a female is at the center of the story (although there is no equivalent male term, such as a "man's film.") Even sad movies, also called "tearjerkers" or "weepies," could often make women feel better by comparing their daily lives to those of tragic onscreen heroines.

During the postwar

Film star Marilyn Monroe became the top female sex symbol of the postwar era. Although other movie studios tried to come up with their own blonde bombshells, none of them came close to Monroe, who seemed to personify the 1950s. Some observers state that only amid the expanding tastes and relaxed morality of postwar era could she have made such an impact. (The Illustrated London News Picture Library)

era, most small towns had at least one movie theater. Large cities had enormous, opulent "picture palaces," where patrons were surrounded by décor in exotic themes such those with Egyptian, Oriental, Mediterranean, or Moorish designs.

For those women who took their young children with them, many theaters had a soundproof "cry room" at the rear of the auditorium where the mother could take her wailing baby and still watch the movie through a glass window without disturbing other patrons. Before home air conditioning became commonplace, women could escape the heat of summer at air-cooled movies theaters.

But as the postwar era of the 1950s progressed, things began to change radically for the movie industry as well as the way Hollywood studios interacted with female moviegoers. Supreme Court decisions hampered the film industry's block booking system, an arrangement that was thought to violate anti-trust laws. Studios had a harder time releasing films to independent theater owners who might not care about showing a women's "weepie" when action films such as westerns and war movies would attract hordes of men.

The film studios themselves were in disarray during the postwar era as powerful movie moguls retired or were aged out of the companies they created. With them went an overall vision for the industry as well as the studio contract system, an arrangement that was not without its downside but that also nurtured female stars.

As the postwar era wore on, movie financing came increasingly from bankers or other outside investors who were intent on earning the largest possible profit. Women, either as stars or audience members, were not a top priority for the men who were in control. Without the contract system, individual performers were free to make independent deals to star in a movie. Among investors, male stars and movies that appealed to men were greatly favored since they were considered to be better moneymakers, especially in foreign markets.

Another blow to the movie industry was the onslaught of television. In the prosperity of the postwar era and the steady flow of bigger, better TV sets, more and more American women stayed home for free entertainment right in their living room. As a part of their daily lives, women could watch television with the whole family in "togetherness" mode.

To combat the juggernaut of television, the movie industry responded by producing epic films that were bigger and splashier than anything audiences could find at home on television. While most had males in leading roles, the epic movies usually had elements of a love story that producers felt would have some appeal for the average woman.

Top films of the 1950s included colorful musicals such as *An American in Paris, Kiss Me Kate, Oklahoma*, and *Singin' in the Rain*. There were spectacles including *Around the World in 80 Days* and *The Greatest Show on Earth*. In many of the big-screen extravaganzas, among the males, there was usually some kind of role for a female character as "the girl."

In the wake of accusations about having atheistic Communists in their midst, Hollywood studios also turned out extravagant biblical epics. Roles for women were often pious Christian maidens such as in the 1951 drama, *Quo Vadis*. Others focused on the other end of the spectrum with seductive biblical temptresses such as Bathsheba, Delilah, or Jezebel who destroyed men before meeting their own doom.

There were usually parts for "the girl" in the deluge of postwar monster movies, science fiction films, and motion pictures that appeared to be in three dimensions, called "3-D."

With more women moving with their families to the new suburbs, there was often not yet a movie theater nearby. They could not simply walk to movie theaters, as urban women had done for decades. Nor did they necessarily wish to travel into the city with its attendant costs. America's love of big, roomy postwar-era automobiles came to the rescue by spurring the growth of drive-in movies.

With drive-ins, the family car could serve as a family's personal theater on wheels. Thousands of drive-in movies were carved out of inexpensive suburban land across the country during the 1950s, enhancing daily life for many average suburban women. At drive-ins, mothers did not have to worry about dressing the children, feeding them when they got hungry, or keeping cranky kids out past their bedtime. They could simply get the children into pajamas, bring snacks from home, and let kids fall asleep in the back seat whenever they dozed off.

Generally, movies being shown at drive-ins had to appeal to the entire family. Therefore, as they were in mainstream theaters, "women's films" were sidelined.

As noted in Malone (2017), traditional women's films often involved a woman being forced to choose between the liberation of a career or some other form of independence versus giving it up for a husband, motherhood, and domesticity. By the end of the traditional woman's film, there is the reaffirmation that sacrificing for a man or a child is more important than independence. Malone claims, "She absolutely cannot have both" (65). This was a significant lesson for average postwar women to absorb from the movies as they lived their daily lives, compounding the messages all around them.

Haskell (1987) claims that movies of the postwar era promoted children as "a woman's ultimate *raison d'etre*, her only worth-confirming 'career'" (169). It was the same message about American women that was promoted by the U.S. government as the nation squared off against the Soviet Union.

The anti-Communism hearings of the 1950s era often targeted members of the movie industry for having alleged socialist leanings. Therefore, in the postwar era, the major Hollywood studios tried to distance themselves from anything that ran counter to the message of happy domesticity that the government wished to project to the world. The image of contented housewives spending their daily lives nurturing ideal families became an important part of the cinematic depiction of the American way of life.

Despite that, after World War II, another type of popular movie emerged from independent studios—called "film noir," the genre consisted of dark movies with flawed heroes and women called "femmes fatales." These "fatal dames" frequently brought about the downfall of the male. Often, the plot involved men who came home from the war to find their wives and girlfriends had become independent women who had a new sense of power that was often used to the male's detriment.

The film noir genre fostered suspicion about this new type of woman. While she was physically attractive, her allure was fatal for men. After bringing disaster for the male, she was generally punished by dying at the end of the film.

The Postman Always Rings Twice (1946) is a classic in the film noir genre. Lead actress Lana Turner first appears onscreen angelically dressed all in white, but she dies by the end of the film for her devilish deeds. Another, *Kiss Me Deadly* (1955), ends with a hellish vision of the femme fatale actually bursting into flames after opening a box of radioactive materials, something she had been forbidden to do. The cautionary message about film noir temptresses was not lost on average American women.

Most major studios released movies involving cheerful, devoted housewives who might be a bit high-spirited but inevitably put their man first. These included films made by such popular actresses as June Allyson and Doris Day who provided role models for postwar housewives as they lived their daily lives.

However, there was another American actress, quite different from June Allyson and Doris Day, who lit up the screen in movies of the postwar era. She was the ultimate fantasy for men along with having a sweet underlying vulnerability that also made her likeable to women. Starting out as brown-haired Norma Jeane

Dougherty, she became a 1950s icon as the blonde bombshell renamed Marilyn Monroe.

Malone (2017) calls the standard characters Monroe played to be "a cartoonish version of a sexy woman—platinum blonde, wide-eyed, childlike, speaking in a whisper, always ready to fulfill a man's needs without asking anything in return" (95).

But average postwar women seemed to like her too, even if she was far beyond the reality of their daily lives or their ability to replicate her massive sex appeal. Audiences came out in droves to see Monroe in movies such as *How to Marry a Millionaire* (1953), *Bus Stop* (1956), and *The Prince and the Showgirl* (1957). Her 1955 movie, *The Seven Year Itch*, featured the iconic shot of Monroe's silky white dress billowing around her waist, a classic moment of postwar-era naughtiness.

But the film that rocketed Monroe to superstardom was *Gentlemen Prefer Blondes* (1953), in which she wriggled onscreen in a tight, hot-pink satin gown singing "Diamonds Are a Girl's Best Friend." As Leaming (1998) writes, it was the birth of "an entirely new character named 'Marilyn Monroe'" (76).

Although other movie studios tried to come up with their own incendiary blondes, none of them came close. Monroe was unique, very much a product of her time, amid the expanding tastes and morality of the postwar era. According to Wagner (2016), "Marilyn Monroe would never have been accepted in the 1940s" (177).

During the postwar era, the movies' production code eased. New technologies such as Technicolor accentuated visuals like Monroe's platinum hair and costumes like the hot-pink dress. After the dreariness of the Great Depression in the 1930s and the solemnity of a nation at war in the 1940s, Monroe seemed to personify a breath of fresh air and a spirit of fun-loving naughtiness in the 1950s for average women.

There was another form of naughtiness in the movies that was not necessarily fun loving but still made an impact among women in postwar America. The "earthiness" of foreign actresses such as Brigitte Bardot and Sophia Loren gave American women something to think about even if they did not know how to achieve the same effect in their daily lives.

If average white American housewives had a hard time seeing their daily lives represented onscreen in more than a narrow depiction, black women had even more of a challenge. Since the very beginning of the motion picture business, if they could get acting jobs at all, African American women were cast almost exclusively as maids or "mammies."

The first black actress to win an Academy Award was Hattie McDaniel for her portrayal of the role of "Mammy" in the 1939 blockbuster *Gone with the Wind*. Best Supporting Actress nominee McDaniel had to sit at a table hidden in the back of the Los Angeles ballroom where the event was held, far away from the rest of the *Gone with the Wind* cast who were her fellow Oscar nominees. After McDaniel's Oscar win, no new types of roles opened up for her. She went back to being cast as maids and mammies.

In 1954, two years after Hattie McDaniel's death, a postwar-era black actress became the first female African American contender for an Oscar since McDaniel had been in 1939. Dorothy Dandridge was nominated as Best Actress for her title role in the movie *Carmen Jones* (1954). Dandridge lost the award to Grace Kelly, but her treatment on Oscar night at New York's Century Theatre was a step forward from what McDaniel's had been. Dandridge was not only seated in the auditorium along with the other nominees, but she also became the first black female to ever take part in the Academy Awards ceremony itself when she presented the Best Film Editing award on nationwide television.

Like McDaniel, Oscar nominee Dandridge would discover that there were still few roles for black women even a generation later, in the years following World War II. According to Malone (2017), when Dandridge died in 1965, she had "two dollars in her bank account" (94).

A number of talented African American actresses such as Lena Horne also had difficulty being cast in mainstream movies. When she was hired at all, Horne was often simply cast as herself in musical scenes. In the 1951 movie *Showboat*, she was turned down in favor of a white actress for the role of a light-skinned black woman, even though that is exactly what she was.

One director stood apart. Douglas Sirk spotlighted women at the center of his storytelling and even expanded roles for black actresses. Sirk's films, including *All That Heaven Allows* (1955), *Magnificent Obsession* (1954), and *Written on the Wind* (1956), were throwbacks to the women's pictures of earlier decades. His lead actress's onscreen "problems" included falling in love with a younger man or being a female who seemed to enjoy sex too much.

One of Sirk's movies, *Imitation of Life* (1959), not only dealt with women's issues but racial ones as well. Fischer (1991) states that the film focuses on the struggles of two single working mothers, one

African American and one white. It is elevated by "its inclusion of prominent black characters" (5) in more than token roles.

Imitation of Life was the top-grossing film that year for its studio. Many average female filmgoers, both black and white, responded to the theme of women forming close friendships in their daily lives regardless of race or other boundaries, especially when working together to provide for their children.

Even in the male-dominated movie industry itself, the few women in jobs such as screenwriters tended to help each other. According to Welch (2018), as opposed to male moguls, many of the women employed at film studios supported each other's careers, adding, "these women saw the value in each other, which is perhaps the greatest lesson of their lives" (10).

Somewhere between movie housewives and cinematic temptresses, it was a lesson that many average women in postwar America could begin to absorb.

MUSIC

With the music industry enjoying the same kind of postwar prosperity as the rest of American business in the 1950s, it played more of a role in the daily lives of the nation's women. Due to advancing technology and other factors, a number of average women who daydreamed about a career in music discovered that their vision might conceivably go beyond fantasy to reality.

Recording technology produced superior sound quality that could be played on the home phonographs of the postwar era that were continually being improved. Affordable tape recorders allowed women to record the kind of music they liked from the radio or other sources and play it as often as they wished. Many learned to sing and play instruments by accompanying recorded sound.

The large console radios that had been the centerpieces of American living rooms from the 1920s through the 1940s were increasingly being replaced in the 1950s by a television set as the family's main source of entertainment. However, housewives could listen to the radio while they went about their daily chores when improved technology produced smaller, portable radios that could be placed in any room of the home.

As part of their daily lives, women regularly gathered with their families around the television set. In that way, many were exposed to new types of music that they might not ordinarily have discovered. Variety shows such as Ed Sullivan's presented musical acts of all kinds, everything from classical to the newly emerging genre called rock and roll. More and more, an average woman could see female singers in the spotlight, causing some to wonder if a person like herself might also have a career in show business.

There had been a few female singers who earned great fame in the late 19th and early 20th centuries such as Mary Garden, Jenny Lind, and Nellie Melba. However, their repertoire was based in the classical world of opera, requiring years of training.

In the 1920s and 1930s, with the sudden rise of the home phonographs and radio, African American blues singers such as Ma Rainey, Bessie Smith, and Ethel Waters found appreciative audiences across racial lines.

The male-dominated big bands of the 1940s usually had a "girl singer" such as Doris Day or Helen O'Connell to perform a few numbers. The Andrews Sisters were a big hit with wartime fans. The biggest female solo act of the 1940s was Kate Smith whose version of "God Bless America" inspired a nation at war.

But women understood that it took years of hard work and lucky breaks for all those ladies to reach the limited spots for females at the top. However, in the postwar era, the coming of television provided a pathway to success that could in some cases be virtually instantaneous. Women did not necessarily need years of operatic training or the long-term struggle of singing in small nightclubs hoping to be discovered. Exposure on television provided a quicker route to success by showcasing their talent for millions of viewers.

The growth of television also coincided with the postwar recording industry's need for a steady supply of fresh talent. For recording studios, the process was no longer prohibitively expensive due to the decreasing costs of production through the 1950s. If a female singer with a good voice also had the kind of sex appeal for men that could be displayed on album covers, she might have a chance.

One postwar TV show that was popular with women as they lived their daily lives provided a shortcut to an entertainment career. *Arthur Godfrey's Talent Scouts* ran from 1948 to 1958 on both radio and television. The winning performer was determined by a meter that allegedly measured the level of applause from the studio audience. Being showcased from coast to coast on *Talent Scouts*, along with positive word of mouth from Godfrey, could provide an early boost to the winner's career.

Would-be performers on *Talent Scouts* had to audition to earn a spot on the program. This audition system was not infallible; both Buddy Holly and Elvis Presley were turned down.

Contestants on the program included female singers such as Rosemary Clooney, Connie Francis, the McGuire Sisters, and Leslie Uggams, all of whom went on to have long, successful careers.

Reflecting a renewed interest in country music during the postwar era, Patsy Cline gained national attention on *Talent Scouts* in 1957. Many average women across the nation found that the reality of their daily lives could be found in country music.

One of the biggest factors in providing a showcase for female country singers began in 1955 when the *Grand Ole Opry*, broadcast from Nashville, Tennessee, made its television debut. The *Opry* was a showcase for country talent. Until that time, there were not many women country singers apart from a few exceptions such as Kitty Wells.

Wells's 1952 hit, "It Wasn't God Who Made Honky Tonk Angels," was the first single by a female solo artist to top America's country charts. In the course of their daily lives, many average women all across the country related to Wells's plaintive lyrics about "trustful wives" and "good girls gone wrong." Called the "Queen of Country Music" in the postwar era, Kitty Wells was country music's first female superstar. Her continued success proved to the music industry that records by women country singers would sell.

Patsy Cline scored a major success in 1957 with her nationwide television appearance on *Talent Scouts*. The song she performed, "Walkin' after Midnight," became her first big hit. Later, "I Fall to Pieces" (1961) topped both the country and the pop charts, which was highly unusual for any singer, male or female.

A number of average postwar women were inspired to try their luck as country singers, more than at any time in the history of the genre. Housewife Loretta Lynn hit the top after teaching herself to play a $17 guitar while staying at home with the children.

Since the 1920s, African American women had popularized the traditional sound of the blues. They are often acknowledged as performing the first "soul" music to be recorded. These blues women, such as Alberta Hunter, Ma Rainey, and Bessie Smith, became known among white blues fans as well as African Americans. However, due to a number of factors in the first half of the 20th century, from primitive technology to racial discrimination, the success of these early blues women was limited.

But the postwar era brought the ability to produce high-quality recordings, including "live" albums that captured the stirring vocals of African American songstresses whose voices ranged from blues to jazz. Black women could see themselves represented in such iconic singers of the postwar era as Ella Fitzgerald and Sarah Vaughan. Another, Billie Holiday, gained a legion of new fans after her death in 1959.

Another showcase in the postwar era for African American women with musical talent was the legendary Apollo Theater in New York's Harlem. The Apollo was one of the first theaters to allow black performers onstage as well as welcoming mixed-race audiences. Its Amateur Night contests provided a showcase for then-unknown female singers such as Ella Fitzgerald and Sarah Vaughan.

In 1955 came the first television broadcast of *Show Time at the Apollo*, taped before a live audience. According to Moore (2010), one audience member who attended a performance at the Apollo in 1955 was said to be notably captivated by Bo Diddley's "driving guitar beat and swinging hips: 20-year-old Elvis Presley" (n.p.). Some say it was the showmanship on display at the Apollo that influenced Presley's hip-shaking style that enthralled women in postwar America across the country.

In the mainstream type of popular music called "pop" that was at the forefront of the early 1950s, the field was dominated by handsome male vocalists known as crooners. But there were also female pop singers who were favorites among postwar listeners. Some women who released million-sellers in the 1950s included Rosemary Clooney, Doris Day, Peggy Lee, Patti Page, and Dinah Shore. Apart from enjoying their music, average women of the 1950s could not often see their daily lives reflected in the slick presentations by women pop singers, who were essentially female versions of male crooners.

However, all that was about to change with a new sound emerging in the postwar era, called rock and roll. Hirshey (1984) claims, "At its most dangerous, rock is a scream. . . . Crooners were too tame" (5). Some postwar American housewives were slow to embrace rock and roll, but others saw a potential place for themselves out of the house and into the spotlight.

One way to do it was in the relative safety of "girl groups" in the early rock and roll era. During the early 1950s, groups such as the Chordettes and the McGuire Sisters sang standard pop music. However, the rock and roll revolution led to a sound for women that was more raw and less polished than simply being female versions of male crooners.

Some early female rock groups consisted of young African American women who transitioned the rhythm-and-blues sound into success on the rock charts. They included the Teen Queens with 1954's "Eddie My Love," the Bobbettes with 1957's "Mr. Lee," and the Chantels with "Maybe" in 1958.

Most sources cite the Shirelles as the prototype for the most successful girl groups of the postwar era. The Shirelles continued to maintain their popularity after their classic "Will You Love Me Tomorrow" (1960) became the first recording by an African American girl group to reach number one on the charts.

Young women of the postwar era, both black and white, saw their potential chance for success in the music industry increase with each new female act that had a hit. Record producer Phil Spector found a way to create a more powerful impact for girl groups by utilizing his "wall of sound" that layered different levels of voices and instruments, creating a stronger effect.

Most record producers were male, but there were a few outliers. Lillian McMurry was the founder of Trumpet Records in 1951. Cordell Jackson founded Moon Records in 1956. One of the most successful labels, Stax Records, was cofounded by Estelle Axton in 1957. Stax, located in segregated Memphis, was renowned not only for its music but also for its racially integrated staff and its artists, including the house band, Booker T. & the M.G.'s.

During the latter part of the postwar era, there was some potential for women in areas of the music business that had traditionally been exclusively male. For example, songwriting was not usually open to women until the success of women in postwar America such as Ellie Greenwich and Carole King.

Both began writing songs with their respective husbands. King earned songwriting credit for such hits as "Up on the Roof" and "Will You Love Me Tomorrow." Greenwich was recognized for "Be My Baby" and "Then He Kissed Me."

It was the work of Carole King that enlivened the daydreams of many average young women of the latter postwar era with the success of a song she wrote called "The Locomotion." In 1962, Eva Boyd, the 19-year-old babysitter for King's children, was enlisted to step out of her daily life around the house and into the recording studio. According to Weller (2008), Boyd was renamed "Little Eva." She recorded the tune and "in weeks, the song reached #1" (114).

In 1958, a young woman emerged who is considered the first bona fide female rock star: Connie Francis. Following her recording of "Who's Sorry Now" (1958), she followed up with one hit after another. Many average young women of the postwar era dreamed of having a career like Francis's.

Still, in the course of their daily lives, some American women continued to listen to a more traditional sound that was worlds apart from the postwar rock and roll era. Amid the roar of rock, classical music remained beloved by many.

African American opera star Marian Anderson continued her successful career in the classics. In 1955, Anderson became the first African American to perform at New York City's Metropolitan Opera.

With the rise of television, a new kind of female opera singer took center stage in the postwar era. Maria Callas was treated like a movie star by the mainstream media, an unusual occurrence for a classical artist. Callas made her debut at New York's Metropolitan Opera in 1956, continuing to perform at the highest level of the operatic field until her retirement in 1965. By appearing on television's *Ed Sullivan Show* in 1956, Callas was introduced to millions of average women across America who, in the course of their daily lives, might never set foot in an opera house.

Television also boosted the operatic career of Leontyne Price in the postwar era. In 1955, Price sang the title role of Tosca on NBC Opera Theatre, becoming the first African American to play a leading role in a televised opera. During the late 1950s, she returned to perform on the program several more times. However, in certain parts of the country, those later broadcasts by Price on NBC Opera Theatre were boycotted by some affiliates because of her race.

There continued to be very few female musicians in major symphony orchestras during the postwar era. Therefore, the dreams of young women who hoped to perform in that area of classical music were generally quashed if they did not play the harp, which was virtually the only instrument that was traditionally allowed for women in a symphony orchestra. According to Pendle (2001), "Some female classical musicians were told they should not play orchestral instruments other than the harp because they did not look good playing them" (206).

Eventually, violins became acceptable instruments for female musicians. Still, it was not until the 1990s that some orchestras began holding tryouts for new members behind a screen to reduce the prevalence of gender bias so the audition panel could not see if the performer was male or female.

Even if many opportunities for females were limited in the postwar era, there were women who found a place for themselves in the music industry by performing traditional jobs such as secretarial work.

One woman of the postwar era is rarely known but might arguably be called the person who ignited the spark of the rock and roll revolution. Working as a secretary at Sun Records in Memphis, Tennessee, Marion Keisker neither sang nor played an instrument. Guralnick (1994) states that she was alone in the office of Sun Records one day in 1953 when a young man who hoped to make a recording stopped by on break from his job as a truck driver. Keisker asked what kind of singer he was and who he sounded like. According to Guralnik, the young man said, "I don't sound like nobody" (2).

Marion Keisker's daily life was spent working as a secretary. But she saw something in the raw teenager. She not only arranged a recording session but also went an extra step by taking him at lunchtime "down the street to the *Press-Scimitar* [newspaper] building" for an interview with an old friend (Guralnik, 108). It was the first press coverage for the young man, whose name was Elvis Presley. If it were not for Marion Keisker, an unsung secretary who recognized raw talent, it is hard to know when—or if—the rock and roll revolution led by Presley would have begun its postwar conquest of the world.

TELEVISION

It is virtually impossible to overstate the impact of television on average women in postwar America. After all, it was the housewife who spent the greatest amount of time in her daily life with this electronic companion that resided permanently in her home. The average housewife spent large portions of her daytime hours with television, being exposed to programs that were aimed directly at women like her. She was also in front of the television during evening prime-time hours when she watched televised images of the ideal American family as she sat amid the "togetherness" of her own family unit.

Maurer (2016) states that at the dawn of the television age just after World War II, the new phenomenon of TV was perceived by average Americans in simple terms: "Television is like radio—but with pictures" (n.p.). Maurer adds, "Dozens of popular radio programs migrated to television, bringing their sponsors and established audience demographics with them" (n.p.). Many of those sponsors and demographics related directly to average women.

I Love Lucy, which premiered in 1951, was the highest-rated situation comedy on television during the postwar era. Lucille Ball's physical comedy and slapstick humor made the show a hit with the whole family. Some of her antics became iconic, as this U.S. postage stamp attests. (Olga Popova/Dreamstime.com)

However, for American women, television became much more than simply adding visual images to what they heard on the radio.

As opposed to going out and paying to see movies, most viewers considered entertainment on their family's television set to be free of charge after they made the initial purchase. What few realized was that the commercials regularly interrupting their favorite programs were more than just minor intrusions. Viewers were targeted very strategically, with an almost military precision. Without remote controls available on early television sets, viewers were essentially a captive audience. Unless they wanted to get up from their chair to change channels by hand during commercials, or manually lower the sound, their eyes and ears absorbed what the sponsor wanted to promote.

Television interacted on a daily basis with the men, women, and children of America in very specific ways. Women were an especially prized consumer group, being targeted accordingly.

Advertising experts felt they could take aim at the average woman's insecurity, vulnerability, and feeling of being unappreciated for the things she did in her daily life. Marketers sought to plant the idea in her mind that by purchasing a certain product, she would feel better about herself.

During the course of their daily lives, many women turned on the television for company as they went through their household routines. Some felt isolated in the newly developed suburbs. Many young mothers had only toddlers for daytime companionship. Some women began to feel estranged from their husbands, whose busy workday life did not permit a lot of time for their wives.

Therefore, television producers delivered what Cassidy (2005) called the "charm boys . . . wooing the unseen thousands of women watching at home" (6). One of the most popular was the avuncular Arthur Godfrey who hosted a weekday morning show, *Arthur Godfrey Time*. As his ratings increased, networks allowed him to regularly go off script as if in a droll conspiracy with his female "friends," drawing them into a bit of fun during the day with a charismatic male.

Cassidy (2005) also quotes fellow daytime "charm boy" Garry Moore, who believed his role for his loyal army of housewives was to supply "the sounds of merriment while they worked" (6). On the popular daytime program *Art Linkletter's House Party*, Linkletter, another "charm boy," offered heartwarming and often hilarious interviews with children, guaranteed to resonate with the mothers of postwar America.

Around lunchtime or early afternoon, when women might take a break from their daily housework, there were daytime dramas. With all the advertisements for cleaning products on this type of program, most had commonly been called "soap operas" since the days of radio. Televised postwar-era "soaps" aimed at the daily lives of the female viewing audience included *Love of Life* and *Search for Tomorrow*.

According to Cassidy (2005), networks tried a wide assortment of inexpensive daytime programming directed at women, including "shopping shows, homemaking shows, variety-vaudeville combinations, live anthology drama, films edited for television, and audience participation shows" (5). The latter included stunt shows, human interest shows, and so-called misery shows.

Misery shows were personified by *Queen for a Day*, which made its television debut in 1956. Four contestants competed daily for prizes by telling their pathetic life stories. For example, a badly underprivileged woman might plead for a wheelchair needed by a disabled child. The contestant who received the most audience sympathy applause was granted her wish. She was crowned "Queen," wrapped in royal robes, and awarded gifts such as a refrigerator or washing machine. Although some critics said the show exploited the deprivation of the poor for the entertainment of the prosperous, *Queen for a Day* reached millions of viewers, running for years throughout the postwar era. Eventually, the half-hour show was expanded to 45 minutes, with the producers claiming it was to accommodate a fifth contestant, although some observers said it was actually in order to add more commercials.

American mothers were sometimes condemned by cultural critics for utilizing television as an "electronic babysitter," particularly while women were occupied with daily household tasks such as making dinner.

In the evening hours, called "prime time," the daily lives of average American women were usually spent gathered in front of the television set watching programs together with the family. Mom was often the one who decided what the family would watch on one of the three networks (ABC, CBS, and NBC).

Frequently, the choice was a mild situation comedy. This type of program, abbreviated as a "sitcom," idealized the average American family for the nation and the world to see. After some sort of dilemma that would be resolved in the half-hour format (including commercials), each episode usually ended with a hug, a kiss, and a moral. Amid the flood of male-centered westerns on postwar television, housewives at least had the chance to see people like themselves portrayed in domestic sitcoms.

One of the most popular domestic situation comedies began in 1952. The debut of *The Adventures of Ozzie & Harriet* set the sitcom template for the postwar years. It was also one of the earliest of today's so-called reality shows because audiences in the 1950s knew that the married couple of Ozzie and Harriet Nelson, along with their two boys, David and Ricky, were a real-life family. Harriet Nelson, which was also her character's name on the show, was always nearby to answer the telephone or offer a comforting slice of pie. It was husband Ozzie who imparted family values not only to his boys but also to the rest of America.

Father Knows Best began its run in 1954, with a title that was a giveaway as to its content. Jane Wyatt's portrayal of the show's Margaret Anderson character, a housewife and mother, was calm, reassuring, and supportive of her husband who always "knew best."

Leave It to Beaver premiered in 1957, the same night that Americans were stunned by the shocking news that the Russians had launched the Sputnik space satellite. It was orbiting above the earth, including the United States, at the very moment when the comforting *Beaver* made its debut. Barbara Billingsley as June Cleaver wore pearls, attractive dresses, and high-heeled shoes while doing her daily chores. She also managed to be a wise, calming influence in her all-male household.

In 1958, Academy Award–winning actress Donna Reed reached her 40th birthday, a milestone that could be career suicide for a female movie star during the postwar era. Moving to television, Reed headlined *The Donna Reed Show* as Donna Stone, an ideal postwar wife and mother. The program varied somewhat by showing housewife Donna Stone staying busy in her daily life doing things apart from housework by participating in charity drives and projects with the local community theater. Along with her other television sitcom counterparts, Reed wore high heels and pearls with charming frocks as she performed her household chores.

The highest rated of the postwar-era television sitcoms, *I Love Lucy*, which premiered in 1951, was in some ways an outlier. Former movie star Lucille Ball played housewife Lucy Ricardo who did not accept her daily life as a housewife. The character of Lucy was constantly seeking a way out of the house and into the wider world, preferably in show business. Because Lucy sought to escape, she is considered by many sources not to be an ideal representative of the average 1950s housewife. However, Lucille Ball's physical comedy and slapstick humor made the show a hit with the whole family. It is important to note that even though Lucy was a discontented housewife who tried to escape her prescribed place in the home, she always failed miserably. At the end of each episode, husband Ricky always welcomed Lucy back into her domestic role with a laugh, a hug, and a kiss.

For many female viewers, everything seemed so perfect in TV families. Obviously, there was a reason for that. Advertisers liked their products to be associated with happy people. The government liked the American way of life to be presented in the most glowing terms. They both liked women to be portrayed as happy homemakers, content with being wives and mothers as their highest and best—indeed their only—calling.

As in the movies, television can control the emotions of viewers through close-ups, cutaways, point of view, and so on. Some of the women watching domestic sitcoms were convinced that the shows reflected real life. Rather than questioning, it was a comfort to watch them. There was a reason for that too. Often, pleasurable experiences are addictive, and one of the most pleasurable is the chance to laugh. In addition, sources state that people tend to laugh and enjoy themselves more when they hear other people laughing. The sitcoms might not be terribly funny at all, but laugh tracks and canned applause—what Packard (1957) called "synthetic hilarity" (176)—could make the domestic sitcoms seem much more enjoyable than they might otherwise have been. In the early days of television, few viewers knew about canned laughter. Women who questioned the quality of the shows often felt at odds with the waves of laughter generated by the televised fun.

Ironically, the importance of television at the center of daily life for the average American woman was reinforced through a rival media source: women's magazines.

Although it may seem counterintuitive for one medium to promote another, as women's magazines did for television, there was a symbiotic relationship based upon their mutual advertisers. Spigel (1992) claims that through pictorial displays of television sets at the center of domestic settings, magazines "advised women on the ways to integrate the new medium into the traditional space of the family home" (5).

Apart from male-oriented products such as beer and razor blades, the woman was the one to whom advertisers pitched many of their products. It was therefore important that she place the television in the center of her home, both physically and symbolically. If the whole family watched television as a group within the ideal of "togetherness," they would all be exposed to the same ads, and theoretically, all would want to purchase those items.

The image of American families viewing television together was presented as the standard pastime for the growing middle class. This also pertained to lower-class women in pockets of poverty who could not yet afford a television. Looking through relatively inexpensive magazines, they could see pictures of happy families around a TV set, aspiring to a vision that was firmly planted in their mind for some future time when a television would come into their own home. In this paradigm, television viewing as promoted in women's magazines became more than entertainment—it was a tutorial.

One female image on postwar television planted itself in the minds of baby boom girls. In 1954, actress Gail Davis became the first woman to star in a TV western when she portrayed legendary sharpshooter Annie Oakley in a groundbreaking television series of the same name. Apart from most other women on television, she did not portray a housewife. According to Hendricks (2016), "many young women later said they were influenced by watching Davis as a female character in a traditionally male role" (49).

A number of women in postwar America were influenced in other ways by the electronic marvel they had invited into their homes like a friend. By the late 1950s, however, instead of enjoying a warm mutual friendship, they felt betrayed.

As part of their daily lives, many housewives regularly watched daytime game shows such as *Concentration*, *Dotto*, and *The Price Is Right*. The popularity of the these programs during the daylight hours often led to evening versions, complete with a built-in fan base of women.

The nighttime quiz shows attracted millions more viewers, both male and female. Producers decided that they needed to create heroes and villains whom the audience could root for or against in order to satisfy sponsors who found the programs dull. Ultimately, that pressure for the nighttime shows to be more competitive would have disastrous results.

Because quiz shows were relatively inexpensive to produce, the postwar airwaves were awash in them. Some of the most popular prime-time quiz shows that women and their families watched together included *The $64,000 Question* and *Twenty-One*. Some mothers felt it was educational for their children and an object lesson for kids to see how educated people could be hugely successful.

During the postwar years, the average American woman tended to trust what she saw on television. Millions of women and their families faithfully tuned in to quiz shows. Then came a shockwave in the late 1950s, as the quiz show scandals revealed that many popular programs had been rigged.

One game show, *Dotto*, was abruptly cancelled in 1958 when a notebook was found backstage containing the answers that a contestant was delivering on camera at that very moment. That particular contestant was Marie Winn, who eventually became a journalist. Her books include *The Plug-In Drug*, published in 1977, which was a scathing critique of television's influence and addictive power over children.

The most highly publicized case took place in 1957, becoming the one that proved the most hurtful to many women. It involved a handsome, urbane contestant named Charles Van Doren. He was a Columbia University instructor whom some mothers held up to their children as an example of the power of education. When his cheating became public, many baby boom children learned quite a different lesson from the one their mothers intended.

Ironically, Van Doren had been scripted to lose so that he could move to an on-air network job as "cultural correspondent." The winner was to be a woman, attorney Vivienne Nearing, who was meant to add an interesting new female element to the show when Van Doren's winning run seemed to be getting stale.

Other female fan favorites during the heyday of the quiz shows included Joyce Brothers on *The $64,000 Question*. Preparing for her 1955 appearance, she had gender roles in mind, deciding to add an element of novelty for a woman contestant. She learned everything she could about the male-oriented sport of boxing before announcing that as her special area of expertise. After her successful run, she went on to become a nationally known psychologist who often utilized television as a kind of electronic analyst's "couch."

Barbara Feldon, another winning contestant on *The $64,000 Question*, chose Shakespeare as her field in 1957. She went on to play "Agent 99" on a popular television spy spoof in the 1960s called *Get Smart*.

Television also affected women in postwar America via the realm of politics. In the new television age, politicians and their handlers were "getting smart" by changing tactics.

According to Lessig (2019), before television, information about politics was primarily conveyed through writing. However, "when television became dominant . . . people wanted to watch [politics on] TV" (74). Therefore, television became the way they received their political information.

Television gave political candidates the ability to present their message exactly the way they wanted to. Speaking directly to millions via TV, they bypassed the interpretation of print reporters and the analysis of columnists.

New techniques were fashioned for politics in the age of television. Radio had allowed candidates to be heard, but with television, they could also be seen. Political operatives therefore wanted to create a candidate who was appealing to female voters as well as men.

Even if the candidate was not necessarily a matinee idol in terms of physical appearance, he (it was almost always a "he") could be filmed in short television spots waving to cheering crowds, many of whom were adoring women. Quick "sound bites" could be shaped to reassure the postwar-era mothers of America that their families would be safe under the candidate's leadership.

In the 1950s, Dwight Eisenhower's team utilized these techniques to great advantage. At first, "Ike" resisted a presidential campaign based on televised ads, but later gave in. Candidates who continued to resist did so at their own peril. Adlai Stevenson, Eisenhower's opponent in 1952 and again in 1956, disdained television. Stevenson lost by a landslide both times.

Some televised political pieces were presented by women for women, directly addressing their hopes and fears in the postwar era. A prime example from the 1956 presidential election, called "The Living Room Candidate," can be seen at http://www.living roomcandidate.org/commercials/1956/women-voters.

However, television time was enormously expensive. The cost of campaigning via the powerful new medium of television changed the course of American politics. Potential candidates, often women, with neither personal wealth nor powerful groups backing them often found themselves barred from running due to lack of funds. In addition, successful candidates were forced to spend a large portion of their time raising money to repay debts from their campaign and/or start building a "war chest" for the next election, something many women found difficult to do.

In 1959, a young senator wrote an article for a new postwar-era publication called *TV Guide* that was popular with many women. According to Wattenberg (2016), the senator stated that television "altered drastically the nature of our political campaigns, conventions, constituents, candidates, and costs" (29).

Apparently, the largely unknown senator learned the lesson well. The following year, that same young senator took part in the first televised presidential debate. He was said by many sources to have won the debate in large part because of the charm, charisma, vigorous good looks, and appeal for women that he radiated on television. His name was John F. Kennedy, and he went on to win the 1960 presidential election.

After Kennedy's assassination three years later, his televised funeral was broadcast nonstop by all three networks. For several days, women and their families across the nation were brought together electronically via the television that sat in the center of their living rooms.

THEATER AND DANCE

With the general upsurge in prosperity and the dazzling new technology of the postwar era, several art forms that had previously been the domain of the wealthy soon became accessible to average American women. Among these were the realms of theater and dance.

Amateur theatrical groups had been a part of small-town American life for generations. According to the American Association for Community Theatre (AACT), a burst of new activity occurred after World War II. AACT estimates that in 1959, there were about 3,500 full-scale community theaters in the United States, up from several hundred before the war.

Many of these "little theater" groups were created in the booming postwar suburbs, with a major portion of their organizers being women. Some new female suburbanites had previously lived in the city, where they were used to having some sort of live theater nearby. Others found that the tedium of their daily life, centering around housework, did not provide many creative outlets. Still others, feeling isolated, simply wanted some form of socialization with other adults apart from spending their daily lives in the company of small children and daytime television.

Situation comedies on prime-time television, such as *The Donna Reed Show*, often had episodes centering on the female character being involved with community theater efforts, with varying results that tended toward the comedic.

For decades, top-tier professional theater in America was synonymous with "Broadway," a district in New York City where major playhouses are located. But as part of their daily lives, even women who lived in parts of the country far removed from Manhattan could regularly read about the celebrities who inhabited the "Great White Way," a metaphor for the bright lights of Broadway. Their source of information was gossip columns.

One of the best-known Broadway gossip columnists was Walter Winchell, who attained a national spotlight by being syndicated across the country in the Hearst chain of daily newspapers. Winchell also had a popular radio show, making him the most recognizable name in Broadway gossip. Each day, women across the nation could learn about the hit shows and top celebrities in New York City, a place they might never visit but which felt familiar to them nonetheless.

Even if the average woman never visited New York, the advance of television in the 1950s brought the sights and sounds of Broadway right into her home. In the course of her daily life, a postwar American woman could see the sensational shows she had only read about in newspapers or heard about on the radio.

Television was a massive force in popularizing American theater during the postwar years. As more average Americans purchased a television set in the postwar era, they were exposed to the glittering world of Broadway theater. It is doubtful that many would have experienced it otherwise.

Early television was broadcast live from New York City, so TV shows could conveniently draw on Broadway talent. Late-night variety programs often attracted stage stars on their days off or after they had finished performing in their Broadway show that evening.

Broadway Open House made its debut in 1950, holding the distinction of being network television's first documented late-night variety series. It was broadcast live on weeknights at 11:00 p.m. It not only attracted major Broadway talent but also created its own star, a woman called Dagmar. Born Virginia Ruth Egnor, she had a specific role on the show: to look sexy and act like a "dumb blonde." Dagmar's popularity as the host's sidekick made her a household name, landing her on the cover of *Life* magazine in 1951. Because of her widespread press coverage and name recognition across the country, Dagmar is usually credited with being the first female TV star.

A competitor of Walter Winchell, Broadway columnist Ed Sullivan, began hosting a weekly television variety show in 1948 that was also broadcast from New York. Among everything from animal acts to ventriloquists, *The Ed Sullivan Show* exposed viewers across the country to scenes from current Broadway plays.

Audiences who knew they would probably never make it to the Great White Way were enthralled from the beginning. On Sullivan's very first program in 1948, top theatrical composers Richard Rodgers and Oscar Hammerstein previewed music for the nationwide television audience from their upcoming show *South Pacific*, which opened on Broadway the following year.

Sullivan's program appealed to a number of average American women because it spotlighted the many shows on Broadway in the postwar era that had females in leading roles. For example, Julie Andrews performed songs from her hit production of *My Fair Lady* (1956). She returned to the Sullivan show to sing numbers from her next hit, *Camelot* (1960) in addition to performing a scene with heartthrob Richard Burton. Broadway star Ethel Merman appeared on *The Ed Sullivan Show* regularly, singing hit songs from her postwar-era shows such as *Annie Get Your Gun*, *Anything Goes*, and *Gypsy*.

The snippets on Ed Sullivan's program were popular, but women in postwar America and their families could regularly enjoy full-length Broadway shows in the comfort of their own living rooms via the miracle of television. Often produced with the original cast, frequently centering around the leading lady, dozens of Broadway shows were broadcast on early television networks. They included Ethel Merman in *Anything Goes* and *Panama Hattie* (both in 1954); *Peter Pan* with Mary Martin in 1955; and *Kiss Me Kate* with Patricia Morrison and *Wonderful Town* with Rosalind Russell, both in 1958.

Sullivan's show as well as television itself were often criticized as "low brow." Ironically, however, they preserved much of what we know today as relatively high brow, including the legendary leading ladies of postwar-era Broadway in their prime. These stars usually performed in the same costumes they wore in the actual Broadway productions, giving us a glimpse of the actresses who originated the roles that have now become classics.

Shows starring top actresses often ran for years, with one production having their name in lights frequently following on the heels of another. The names of those female stars were well known to average postwar women. For example, Mary Martin's Broadway success in the postwar era included starring in *South Pacific* (1949), *Kind Sir* (1953), *Peter Pan* (1954), *The Skin of Our Teeth* (1955), and the megahit *The Sound of Music* (1959).

Ethel Merman starred in *Annie Get Your Gun* (1946), *Call Me Madam* (1950), *Happy Hunting* (1956), and *Gypsy* (1959).

The legendary Gwen Verdon sang, danced, and starred in the original productions of *CanCan* (1953), *Damn Yankees* (1955), *New Girl in Town* (1957), *Redhead* (1959), and *Sweet Charity* (1966). By the end of the postwar era, she was still headlining. In 1975, Verdon originated the role of Roxie Hart in the hit musical *Chicago*, on Broadway at age 50, an inspiration for many average women who felt that postwar American society implied that they were "over the hill" by that age.

In addition, advances in recording technology allowed average women to buy original cast albums to play on phonographs at home as part of their daily lives, listening as often as they wished. Some enjoyed singing along as they did their everyday housework; others may have nurtured dreams of leaving the house and seeing their own name in lights.

During the postwar era, there were a few spots that slowly opened for women in the world of theater that did not involve performing onstage. These women, often unsung, changed the landscape of

American theater. In some cases, their work with regional theaters that had a permanent troupe of professional actors allowed many American women to see the kind of live, high-quality theatrical productions that had previously barely existed beyond New York.

Cheryl Crawford was a powerful female producer who cofounded New York's American Repertory Theater, Group Theater, and the Actors Studio, all major groundbreakers in the American theatrical world. Crawford produced postwar Broadway classics such as the musical *Brigadoon* (1947) and the Tennessee Williams drama, *Sweet Bird of Youth* (1959).

In 1950, Zelda Fichandler founded the Arena Stage in Washington, DC, which became one of America's leading regional theaters. It was the first integrated theater in the nation's capital, with Fichandler hiring performers regardless of race. As its original producing organization, Arena Stage was the first regional theater to transfer a show to Broadway, which it did in 1967 with *The Great White Hope*—a controversial drama based on a true story involving racism. The play went on to win the Pulitzer Prize for Drama.

Between 1945 and 1950, Margo Jones directed five Broadway plays in five years. However, it was her work in regional theater set the template for theatrical institutions that are common today but were innovative for their time. These include hiring a resident professional company and staging shows in the round. On Broadway, Jones directed *The Glass Menagerie* in 1945, which today is a classic. She also produced another classic, *Inherit the Wind* (1955), after eight Broadway producers turned it down.

These women were known for their cooperation and mutual admiration, often learning from each other. In 1948, Hildy Parks appeared in the Broadway premier of Tennessee Williams's *Summer and Smoke*, produced and directed by Margo Jones. Following other acting roles, Parks moved into different kinds of work in theater. In 1967, she wrote and produced the first Tony Awards ceremony to be televised. Under her leadership, that event, recognizing outstanding achievements in Broadway theater, could thereafter be seen by average women as part of the nationwide television audience. Some say that today's Tony Awards presentation, having struggled to survive for years before it was televised, owes its existence to Hildy Parks.

As demands for civil rights increased throughout the postwar era, African Americans and other minorities slowly attained greater recognition in the world of theater. Premiering in 1958, the musical *Flower Drum Song* was unique for the time in its casting of Asian

American performers instead of heavily made-up whites to play Asian roles.

In 1950, Juanita Hall became the first African American to receive a Tony Award following her performance in *South Pacific*. Other African American women were also receiving acclaim, in some cases for their nonperformance work, inspiring average black women. A major breakthrough came with the success of Lorraine Hansberry, who was the first African American female playwright to have a show performed on Broadway. Her best known work, the play *A Raisin in the Sun*, made its Broadway debut in 1959. Set in Chicago, the play dramatizes the daily life of an average African American matriarch and her family as they experienced racial segregation.

The cast of *A Raisin in the Sun* included acclaimed performances by African American actresses Ruby Dee, Claudia McNeil, and Diana Sands. The show was a major hit, running almost two years. At the age of 29, Hansberry won the New York Drama Critics' Circle Award, becoming the first African American playwright as well as the youngest to do so. In 1965, Hansberry died at age 34, the same night that her next Broadway play, *The Sign in Sidney Brustein's Window*, closed after more than 100 performances.

Vinnette Carroll became the first African American woman to direct on Broadway. In addition to her work as a performer in four Broadway shows, she served as writer and/or director for six productions beginning in 1956. Carroll became best known on Broadway for her part in developing shows that became classics in the African American theatrical genre such as *Your Arms Too Short to Box with God* and *Don't Bother Me, I Can't Cope*. Micki Grant, one of the few women composers represented on Broadway, frequently collaborated with Vinnette Carroll. Their shows together include *Don't Bother Me, I Can't Cope* and *Your Arms Too Short to Box with God*.

Some African American women in the world of theater sought to address the dual themes of sexism and racism in their works as well as becoming involved with the civil rights movement. They were not insulated from political repercussions in the Cold War era. In the postwar era, politics were never far from the surface. This was especially true in the arts, which was felt to influence the masses and to nurture artists with socialist leanings. For their civil rights activism, the names of playwrights such as Lorraine Hansberry appeared on the FBI's list of suspected Communists.

Another black female playwright, Alice Childress, saw her play *Trouble in Mind* briefly performed off Broadway in 1955. According to Washington (2015), the play's theme of racism was joined by images of the blacklist. Subsequently, Childress was "[b]lacklisted herself by 1956" (124).

It was not only playwrights who found themselves in trouble with the blacklist. For some, it was not for their work onstage, but in personal circumstances, such as the case of actress Lee Grant. As her career was beginning in 1951, she was acclaimed for her talent, earning an Oscar nomination and winning the Best Actress Award at the Cannes Film Festival. However, that same year, remarks that Grant made at the memorial for a fellow stage actor came to the attention of *Red Channels*, the publication that listed suspected Communists.

Grant's actor friend had died of a heart attack while under investigation by the House Un-American Activities Committee. According to Grant (2015), at his funeral she said, "I feel the committee ultimately killed him" (85). Soon her name too was listed in *Red Channels*, resulting in loss of work during what she calls her prime years as an actress, ages 24–36. Grant said, "From that day forward, for twelve years, I was blacklisted" (85).

Riedel (2015) claims that *Camelot*, written in 1959 and opening on Broadway in 1960, "is generally thought to be the last show of the golden age of musical theatre" (64), which had begun with *Oklahoma* in 1943. Like most Broadway productions in the golden age, women featured prominently in *Camelot*. The show boasted a strong female leading role for Julie Andrews who had also headlined *My Fair Lady* in 1956.

Many of Broadway's top leading ladies created a remarkable record of hits in the golden age of the postwar years. But Reidel states that by 1960, in the latter part of the postwar era, Broadway shows "coming on the heels of Elvis Presley sounded hopelessly square" (65). There seemed to be fewer prominent roles for women. Some actresses after that time had a single hit show but were rarely seen in leading roles on Broadway again.

The future of postwar theater was presaged when *Bye Bye Birdie* opened in 1960. It was a satire poking fun at singers such as Elvis Presley in what was quickly becoming the rock and roll era. Soon, a new generation was looking for more excitement in the world of theater.

One way that happened was by the incorporation of new forms of dance into the dramatic action of the play. Modern dance, an unstructured, abstract style popularized by Martha Graham in the postwar era, often took center stage in Broadway musicals. Black female choreographers of the 1950s such as Katherine Dunham and Pearl Primus also became influential by blending African and Caribbean influences with modern dance, creating an exciting hybrid style.

Native American prima ballerina Maria Tallchief was a major star in the world of dance during the postwar years for performances such as in *The Firebird* (1949). She is also known for attracting widespread attention by dancing in *The Nutcracker* during the postwar years. Her fame transformed it from a ballet that was virtually unknown to average Americans into what is probably the nation's most popular ballet today, inspiring girls to perform in annual productions at Christmastime across the country.

However, it may have been some anonymous teenage girls in Florida who inspired the major dance sensation of the postwar era. It was one that many average American women could do, sometimes even by themselves while alone at home with their housework in the course of their daily lives.

According to Capouya (2017), in 1958, musician Hank Ballard noticed high school girls in Tampa, Florida, "doing some kind of new dance . . . they were twisting their bodies" (82). Ballard set about writing a song in an attempt to popularize it. In 1960, Chubby Checker recorded Ballard's tune, called "The Twist." Checker's version was a hit all across the country. The dance did not require taking lessons or learning any special steps, but it became one of the biggest dance crazes not only of the postwar era but of the entire 20th century.

VISUAL ARTS

If the average postwar American woman had studied art history in school, she would certainly have come across the names of world-famous white male artists through the ages including Michelangelo, Rembrandt, and Van Gogh. If that same average woman read popular magazines of the 1950s such as *Life*, she would also have learned about contemporary painters being called the leaders of the postwar art world, also white males such as Willem de Kooning, Jackson Pollock, and Mark Rothko.

Artist Pablo Picasso was a household name for most Americans in the 1950s, helped in no small part by being a punch line among comedians and on situation comedies for his enigmatic abstract work. Throughout the postwar years, Picasso was creating artwork that was not only highly regarded but also commanded high prices.

Most average women in postwar America knew the name of painter Grandma Moses (pictured here at right). She began painting at age 76 and had her first gallery exhibition when she was 80. In the Cold War era, her work was widely promoted for its idealized pastoral scenes that were said to reflect traditional American values. (Library of Congress)

In the course of their daily lives, some average women followed the art world via mainstream newspapers. In that way, they might have heard of an up-and-coming commercial artist in New York City named Andy Warhol who was beginning to show his work in Manhattan galleries during the 1950s.

But it was rare for art history books, magazine articles, or newspaper columns of the postwar era to include even a handful of women painters among the hundreds of men who were represented.

One of the very few female artists whose name was sometimes mentioned in textbooks was Mary Cassatt, who painted in the late 1800s and early 1900s. Cassatt's canvases often portrayed domestic scenes of women and children.

Another female painter, Frida Kahlo, did not earn a great deal of attention during her lifetime, including at the time of her death in 1954. If she was mentioned at all, it was usually in relation to being the wife of Mexican artist Diego Rivera. It was not until the 1970s that Kahlo began to earn critical and popular acclaim for her own artwork, exemplified by her surrealist folk art paintings.

Throughout history, including the postwar era, a number of factors limited women's representation in the visual arts. "Serious art" was considered the realm of males. To develop, an artist generally needs things that were not usually available to average women through the centuries such as education, apprenticeship, patronage, exhibitions, and representation. Women were usually barred even from sketching the human anatomical form from nude models as men did simply as a matter of course.

In addition, for centuries women were expected to marry and have children, just as they were obliged to do in postwar America. After marriage, average women through the ages would spend their daily lives cooking, cleaning, keeping house, doing laundry, and meeting a husband's needs as well as bearing and nurturing children—all the things that were required of a female lest she appear "unnatural." With the demands of their daily lives, most women simply did not have the time to be artists.

Those societal demands on females were still in effect during America's postwar era, even though it was a time of experimentation in a number of other fields. Many male artists adopted a style called abstract expressionism that was widely acclaimed for its nonpictorial content. Pohl (2012) states that artists such as Jackson Pollock spoke of his work as arising out of his inner self, seeing the resulting form as "universal" (470).

Pohl also points out that postwar women artists were engaging in the same explorations of nonpictorial form and content as the male abstract expressionists. However, the artwork of women doing the same thing as the men was often dismissed by critics as "too personal" (470).

Creative works by female artists did not sell as well as those of white males. One reason was that women artists were not accepted into galleries, where their work could be displayed for potential buyers. To surmount this obstacle, some female artists of the 1950s adopted various methods for exhibiting their works. By working under gender-neutral names, Jay DeFeo and Lee Krasner blurred their female given names of "Mary Joan" and "Lenore," respectively. Grace Hartigan occasionally submitted works under the pseudonym "George."

One of the watersheds that led to at least a small degree of change for women in the art world of the postwar era was New York City's Ninth Street Show, which opened in 1951. It was an exhibition by notable avant-garde artists that was held in an empty storefront, rented by the artists themselves.

The exhibit's jury selected 61 male artists and 11 women. Although the women were only a small fraction of the men, it was at least an opportunity to have work by female artists prominently displayed. The exhibition called attention to the burgeoning abstract movement, which was struggling for acceptance. As Pierpont (2018) states, "Even in this renegade atmosphere, there was some initial discussion of whether including women in the exhibition would diminish its chance of being taken seriously" (n.p.).

Five of those women—Elaine de Kooning, Helen Frankenthaler, Grace Hartigan, Lee Krasner, and Joan Mitchell—became known as pioneering female artists in the postwar era. After having their work displayed at the Ninth Street Show in 1951, they were not only taken more seriously but went on to have distinguished international careers. Slowly, over the years, their work came to be accepted by major museums and galleries on par with male artists.

Although the genres in which they painted were different from each other, the women artists shared a common commitment to their art as well as the courage to stand apart from the mainstream of women's daily lives in postwar America. According to Gabriel (2019), "Each would pay a price for selecting art over the life society would have prescribed for her" (11).

Some of the women whose work was accepted for the Ninth Street Show were not married and/or did not have children. Some who were married, such as de Kooning, took their husband's name. Krasner, married to superstar artist Jackson Pollock, did not.

While they differed from each other in their approaches to art, they had one thing in common, something that was apparently the kiss of death in the postwar art world: being perceived as "painting like a girl." Elaine de Kooning, married to leading postwar artist Willem de Kooning, is said by Pierpont (2018) to have taken up portraiture as her specialty, saying it was "one area where she didn't have to compete with her husband, who dismissed portraits as 'pictures that girls made'" (n.p.).

Most average women in postwar America hardly knew the names of such pioneering female artists of the 1950s unless they closely followed the art world as part of their daily lives. However, many could certainly name *one*. She was a woman artist who attained great fame in the 1950s for her novelty: Grandma Moses.

Anna Mary Robertson Moses was born in 1860, two months before Abraham Lincoln was elected president. At age 76, she developed arthritis in her hands, making it painful to do her customary embroidery. Untaught, she switched to painting primitive pastoral scenes, which she could do with her left hand when working with her right hand became too painful.

She began selling her canvases for under five dollars each through local drug stores in upstate New York, where she lived. Eventually, it was discovered by collectors. Her work gained acclaim as much for its primitive style as for the novelty of having been created by a woman who did not have her first gallery exhibition until she was 80. With her quaint grandmotherly looks, she became a media darling. Art critics publicized not only her works but the fact that her art exhibitions also included samples of the homemade preserves and baked goods she made as part of her daily life.

Throughout the postwar era, while in her 90s, Grandma Moses was still painting. Her artwork, which according to Waxman, "sold for as much as $3,000 a piece" (n.p.) in the 1950s, today commands millions of dollars each. In the postwar era, the work of Grandma Moses was widely promoted for its idealized American values—an element that was greatly in demand during the Cold War. Greeting cards, printed fabrics, and other consumer goods were emblazoned with scenes from her paintings. In that way, average women could incorporate her art into their daily lives. Waxman states that almost 50 million Christmas cards printed with Grandma Moses's artwork were sold during that time.

Moses herself became a cultural icon of the 1950s, with a name that was known to most average women. She continued to paint, winning multiple awards, and earning praise from people such as President Harry Truman, who obtained her work for the White House. Her 1952 autobiography became a top seller, and in 1955, she was a guest on the popular television program *See It Now*, hosted by newsman Edward R. Murrow. When Moses died in 1961 at age 101, she was eulogized by President John F. Kennedy. Most obituaries stressed her work's ability to idealize America's simple agrarian past amid the angst of the postwar atomic age.

Some women in postwar America knew not only the name of Grandma Moses but also one of the few other female artists to gain renown, Georgia O'Keeffe. Known for her paintings of flowers and the New Mexico landscape, O'Keeffe's subjects were sometimes dismissed by critics as "girlish."

In the art world, as in many aspects of daily life in postwar America, the Cold War was never far away. In 1950, an exhibit of the primitivistic artworks by Grandma Moses toured Europe. She was considered by the U.S. government to be a Cold War asset for her depiction of idyllic American rural scenes. As quoted in Jentleson

(2020), postwar art critic Lloyd Goodrich reflected the jargon of the atomic age by stating that such art could provide a "fallout shelter for the human spirit" (8).

Other female artists of the postwar era did not fare as well as Grandma Moses. According to Jentleson, "in 1947, Congress called off an international tour of American art for its alleged subversion. . . . American art critics were appalled to see Congress reject even O'Keeffe's beloved botanicals" (9).

Another group of female artists in the postwar era was also struggling for its vision to be recognized. African American women artists battled not only gender bias but also racial prejudice. Starting from the days of slavery, the black experience was portrayed primarily thorough folk arts such as quilting since creating other types of artwork like painting was generally forbidden.

By the mid-20th century, many black female artists felt free to explore more varied genres and subjects. Farrington (2011) states, "A persistent theme in the art of African American women has been the configuration of their own image without racial or gender stereotypes" (8).

But many black women artists also struggled against political allegations amid the anti-Communist fervor of the 1950s. Some took up the cause of civil rights, utilizing their art to spotlight African American lives. For their perceived activism, some aroused the attention of the House Un-American Activities Committee (HUAC).

Elizabeth Catlett's work as a graphic artist and sculptor is best known for depicting the African American experience in the United States, often focusing specifically on the lives of black women like herself. Catlett's support of the civil rights movement in the postwar era led to her being investigated by HUAC.

Much of the work created by Catlett, the granddaughter of slaves, was shaped by personal experiences such as an incident when she taught art in the 1940s at Dillard University in New Orleans. Arranging a field trip to see the Picasso exhibit at a local museum, she found that the museum was closed to African Americans.

Being called to testify before the House Un-American Activities Committee, Catlett renounced her citizenship and moved to Mexico. In her continuing quest to convey social messages, Catlett's artwork included images of strong black women such as Harriet Tubman and writer Phyllis Wheatley.

Lois Mailou Jones was inspired by African and Haitian art. She used bright colors to draw attention to works that spotlighted African American daily life, with both its joys and challenges. Part of the challenge for Jones herself included obstacles that hindered her own work as a black female artist in the postwar era. She was forced to have a white friend submit her artwork in postwar competitions where works by African American artists were not accepted. When one of her paintings won first prize at a prestigious event, Jones was not able to pick up the award herself, opting instead for it to be sent to her in the mail.

In the course of their daily lives, most American women may not have been aware of the transitions involving female artists in the postwar era nor the implications of their artwork for the civil rights movement. But there is one area of visual art in the postwar era that literally stared housewives in the face as they lived their daily lives: their own homes.

Most average American women did not have to go to gallery openings or museum exhibitions in order to experience visual art as part of their daily lives in the postwar era. All they had to do was look around the house. In many cases, they were the ones who actually created it.

According to Boucher (2013), "thanks to the GI Bill, America began the postwar period with an educated and stable workforce, [and] access to cheap home financing" (5). Enjoying widespread prosperity and being part of the rise of suburbia, the energies of many white middle-class women were focused on the home, the place where they lived the bulk of their daily life.

Once an average middle-class woman had a home, she needed to put something in it. A housewife was generally able to decorate their family's "nest" in keeping with her taste and the family budget. For many stay-at-home women, it was one of the few outlets for creative energy in the course of their daily lives. In addition, amid the consumer culture of the 1950s, it allowed them to participate in another postwar mainstay: keeping up with the Joneses.

In the course of their daily lives, postwar women could get decorating ideas from popular women's magazines along with more specialized ones such as *Architectural Digest* and *Better Homes & Gardens*. If they opted not to attempt their home decorating job themselves, women could also seek outside professionals, some of whom were employed by mainstream retail stores such as Sears.

While average women of the 1950s might not have considered the way they decorated their houses to be part of the field of visual art, today postwar-era home décor is ranked among the classics. It is also known for specific trends that reflected the spirit of the times.

The 1950s radiated confidence and optimism for many middle-class American women as they lived their daily lives. Amid the newfound prosperity of the postwar years, the average suburban woman departed from the drabness of previous decades such as the Great Depression and the austerity of the World War II era. She could decorate her new home in ways that provided a safe, happy, comfortable place for her family to love their daily lives.

After World War II, there was also an increasing degree of leisure time to be enjoyed by middle-class Americans. This development was incorporated into the average woman's home. Many had a "recreation room" or specially designated area that needed to be equipped for family fun.

The home décor of the postwar era reflected several trends that were often combined in the homes of average women. One was the bold, futuristic look of the space age. Some furnishings were made from materials such as slick vinyl or shiny chrome. Gleaming new appliances such as stoves, refrigerators, and washing machines came in nontraditional looks painted with a rainbow of colors instead of basic white to brighten up women's daily lives.

A central spot was carved out in living rooms across America for the family television set. Seating had to be arranged accordingly. Comfortable, plush sectional sofas might be combined with the clean lines of a postwar-era Eames chair.

Available after the war in bright patterns and colors, linoleum floors went from utilitarian to trendy in order to accommodate baby boom children at play. Average middle-class women could also usually afford wall-to-wall carpeting throughout the house instead of smaller area rugs as in the past. Thus, the ever-growing population of toddlers in the 1950s could crawl in comfort.

Many decorative fabrics that were inspired by the excitement of postwar-era space exploration and science were embraced by homemakers. Atomic graphics, stylized stars, and planetary imagery joined abstract art and modernistic patterns on drapes, tablecloths, upholstery, and wallpaper all through the house.

The small appliances that women used in their daily lives no longer needed to be strictly utilitarian in appearance. Clocks, lamps, and electric mixers came in bold colors and designs. On bright Formica countertops, the homemaker's array of dishware, glasses, kitchen canisters, and mixing bowls added their own counterpoint in cheerful colors and festive designs.

Entertaining was a top priority for many middle-class women. Cocktail hours and dinner parties became essential postwar pastimes for many average American women and their friends. Living spaces, dining areas, and recreation rooms had to be furnished to accommodate guests in ways that reflected the good taste of the hostess. Women could personalize those areas with décor and accessories as desired, including "entertainment units" with the most up-to-date equipment such as tape recorders and stereophonic phonographs.

Most average women in postwar America generally assumed "art" to be something that was found in a gallery or museum. Few considered it to include the items they selected for daily life in the home. The decorative arts of the postwar era would become a trend that fell out of favor after the 1950s but ultimately came back decades later with "retro" fans.

Future generations would look back on the postwar era as one of prosperity, comfort, and fun. The bold colors, cheerful pastels, sparkling chrome, and space-age designs incorporated by average women in their homes underscored that perception. However, the fun often obscured the reality of daily life in the postwar era for many women who were not part of the prosperous white middle class. In the 1950s, shadows often swirled just beneath the bright, cheery surface.

FURTHER READING

Ackmann, Martha. *Curveball: The Remarkable Story of Toni Stone, the First Woman to Play Professional Baseball in the Negro League.* Chicago: Lawrence Hill Books, 2010.

Billings, Andrew. *Olympic Television: Broadcasting the Biggest Show on Earth.* New York: Routledge, 2018.

Boucher, Diane. *The 1950s American Home.* New York: Shire Publications, 2013.

Capouya, John. *Florida Soul: From Ray Charles to KC and the Sunshine Band.* Gainesville: University Press of Florida, 2017.

Cassidy, Marsha. *What Women Watched: Daytime Television in the 1950s.* Austin: University of Texas Press, 2005.

Farrington, Lisa. *Creating Their Own Image: The History of African-American Women Artists.* New York: Oxford University Press, 2011.

Fischer, Lucy. *Imitation of Life: Douglas Sirk, Director.* New Brunswick, NJ: Rutgers University Press, 1991.

Friedan, Betty. *The Feminine Mystique.* New York: Norton, 50th anniversary edition, 2013.

Gabriel, Mary. *Ninth Street Women: Lee Krasner, Elaine de Kooning, Grace Hartigan, Joan Mitchell, and Helen Frankenthaler: Five Painters and the*

Movement That Changed Modern Art. New York: Back Bay Books, 2019.

Grant, Lee. *I Said Yes to Everything*. New York: Plume, 2015.

Guralnick, Peter. *Last Train to Memphis: The Rise of Elvis Presley*. New York: Little, Brown, 1994.

Haskell, Molly. *From Reverence to Rape: The Treatment of Women in the Movies*. Chicago: University of Chicago Press, 2nd edition, 1987.

Hendricks, Nancy. *Notable Arkansas Women: From Hattie to Hillary, 100 Names to Know*. Little Rock, AR: Butler Center Books, 2016.

Hirshey, Gerri. *Nowhere to Run: The Story of Soul Music*. New York: Crown, 1984.

"Hope for America: Performers, Politics and Pop Culture—Television and Politics." *Library of Congress*. http://www.loc.gov/exhibits/hope -for-america/television-and-politics.html#obj0.

Jentleson, Katherine. "Show of Patriotism." *Smithsonian Magazine*, March 2020, pp. 7–9.

Johnson, Susan E. *When Women Played Hardball*. Seattle, WA: Seal Press, 1994.

Leaming, Barbara. *Marilyn Monroe*. New York: Three Rivers Press, 1998.

Lessig, Lawrence. *They Don't Represent Us: Reclaiming Our Democracy*. New York: Dey Street Books, 2019.

"The Living Room Candidate." *Museum of the Moving Image*. http://www .livingroomcandidate.org/commercials/1956/women-voters.

Lynch, Twink. "From the Top: History of Community Theatre in America." *American Association of Community Theatre*. https://aact.org /community-theatre-history.

Malone, Alicia. *Backwards and in Heels: The Past, Present and Future of Women Working in Film*. Coral Gables, FL: Mango Publishing, 2017.

Maurer, Elizabeth. "Tuning in to Women in Television." *National Women's History Museum*, September 21, 2016. https://www.womenshis tory.org/articles/tuning-women-television.

May, Elaine Tyler. *Homeward Bound: American Families in the Cold War Era*. New York: Basic Books, 2008.

Moore, Lucinda. "Show Time at the Apollo." *Smithsonian.com*, November 2010. https://www.smithsonianmag.com/arts-culture/show-time -at-the-apollo-64658902.

Packard, Vance. *The Hidden Persuaders*. New York: Pocket Books, 1957.

Pendle, Karin. *Women and Music: A History*. Bloomington: Indiana University Press, 2nd edition, 2001.

Pierpont, Claudia Roth. "How New York's Postwar Female Painters Battled for Recognition." *Newyorker.com*, October 1, 2018. https:// www.newyorker.com/magazine/2018/10/08/how-new-yorks-post war-female-painters-battled-for-recognition.

Pohl, Frances. *Framing America: A Social History of American Art*. New York: Thames and Hudson, 2012.

Puglisi, Gabrielle. "The Rough-and-Tumble Sport of Roller Derby Is All about Community." *Smithsonian.com*, March 12, 2020. https://www .smithsonianmag.com/smithsonian-institution/rough-tumble -sport-roller-derby-all-about-caring-community-180974235/.

Riedel, Michael. *Razzle Dazzle: The Battle for Broadway.* New York: Simon & Schuster, 2015.

Schiot, Molly. *Game Changers: The Unsung Heroines of Sports History.* New York: Simon & Schuster, 2018.

Smith, Lissa. *Nike Is a Goddess: The History of Women in Sports.* New York: Atlantic Monthly Press, 1999.

Spigel, Lynn. *Make Room for TV: Television and the Family Ideal in Postwar America.* Chicago: University of Chicago Press, 1992.

Wagner, R. J., with Scott Eyman. *I Loved Her in the Movies: Memories of Hollywood's Legendary Actresses.* New York: Viking, 2016.

Washington, Mary. *The Other Blacklist: The African American Literary and Cultural Left of the 1950s.* New York: Columbia University Press, reprint edition, 2015.

Wattenberg, Martin. *Is Voting for Young People?* New York: Routledge, 4th edition, 2016.

Waxman, Olivia B. "Grandma Moses Didn't Start Painting Until Her 70s. Here's Why." *Time.com*, September 7, 2016. https://time.com /4482257/grandma-moses-history/.

Welch, Rosanne. *When Women Wrote Hollywood: Essays on Female Screenwriters in the Early Film Industry.* Jefferson, NC: McFarland, 2018.

Weller, Sheila. *Girls Like Us: Carole King, Joni Mitchell, Carly Simon and the Journey of a Generation.* New York: Washington Square Press, 2008.

7

RELIGIOUS LIFE

During the postwar years, the mass media made it clear to women that they could derail their husband's career—and thus their family life—in any number of ways. A woman might not be perceived as a good wife or mother or as a happy homemaker. When her husband brought the boss home for dinner, she might not turn out to be a wizard in the kitchen or her clothes might not be fashionable; her appliances might not be shiny nor her conversation sparkling.

In the course of their daily lives, one other area could also be an important one for postwar women to handle successfully. It was in religious life that a woman might inadvertently fall short in the Cold War era, since it combined both faith and patriotism. If she did not already have a house of worship, it was of extreme importance to find one and make sure her family attended regularly. In the postwar years, where appearances and conformity were paramount, it was vital to be seen conspicuously in an attitude of prayer.

That is not to say that most women in postwar America did not sincerely value their religion. Most considered it to be an important part of their lives, to be highly cherished. However, churchgoing took on a new significance in the postwar era as a lynchpin for America's strength against Communism during the Cold War.

That message came right from the top of the country's hierarchy. In 1953, the president of the United States, 62-year-old Dwight

Eisenhower, who had claimed no previous church membership, was baptized and confirmed into the Presbyterian Church. He was the only U.S. president to be baptized while in office.

The following year, Eisenhower added the phrase "Under God" to the nation's Pledge of Allegiance. He also oversaw the requirement that all U.S. coins and currency would bear the slogan "In God We Trust." In 1956, Eisenhower signed a joint resolution from the U.S. Congress declaring "In God We Trust" to be the national motto of the United States. That resolution passed both the House of Representatives and the Senate unanimously, without debate.

As president, Eisenhower began his cabinet meetings with a moment of silent prayer, initiated the National Prayer Breakfast, and welcomed Reverend Billy Graham into the White House as a spiritual adviser. Eisenhower both reflected and responded to America's religious life during the postwar years. America would fight the Communist aggressor on any battleground, including the nation's pews and pulpits.

Women often spearheaded their family's membership in a house of worship. It was something at which they were very effective. Robert Ellwood (1997) writes, "In the Fifties, church membership nationwide grew at a faster rate than the national population, from 57 percent of the U.S. population in 1950 to 63.3 percent in 1959" (5).

There were many choices. Ellwood adds that within the sphere of Christianity alone, people could choose "between 'highbrow' theology and 'lowbrow' popular taste" (6). Reflecting the consumerism of the decade, Ellwood's book title, *The Fifties Spiritual Marketplace*, underscores the decade's abundance of choice. There was something for everyone, as long as they found *something* and, most importantly, were *seen* worshipping.

It was not just appearances that drove the move toward religion. In a later book, Ellwood (2000) states that "young families, their husbands and fathers back from the war, wanted the solace and, in a word of the time, 'togetherness' of churches and synagogues" (2). It was not only a way for women to strengthen the family unit against Communism, but it also offered spiritual comfort against the constant threat of nuclear annihilation that hung over the heads of postwar Americans.

One of the factors spurring the growth of a religious mix was the rise of the suburbs where some of the first buildings to be constructed were houses of worship. With the publication of his book *Protestant-Catholic-Jew: An Essay in American Religious Sociology* in 1955, Will Herberg was one of the first to comment on America's religious framework in the postwar era, stating that factors such as population trends and the rise of the automobile had to be considered "in an effort to estimate the reasons for the growing proportions of Americans in the churches" (48).

Some women also found a comforting social structure through membership in a house of worship, one that enriched their lives and helped keep the family unit strong. Women who felt isolated in the suburbs, far from their original home, sometimes found much-needed socialization through church-sponsored activities that extended beyond religious rites on the Sabbath. With opportunities for social pursuits, they could make new friends and promote a sense of belonging.

Based on the messages all around them, women also felt they were contributing to the Cold War effort as an important part of their daily lives. In the postwar years, religiosity was equated with Americanism, which to some observers constituted a kind of national revival in the evangelical Christian tradition.

For women, there were other concerns as well. Many felt it was important to provide their baby boom offspring with religious training. Others wanted to protect their children from the godlessness of Communism, a recurrent theme in postwar society. Above all, many women absorbed the expression they would have heard often in their daily lives: "The family that prays together, stays together."

FEMALE PRESENCE IN RELIGION

Although women in postwar America were usually denied entry—and certainly power—in professional careers, they started to become more of a significant presence in religion during that era. This was due in great part to the large number of churchgoing women within various denominations.

Their sheer numbers began to exert an influence beyond their traditional roles in church sewing circles, women's guilds, and "hospitality committees" (cooks). In the postwar years, some women rose to positions of power in the religious realm that had almost always been reserved for males.

Georgia Elma Harkness was an important figure in the movement toward the ordination of women in American Methodism. Serving at the Pacific School of Religion from 1950 to 1961, she was the first woman to obtain a full professorship in an American theological seminary. She became the first female member of the American

Some historians call the postwar era a high point for African American churches, with a number of popular singers starting out in their church choir during that time. Most notable was Aretha Franklin (pictured here), who began singing solos in her father's church during the 1950s and remains one of the top-ranked female singers in history. (Joe Sohm/Dreamstime.com)

Theological Society and published 16 books, 5 of them between 1952 and 1959 alone. Among her works was the seminal *Women in Church and Society: A Historical and Theological Inquiry.*

Maud Keister Jensen was the first woman to receive full clergy rights in the Methodist Church of the United States. A bishop in the Central Pennsylvania Conference approved her for local clergy ordination in 1952. When the Methodist Church voted to allow women to have full clergy rights in 1956, Jensen was given temporary full clergy rights for two years and obtained permanent clergy status in 1958.

In 1950, Mary Ely Lyman was appointed to the Union Theological Seminary as the first woman to hold a full professorship and an endowed chair at Union. She also held the inaugural deanship for women students until 1955. Her journey reflected increased opportunities for women in organized religion during the postwar years, especially when compared to her own experiences. She had been the only female student at Union, graduating first in her class in 1919. However, being a woman, she was not allowed to march with her class at commencement or to sit with them, being relegated to the balcony with faculty wives.

Edith Lowry spent three decades as the national director of interdenominational Protestant work among agricultural migrants. Starting in 1950, she was director of the Home Mission for the

National Council of Churches. Lowry was one of the first Americans of any religious denomination to draw attention to the plight of migrant workers, a group who few Americans ever really thought about. Most women did not stop to consider how their food arrived on grocery shelves. The condition of many migrant workers was summed up succinctly in the title of Lowry's 1938 publication, *They Starve That We May Eat.*

With the advent of television during the postwar era, the public preaching of Christian gospel, called evangelism, was widely available. One particular female evangelist became a household name, one that was familiar to most women in the course of their daily lives. Kathryn Kuhlman, originally from rural Missouri, was one of the most well-known "healing ministers" or "faith healers" in the world. She traveled extensively around the United States and in many other countries with what were called her healing crusades from the 1940s into the 1970s. She was the star of a half-hour nationwide radio ministry in which she taught from the Bible and frequently featured recordings from her healing services. Along with locally televised excerpts from her crusades during the postwar years, in 1966, Kuhlman launched her own weekly television program *I Believe in Miracles*, which was aired nationally. Kuhlman's mainstream success also made her a popular guest on such television offerings as *The Mike Douglas Show*, Dinah Shore's daily variety program, and *The Tonight Show with Johnny Carson*.

Although Ida B. Robinson died in 1946, as the postwar era was beginning, her influence on the postwar world was profound. As an African American Pentecostal Holiness and Charismatic denominational leader, she was the founder, first senior bishop, and president of the Mount Sinai Holy Church of America. Robinson formed the organization in response to her divine vision of securing an ecclesiastical home where women would be welcomed and encouraged as preachers. Mount Sinai Holy Church of America is the only organization founded by an African American woman that held consistent female leadership from its founding in 1924 until February 2001. When Robinson died in 1946, the denomination consisted of 84 churches, with more than 160 ordained ministers. Of that number, 125 were women.

Churches have traditionally held an important place in the lives of African Americans, especially black women. Along with regular religious services in both cities and rural areas, traditionally black churches held a number of other activities, many generally organized by women. These included missionary societies, musical concerts, prayer meetings, public lectures, sewing circles, women's clubs, and youth groups. Revivals, often a week long, attracted large, appreciative crowds among the faithful.

Collier-Thomas (2010) states that although often overlooked, an important factor in the development of the African American religious culture has always been the black woman. Women were "the glue that held the family and community together, and a significant part of the foundation for the development of black religious institutions" (4).

Woodward (2016) concurs, stating that the postwar era "was the day of urban black religion . . . of praying mothers who virtually lived at the church and of young women who sang in the choir" (179). A number of singers who later joined the popular music field started in their church choir during the postwar years. Most notable was Aretha Franklin (1942–2018) who began singing solos in her father's church as a child in the 1950s and remains the most charted female artist in history.

There was one group of postwar women who exerted a highly significant, long-lasting influence over people of the time, especially baby boom children. As Woodward (2016) states, American nuns were "the face of Catholicism in countless hospitals and parochial school classrooms" (2).

According to McGuinness (2013), "Women entering a religious community in the 1950s were introduced to a lifestyle that had changed very little over the past several centuries" (156). Female religious communities steadily made gains during the postwar period, with their numbers peaking at about 180,000 in 1965.

Jewish women gained a greater presence in their congregations during the postwar years. A Reform movement in Judaism brought a more liberal slant to the religious role of women, a trend that gained momentum through the postwar years. In 1953, about a fifth of Reform synagogues allowed women to be called up to read from the Torah, the first five books of the Old Testament, which was the highest honor for laypeople. In 1972, Sally Jane Priesand was ordained as the country's first female rabbi. Within 10 years, there were almost 100 women rabbis among non-Orthodox Jewish congregations in America.

While it was not a religious event per se, after the horrors of World War II, there was cause for rejoicing in America's postwar Jewish community in 1945. That year, Bess Myerson became the first Jewish woman to be crowned Miss America. As of this writing, Myerson remains the only Jewish woman to win the title.

A number of middle-class Jewish women who had moved to the suburbs after World War II enhanced their daily lives by adopting a wide range of volunteer activities for what they felt would be the betterment of the community, or "giving back." Many supported peace groups, organizations to strengthen public schools, equal rights for women, and causes seeking civil rights for minorities.

In the postwar era, there were Jewish women who joined their efforts, with the movement grounded in black churches that formed the foundation of the civil rights movement. Ministers including Martin Luther King Jr. and Ralph David Abernathy provided the faith-based framework that led many people to describe the civil rights movement as a religious crusade. Much of that work, though often unheralded, was performed by women. Gospel singer Aretha Franklin joined Dr. King on his speaking tours, events where church leaders often drew on stories from the Old and New Testaments as parables. Especially popular in the civil rights movement was the Old Testament narrative of Exodus, with its themes of liberation and rallying cry of "Let my people go."

RELIGION AND SECULAR LIFE

In 1957, American women were stunned when the Soviet Union launched an orbiting space satellite, Sputnik. Adding to the anxiety over nuclear war in postwar America, there was the fear that there might now be an attack from the skies. Many found it to be a compelling reason for affiliation with a religious denomination and the attendant spiritual comfort. In the postwar years, organized religion was the moral equivalent to patriotism. With the world becoming more uncertain, many women feared their children might never have the chance to grow up. They prayed for holy intervention in preventing catastrophic warfare.

There were few areas of daily life in postwar America where the merging of religion and patriotism could not be found. Even if it was called a "Cold War" that did not take place on a battlefield, it was still a war for control of people's hearts and minds over the atheistic Communists. This included the secular realm, which is defined as things that are not deemed to be religious or sacred in nature.

To win the Cold War, messages from the U.S. government and the mass media stressed that America's people must be dedicated to faith-based principles. In the course of their daily lives, women would be the vanguard. The struggle against Communism was often called a "crusade," adapting religious symbolism to the secular world.

Women in postwar America were often involved in organizing regular church-sponsored activities for children. In the Cold War era, the government and mass media stressed that the mothers of America must be dedicated to faith-based principles in the battle against Communism so their children could grow up to live in freedom. (Library of Congress)

The advent of television as part of daily life became a powerful tool in advancing America's postwar religious life. From the early days of radio that began in the 1920s, evangelism, or the public preaching of Christian gospel, could be heard on the airwaves. However, beginning in the 1950s, the visual medium of television allowed viewers to feel a more personal connection with religious personalities. As with critiques of female voting habits in the early 20th century, some felt that the more attractive the TV preacher, or "televangelist" was, the more power he exerted over women, which translated into increased donations.

In the secular realm, along with the spiritual rewards of religious affiliation, postwar women were often involved in regular church-sponsored pursuits such as activities for children, church picnics, women's groups, and holiday celebrations in their respective houses of worship. Such social events were often organized by women as ways to enjoy a sense of connection with others of their denomination. In keeping with the spirit of "togetherness" as promoted in women's magazines, church-sponsored activities could be enjoyed by the entire family.

Religious rites and rituals took on a new importance in the postwar years, with women often at the forefront. America generally sought to present itself like the popular World War II movies of the era, in which Catholics, Protestants, and Jews were portrayed as fighting side by side with no animosity or divisiveness. Those diverse fictional characters had just one goal: victory for the United States. This was the theme that was presented to the world in the postwar era. It was a way of demonstrating how embracing religion in America was far superior to atheistic Communism.

In postwar America, Christmas grew to immense proportions as marketers transformed this religious holiday into a multimillion-dollar industry. Women were generally presumed to do the shopping for Christmas presents, Christmas ornaments, and Christmas cards, as pictured in this advertisement. (Vintage Literature Reproductions)

One way to do that was by bringing what were formerly religious rites into the secular mainstream, with an influence that was often magnified on a national scale by television.

For example, the celebration of Mardi Gras, the Tuesday before the Christian season of Lent begins, had traditionally been marked by festive parades in a few places such as Mobile, Alabama, and New Orleans, Louisiana. Occurring early in the calendar year, Ash Wednesday ushers in a time of penitence. Therefore Tuesday, the day before, is the last opportunity to eat rich foods before the ritual fasting period of Lent begins. In formerly French-speaking regions of the American South, "Mardi Gras" translates to "Fat Tuesday."

Mardi Gras became a time of parades, costumes, and festivity that gained an even more animated spirit when television cameras recorded the revelry for broadcast all across the nation. Although Mardi Gras is not an actual holy day, many men and women began to treat it as a date with religious undercurrents that demanded to be celebrated, albeit usually in ways that were hardly spiritual.

Traditional Catholic celebrations entered the mainstream. These included St. Patrick's Day, which honored the patron saint of Ireland. In the postwar era, once again under the watchful eye of television cameras, it grew into a tradition of large parades and "the wearing of the green" even for non-Irish Catholics. Although honoring the feast day of St. Patrick began as a religious rite, national television helped cement its status as a secular event.

Several holy days were celebrated at approximately the same time by both Christians and Jews. Hanukkah, the Jewish Festival of Lights, usually fell during the Christmas season. Passover came in the springtime, around the coming of Easter.

Easter celebrated the Resurrection of Jesus Christ, one of the central tenets of Christianity. With the prosperity and consumerism of the era, its traditions expanded to what was promoted as the obligatory purchase of certain items, many of which were the responsibility of women. These included the purchase of Easter baskets, Easter dresses, Easter bonnets, and a bounty of foods for sumptuous Easter dinners.

However, in postwar America, nothing grew to such immense proportions as Christmas. Christmas is traditionally based on the events surrounding the birth of Jesus. Wise men were said to have brought gifts to the newborn king. This was impetus enough for American businesses in the postwar era to shift into high gear. Aveni (2003) maintains that American culture refashioned Christmas "to resonate with the desires of a commercially driven society" (5).

Women, especially mothers, were often the driving force for making Christmas the kind of event that was said to be "making lifelong memories" for families.

In the postwar consumer culture, gift-giving was not limited to children. Women found themselves foraging for presents for everyone, along with Christmas cards, Christmas ornaments, and Christmas trees. What started as a religious holiday became a multimillion-dollar industry.

Religion was a common factor in many aspects of everyday secular life. Civic meetings often began with a prayer, as did the start of classroom time each day for many schoolchildren. In 1955, the state of New York developed a prayer recommended for the school districts in that state. The daily prayer was relatively nonsectarian: "Almighty God, we acknowledge our dependence on Thee, and we beg Thy blessings upon us, our parents, our teachers, and our country." The stated purpose of the prayer was to combat juvenile delinquency and to counter the threat of Communism.

Other school districts started their day with the Lord's Prayer ("Our Father, who art in Heaven, hallowed be thy name . . . ").

Amid the atmosphere of the postwar era, it was important to be seen observing religious rituals, even those such as Christmas, which mushroomed into a commercial enterprise. With possible political implications attached, the postwar era was not a good time for Americans to declare themselves as atheists or agnostics.

An atheist is defined as a person who denies the existence of a deity, while an agnostic believes it is impossible to know anything about God and does not commit to any religious doctrine. Neither was popular in the postwar era.

One of the most unpopular was a woman named Madalyn Murray O'Hair, whose name would have been familiar to many women of the postwar era as they lived their daily lives. *Life* magazine dubbed O'Hair "the most hated woman in America." Church groups condemned her. She was an outspoken supporter of atheism and the strict separation of church and state. In 1960, she filed a lawsuit against the Baltimore City Public School System, challenging the requirement that students participate in Bible readings. Ultimately, the suit was heard by the U.S. Supreme Court in 1963. The court declared mandatory Bible readings by students to be unconstitutional. This followed a previous Supreme Court decision in 1962 that ruled school prayer other than Bible readings was unconstitutional.

O'Hair also filed suit to have the phrase "In God We Trust" removed from United States currency as well as seeking to have the words "Under God" removed from the Pledge of Allegiance. At the time of this writing, both phrases still remain.

O'Hair found that television gave her a national forum for her views. Between those who supported her and those who reviled her, high ratings usually followed as people tuned in to see what she might say. On television, O'Hair gleefully debated evangelists and could be found as a guest on Phil Donahue's program as well as *The Tonight Show with Johnny Carson*.

Another postwar American woman was perceived as slightly less abrasive. Although not as well known today, Elinor Goulding Smith was a postwar writer and illustrator known for such quotes as "People of accomplishment rarely sat back and let things happen to them. They went out and happened to things." Smith wrote an article for *Harper's Magazine* in 1956 titled "Won't Somebody Tolerate Me?" from her viewpoint as an agnostic. She wrote that in the postwar era, America's interpretation of freedom of religion meant that people were free to choose the religion they wanted but that they had to choose one. She concluded with the statement, "I speak in what I fear is a lonely voice for a return to a real respect for one another's beliefs—or disbeliefs" (38).

Such viewpoints, while relatively rare in the postwar era, found a place in magazines and on television, gaining a wide audience if not an entirely sympathetic one. Religious concerns were a part of most women's daily lives as well as the popular entertainment of the time.

Many mainstream books with religious themes became bestsellers during the postwar era. Some of these included *The Cardinal* (1950) by Henry Morton Robinson, *East of Eden* (1952) by John Steinbeck, *Moses* (1951) by Sholem Asch, and *The Silver Chalice* (1952) by Thomas Costain.

Most of the bestsellers conveyed a mainstream Christian outlook, although the postwar era saw Jewish themes being expressed more openly. Jewish American writer Harry Golden scored popular hits in 1958 with the gentle humor of the books *Only in America* and *For 2¢ Plain*. Also in 1958, *Exodus* by Leon Uris told a fictionalized version of the founding of the Jewish state of Israel, which had taken place just 10 years before, in 1948.

Many women across denominational lines found an uplifting message in such books as *The Power of Positive Thinking* (1952) and *Stay Alive All Your Life* (1957) by Protestant minister Norman Vincent Peale as well as *Life Is Worth Living* (1953) by the Catholic bishop Fulton J. Sheen.

Several postwar women authors published bestsellers that were centered in the spiritual realm. Anne Morrow Lindbergh's *Gift from the Sea* (1955) was a popular inspirational book of the postwar years, reflecting on the lives of American women.

Catherine Marshall's husband had been a Presbyterian pastor and Chaplain of the U.S. Senate before his death. Her book honoring him, *A Man Called Peter*, was a nationwide success when it was published in 1951 and again as a Hollywood movie of the same name, released in 1955.

Television was, of course, the most pervasive form of secular entertainment. Many authors whose books made the bestseller list became known to audiences across the country through TV appearances.

In addition to televangelists such as Kathryn Kuhlman, there was often a subtle religious message in many television programs of the postwar era that women regularly watched with their family. They all understood that religion in a popular format was equated with basic patriotism. The suburban middle-class families on TV's *Ozzie and Harriet, Father Knows Best,* and *Leave It to Beaver* may not have been not seen attending a specific church. But the unspoken message was that they were white Anglo-Saxon Protestants who were living the American Way by upholding *some* religious faith, all part of the ideal that separated the United States from Communism.

Nowhere was the religious influence in secular life more evident than in the movies of the postwar era. Hollywood moguls were doing their best to ensure their own happy ending. In the early 1950s, the movie business was devastated by the advent of television. Movie studios felt they had to offer something people could not get at home for free.

A tremendous factor was also the McCarthy "Red Scare" investigations around the same time that targeted the entertainment industry. Actors, writers, and directors who were suspected of left-wing leanings were being targeted and blacklisted. Hollywood was determined to prove that the film industry was not Communistic "red" but good All-American "Red, White, and Blue."

One way in which they did that was by producing big-budget biblically based movies. Shaw and Youngblood (2010) write that historical heroes, religion, and the Cold War came together in one of the defining genres of this era, the biblical epic. They state that "at least one of these epics, Cecil B. DeMille's multi-million-dollar grossing extravaganza *The Ten Commandments* (1956), was designed to give scriptural authority to the ideology of America's Cold War" (26).

Moviegoers of the postwar era demonstrated their own religious faith by purchasing tickets in droves. Women often made the entertainment choices for the family. Sometimes, entire church groups attended showings together. Along with *The Ten Commandments,* big biblical epics of the era included *Ben-Hur, The Big Fisherman,*

Demetrius and the Gladiators, Martin Luther, Quo Vadis, The Robe, and *The Silver Chalice.*

A genre that was separate from big-budget biblical epics would have been familiar in the daily lives of women in postwar America. Popular science fiction movies of the Cold War era often contained prevalent religious themes. It was convenient that the planet Mars was called the "Red Planet," just as Communists were termed "reds."

In one science fiction movie, *Red Planet Mars,* released in 1952 during the height of McCarthyism, a group of Christian American rebels overthrow godless Communism in the Soviet Union. In the film's story line, Christian governments are established in both Russia and the United States. According to the movie script, this would prevent either side from destroying the world with nuclear weapons.

There were overt religious references in many other science fiction films of the postwar era, especially the early years when the McCarthy investigations were in vogue. Facing giant insect invaders in the movie *Them!* a scientist states, "We may be witnessing a Biblical prophecy come true. . . . The beast will reign over the Earth."

In *The War of the Worlds,* a small American town is attacked by invaders from the "Red Planet." After praying for God's intervention, the townspeople are provided with the weapon that turns out to be able to defeat the Martian invaders: bacteria. The film's narrator states, "After all that men could do, victory came through the littlest things which God in His wisdom had put on this Earth."

Films of the postwar era emphasized that God-fearing Americans were better guardians of the atomic arsenal than godless Communists. Any antinuclear sentiment in the script was often counteracted by optimistic suggestions of redemption. In *The Day the Earth Stood Still,* one of the most highly rated science fiction films of all time, there was a message of faith amid the threats of atomic weapons and Communism that faced the nation. An extraterrestrial, the movie's main character, assumes the name "Mr. Carpenter," evoking Jesus, the Carpenter of Nazareth. His greeting to Planet Earth— "We have come to visit you in peace and good will"—echoes the biblical angel who announces Christ's birth in Luke 2:14 with "Glory to God in the highest and on earth peace, good will toward men." Mr. Carpenter brings a messiah-like message of peace but is killed by the authorities. It was a woman, famously played by actress Patricia Neal, who saved the planet by overcoming her fear and disarming the threat with the immortal words *"Klaatu Barada Nikto."* After Mr. Carpenter is resurrected by his robot companion, some saw a vision of Christ's return.

The secular life of the postwar era suggests that even in facing the Communist menace and the nuclear threat, America would prevail because of the nation's values, including freedom of religion. In the course of their daily lives, women in postwar America were a significant frontline contingent in that battle. Along with a widespread internal fear that a perceived lack of religion by individual Americans meant their lack of patriotism, Miller and Nowak (1977) state, "People turned to religion in record numbers to find hope in an anxious world. . . . [postwar] Americans saw the world in terms of good and evil, godly and godless" (92).

FURTHER READING

Aveni, Anthony. *The Book of the Year: A Brief History of Our Seasonal Holidays*. New York: Oxford University Press, 2003.

Collier-Thomas, Bettye. *Jesus, Jobs, and Justice: African American Women and Religion*. New York: Knopf, 2010.

Ellwood, Robert. *1950: Crossroads of American Religious Life*. Louisville, KY: Westminster John Knox Press, 2000.

Ellwood, Robert. *The Fifties Spiritual Marketplace: American Religion in a Decade of Conflict*. New Brunswick, NJ: Rutgers University Press, 1997.

Herberg, Will. *Protestant-Catholic-Jew: An Essay in American Religious Sociology*. Chicago: University Of Chicago Press reprint edition, 1983.

McGuinness, Margaret M. *Called to Serve: A History of Nuns in America*. New York: New York University Press, 2013.

McKee, Gabriel. *The Gospel According to Science Fiction*. Louisville, KY: Westminster John Knox Press, 2007.

Miller, Douglas T., and Marion Nowak. *The Fifties: The Way We Really Were*. New York: Doubleday, 1977.

Shaw, Tony, and Denise Youngblood. *Cinematic Cold War: The American and Soviet Struggle for Hearts and Minds*. Lawrence: University Press of Kansas, 2010.

Smith, Elinor Goulding. "Won't Somebody Tolerate Me?" *Harper's Magazine*, August 1956, pp. 36–38.

Woodward, Kenneth L. *Getting Religion: Faith, Culture, and Politics from the Age of Eisenhower to the Era of Obama*. New York: Convergent Books, 2016.

APPENDIX A:
BOOKS CITED IN
LITERATURE SECTION
(CHAPTER 3)

Advise and Consent (1959)—Allen Drury
Affluent Society, The (1958)—John Kenneth Galbraith
Another Country (1962)—James Baldwin
Atlas Shrugged (1957)—Ayn Rand
Bell Jar, The (1963)—Sylvia Plath
Best of Everything, The (1958)—Rona Jaffe
Black Like Me (1961)—John Howard Griffin
Bonjour Tristesse (1954)—Françoise Sagan
Catcher in the Rye, The (1951)—J. D. Salinger
Daisy Kenyon (1945)—Elizabeth Janeway
Désirée (1951)—Annemarie Selinko
Doctor Zhivago (1957)—Boris Pasternak
East of Eden (1952)—John Steinbeck
Fahrenheit 451 (1953)—Ray Bradbury
Faithful Are the Wounds (1955)—May Sarton
Feminine Mystique, The (1963)—Betty Friedan
Forever Amber (1944)—Kathleen Winsor
From Here to Eternity (1953)—James Jones
Gone with the Wind (1936)—Margaret Mitchell
Guns of August, The (1962)—Barbara Tuchman
Haunting of Hill House, The (1959)—Shirley Jackson
Hidden Persuaders, The (1957)—Vance Packard
Howl (1956)—Allen Ginsberg

Invisible Man (1952)—Ralph Ellison

Lady Chatterley's Lover (1959)—D. H. Lawrence

Lolita (1958)—Vladimir Nabokov

Lord of the Flies (1954)—William Golding

"Lottery, The" (1949)—Shirley Jackson (short story)

Man in the Gray Flannel Suit, The (1955)—Sloan Wilson

Man's World, Woman's Place: A Study of Social Mythology (1971)—Elizabeth Janeway

Marjorie Morningstar (1955)—Herman Wouk

My Cousin Rachel (1951)—Daphne du Maurier

Naked Lunch (1959)—William S. Burroughs

Notes of a Native Son (1955)—James Baldwin

On the Road (1957)—Jack Kerouac

Organization Man, The (1956)—William H. Whyte

Other America, The: Poverty in the United States (1962)—Michael Harrington

Peyton Place (1956)—Grace Metalious

Prime of Miss Jean Brodie, The (1961)—Muriel Spark

Raisin in the Sun, A (1959)—Lorraine Hansberry

Secrets We Kept, The (2019)—Lara Prescott

Sex and the Single Girl (1962)—Helen Gurley Brown

Ship of Fools (1962)—Katherine Anne Porter

Shower of Summer Days, A (1952)—May Sarton

Silent Spring (1962)—Rachel Carson

Song of Solomon (1977)—Toni Morrison

Star Money (1950)—Kathleen Winsor

Strangers on a Train (1950)—Patricia Highsmith

Their Eyes Were Watching God (1937)—Zora Neale Hurston

To Kill a Mockingbird (1960)—Harper Lee

Ugly American, The (1958)—William J. Lederer and Eugene Burdick

APPENDIX B: BESTSELLING BOOKS OF THE 1950s

1950

Fiction: *Across the River and into the Trees* by Ernest Hemingway, *The Cardinal* by Henry Morton Robinson, *Joy Street* by Frances Parkinson Keyes

Nonfiction: *Kon-Tiki* by Thor Heyerdahl; *Look Younger, Live Longer* by Gayelord Hauser; *The Pocket Book of Baby and Child Care* by Dr. Benjamin Spock

1951

Fiction: *The Caine Mutiny* by Herman Wouk, *From Here to Eternity* by James Jones, *Moses* by Sholem Asch

Nonfiction: *Better Homes and Gardens Handyman's Book, Betty Crocker's Picture Cook Book, Washington Confidential* by Jack Lait and Lee Mortimer

1952

Fiction: *East of Eden* by John Steinbeck, *My Cousin Rachel* by Daphne du Maurier, *The Silver Chalice* by Thomas Costain

Nonfiction: *A Man Called Peter* by Catherine Marshall, *The Sea around Us* by Rachel Carson, *Tallulah* by Tallulah Bankhead

1953

Fiction: *Battle Cry* by Leon Uris, *Désirée* by Annemarie Selinko, *From Here to Eternity* by James Jones, *The Robe* by Lloyd Douglas

Nonfiction: *Life Is Worth Living* by Fulton J. Sheen, *The Power of Positive Thinking* by Norman Vincent Peale, *Sexual Behavior in the Human Female* by Alfred Kinsey

1954

Fiction: *Love Is Eternal* by Irving Stone, *Mary Anne* by Daphne du Maurier, *Not as a Stranger* by Morton Thompson

Nonfiction: *Better Homes and Gardens New Cook Book, Betty Crocker's Good and Easy Cook Book, The Tumult and the Shouting* by Grantland Rice

1955

Fiction: *Andersonville* by MacKinlay Kantor, *Auntie Mame* by Patrick Dennis, *Bonjour Tristesse* by Françoise Sagan, *The Man in the Gray Flannel Suit* by Sloan Wilson, *Marjorie Morningstar* by Herman Wouk

Nonfiction: *The Family of Man* by Edward Steichen, *Gift from the Sea* by Anne Morrow Lindbergh

1956

Fiction: *Don't Go Near the Water* by William Brinkley, *The Last Hurrah* by Edwin O'Connor, *Peyton Place* by Grace Metalious

Nonfiction: *Better Homes and Gardens Barbecue Book, Betty Crocker's Picture Cook Book, Etiquette* by Frances Benton

1957

Fiction: *By Love Possessed* by James Cozzens, *Compulsion* by Meyer Levin, *Rally Round the Flag, Boys!* by Max Shulman

Nonfiction: *The FBI Story* by Don Whitehead, *Kids Say the Darndest Things!* by Art Linkletter, *Stay Alive All Your Life* by Norman Vincent Peale

1958

Fiction: *Anatomy of a Murder* by Robert Traver, *Doctor Zhivago* by Boris Pasternak, *Exodus* by Leon Uris, *Lolita* by Vladimir Nabokov

Nonfiction: *Only in America* by Harry Golden, *Please Don't Eat the Daisies* by Jean Kerr, *Twixt Twelve and Twenty* by Pat Boone

1959

Fiction: *Advise and Consent* by Allen Drury, *Hawaii* by James Michener, *Lady Chatterley's Lover* by D. H. Lawrence
Nonfiction: *Act One* by Moss Hart, *For 2¢ Plain* by Harry Golden, *The Status Seekers* by Vance Packard

Other books published during the 1950s that were not bestsellers but became culturally significant:

1950

I, Robot by Isaac Asimov

1951

The Catcher in the Rye by J. D. Salinger

1952

Charlotte's Web by E. B. White, *Invisible Man* by Ralph Ellison

1953

Fahrenheit 451 by Ray Bradbury, *Go Tell It on the Mountain* by James Baldwin

1954

Lord of the Flies by William Golding

1955

Notes of a Native Son by James Baldwin

1956

Howl by Allen Ginsberg, *The Organization Man* by William H. Whyte

1957

Atlas Shrugged by Ayn Rand, *The Cat in the Hat* by Doctor Seuss, *The Hidden Persuaders* by Vance Packard, *On the Road* by Jack Kerouac

1958

The Affluent Society by John Kenneth Galbraith, *The Ugly American* by William J. Lederer and Eugene Burdick

1959

Naked Lunch by William S. Burroughs

Source: Publishers Weekly

APPENDIX C: AWARD WINNERS OF THE 1950s

ACADEMY OF MOTION PICTURE ARTS AND SCIENCES (OSCAR) FOR BEST MOVIE

1950 *All About Eve*
1951 *An American in Paris*
1952 *The Greatest Show on Earth*
1953 *From Here to Eternity*
1954 *On the Waterfront*
1955 *Marty*
1956 *Around the World in 80 Days*
1957 *The Bridge on the River Kwai*
1958 *Gigi*
1959 *Ben-Hur*

ACADEMY OF TELEVISION ARTS & SCIENCES (EMMY)

1950 *The Ed Wynn Show/Texaco Star Theatre*
1951 *The Alan Young Show/Pulitzer Prize Playhouse*
1952 *Your Show of Shows/Studio One*
1953 *I Love Lucy/Your Show of Shows*
1954 *I Love Lucy/ U.S. Steel Hour/Omnibus*
1955 *Make Room for Daddy/U.S. Steel Hour/Walt Disney's Disneyland*
1956 *The Phil Silvers Show/Toast of the Town* (later called *The Ed Sullivan Show*)

1957   *The Phil Silvers Show/Playhouse 90*
1958   *The Phil Silvers Show/Dinah Shore Chevy Show/Gunsmoke*
1959   *The Jack Benny Program/Dinah Shore Chevy Show/Alcoa Hour*

EXCELLENCE IN BROADWAY THEATRE (TONY)

Best Musical

1950   *South Pacific*
1951   *Guys and Dolls*
1952   *The King and I*
1953   *Wonderful Town*
1954   *Kismet*
1955   *The Pajama Game*
1956   *Damn Yankees*
1957   *My Fair Lady*
1958   *The Music Man*
1959   *Redhead*

Best Play

1950   *The Cocktail Party*
1951   *The Rose Tattoo*
1952   *The Fourposter*
1953   *The Crucible*
1954   *The Teahouse of the August Moon*
1955   *The Desperate Hours*
1956   *The Diary of Anne Frank*
1957   *Long Day's Journey into Night*
1958   *Sunrise at Campobello*
1959   *J.B.*

GRAMMY AWARDS

Honoring the music industry, the Grammy Awards were first held in 1959 with winners that year including the following:

Album of the Year: *Music from Peter Gunn* by Henry Mancini
Best Female Pop Performance: Ella Fitzgerald
Best Male Pop Performance: Perry Como
Best New Artist: Bobby Darin
Record of the Year: "Volare" by Domenico Modugno

APPENDIX D: MOST POPULAR ENTERTAINMENT OF THE 1950s

TOP-GROSSING MOVIES

1950 *Cinderella*
1951 *Quo Vadis*
1952 *The Greatest Show on Earth*
1953 *Peter Pan*
1954 *Rear Window*
1955 *Lady and the Tramp*
1956 *The Ten Commandments*
1957 *The Bridge on the River Kwai*
1958 *Auntie Mame*
1959 *Ben-Hur*

Source: Internet Movie Database

TOP-SELLING RECORDS

1951 "It's All in the Game"—Tommy Edwards
1952 "Blue Tango"—Leroy Anderson
1953 "The Song from Moulin Rouge"—Percy Faith
1954 "(We're Gonna) Rock Around the Clock"—Bill Haley and His Comets
1955 "Autumn Leaves"—Roger Williams
1956 "Don't Be Cruel" / "Hound Dog"—Elvis Presley
1957 "Love Letters in the Sand" / "April Love"—Pat Boone

1958 "To Know Him Is to Love Him"—The Teddy Bears
1959 "Mack the Knife"—Bobby Darin

Source: Billboard Magazine

TOP-RATED PRIME-TIME TELEVISION SHOWS

1950–1951 *Texaco Star Theater*
1951–1952 *Arthur Godfrey's Talent Scouts*
1952–1953 *I Love Lucy*
1953–1954 *I Love Lucy*
1954–1955 *I Love Lucy*
1955–1956 *The $64,000 Question*
1956–1957 *I Love Lucy*
1957–1958 *Gunsmoke*
1958–1959 *Gunsmoke*
1959–1960 *Gunsmoke*

Source: Nielsen Media Research

BIBLIOGRAPHY

The following materials will prove useful to the reader in assessing a full picture of the daily lives of women in postwar America. Each entry below was helpful to the author in its own way by offering a deeper understanding of that era. Some sources might especially appeal to readers according to particular areas of interest, such as advertising, athletics, consumerism, science, and television.

INTRODUCTION

Anderson, Becca. *The Book of Awesome Women: Boundary Breakers, Freedom Fighters, Sheroes and Female Firsts*. Coral Gables, FL: Mango, 2017.

Boorstin, Daniel. *The Americans: The Democratic Experience*. New York: Vintage, 1974.

Collins, Gail. *America's Women: 400 Years of Dolls, Drudges, Helpmates, and Heroines*. New York: William Morrow, 2007.

Collins, Gail. *When Everything Changed: The Amazing Journey of American Women from 1960 to the Present*. Boston: Little Brown, 2009.

Cooke, Alistair. *Alistair Cooke's America*. New York: Alfred A. Knopf, 1977.

DuBois, Ellen Carol, and Lynn Dumenil. *Through Women's Eyes: An American History with Documents*. Boston, MA: Bedford/St. Martin's, 2019.

Edgerton, Gary. *The Columbia History of American Television*. New York: Columbia University Press, 2009.

Galbraith, John Kenneth. *The Affluent Society*. New York: Mariner Books, 1998.

Girard, Jolyon, ed. *The Greenwood Encyclopedia of Daily Life in America: Volume 4, Wartime, Postwar, and Contemporary America, 1940–Present.* Westport, CT: Greenwood, 2008.

Greer, Germaine. *Shakespeare's Wife.* New York: Harper Perennial, 2009.

Halberstam, David. *The Fifties.* New York: Villard, 1993.

Hendricks, Nancy. *Daily Life in 1950s America.* Santa Barbara, CA: Greenwood, 2019.

Lamphier, Peg, and Rosanne Welch, eds. *Women in American History: A Social, Political, and Cultural Encyclopedia and Document Collection.* Santa Barbara, CA: ABC-CLIO, 2017.

Lupiano, Vincent Depaul. *It Was a Very Good Year: A Cultural History of the United States from 1776 to the Present.* Fairfield, OH: Adams Media, 1994.

Mittell, Jason. *Television and American Culture.* New York: Oxford University Press, 2009.

Patterson, James T. *Grand Expectations: The United States, 1945–1974.* New York: Oxford University Press, 1997.

Roberts, Cokie. *Founding Mothers: The Women Who Raised Our Nation.* New York: Harper Perennial, 2005.

Samuel, Lawrence R. *Brought to You by: Postwar Television Advertising and the American Dream.* Austin: University of Texas Press, 2002.

Young, William, and Nancy K. Young. *The 1950s.* Westport, CT: Greenwood, 2004.

CHAPTER ONE: DOMESTIC LIFE

Barrett, Duncan, and Nuala Calvi. *GI Brides: The Wartime Girls Who Crossed the Atlantic for Love.* New York: William Morrow, 2014.

Brown, Claude. *Manchild in the Promised Land.* New York: New American Library, 13th edition, 1965.

Canine, John. *The Psychosocial Aspects of Death and Dying.* New York: McGraw Hill, 1996.

Celello, Kristin. *Making Marriage Work: A History of Marriage and Divorce in the Twentieth-Century United States.* Chapel Hill: University of North Carolina Press, 2009.

Coontz, Stephanie. *Marriage, A History: From Obedience to Intimacy or How Love Conquered Marriage.* New York: Penguin Books, 2006.

Costa, Dora L. *The Evolution of Retirement: An American Economic History, 1880–1990.* Chicago: University of Chicago Press, 1998.

Cott, Nancy F. *Public Vows: A History of Marriage and the Nation.* Cambridge, MA: Harvard University Press, 2002.

D'Emilio, John, and Estelle Freedman. *Intimate Matters: A History of Sexuality in America.* Chicago: University of Chicago Press, 1988.

DeMeyer, Trace. *One Small Sacrifice: Lost Children of the Indian Adoption Projects.* Greenfield, MA: Blue Hand Books, 2012.

Douglas, Susan J. *Where the Girls Are: Growing Up Female with the Mass Media*. New York: Three Rivers Press, 1995.

Edwards, Elisabeth. *I Love Lucy: A Celebration of All Things Lucy—Inside the World of Television's First Great Sitcom*. New York: Running Press, 2011.

Eskridge, William. *Gaylaw: Challenging the Apartheid of the Closet*. Cambridge, MA: Harvard University Press, 2002.

Gerber, Robin. *Barbie and Ruth: The Story of the World's Most Famous Doll and the Woman Who Created Her*. New York: Harper, 2010.

Hardy, Sheila. *A 1950s Housewife: Marriage and Homemaking in the 1950s*. Charleston, SC: The History Press, 2016.

Hart, Elva Treviño. *Barefoot Heart: Stories of a Migrant Child*. Tempe, AZ: Bilingual Press, 1999.

Harvey, Brett. *The Fifties: A Women's Oral History*. New York: HarperCollins, 1993.

Jackson, Kenneth T. *Crabgrass Frontier: The Suburbanization of the United States*. New York: Oxford University Press, 1987.

Kübler-Ross, Elisabeth. *On Death & Dying*. New York: Scribner, reprint edition, 2014.

Maier, Thomas. *Dr. Spock: An American Life*. New York: Houghton Mifflin Harcourt, 1998.

May, Elaine Tyler. *America and the Pill: A History of Promise, Peril, and Liberation*. New York: Basic Books, reprint edition, 2011.

Miles, Rosalind. *Who Cooked the Last Supper? The Women's History of the World*. New York: Three Rivers Press, 2001.

O'Neill, William. *American High: The Years of Confidence, 1945–60*. New York: Simon and Schuster, 1986.

Sanvidge, Susan. *Penny Loafers and Bobby Pins: Tales and Tips from Growing Up in the '50s and '60s*. Madison, WI: Wisconsin Historical Society Press, 2010.

CHAPTER TWO: ECONOMIC LIFE

Berry, Daina, and Kali Gross. *A Black Women's History of the United States*. Boston, MA: Beacon Press, 2020.

Brown, D. Clayton. *Electricity for Rural America: The Fight for the REA*. Westport, CT: Greenwood, 1980.

Cohen, Deborah. *Braceros: Migrant Citizens and Transnational Subjects in the Postwar United States and Mexico*. Chapel Hill: University of North Carolina Press, 2011.

Feather, Carl E. *Mountain People in a Flat Land: A Popular History of Appalachian Migration to Northeast Ohio, 1940–1965*. Athens: Ohio University Press, 1998.

Harrington, Michael. *The Other America: Poverty in the United States*. New York: Touchstone, first Touchstone edition, 1997.

Hartigan, John. *Racial Situations: Class Predicaments of Whiteness in Detroit.* Princeton, NJ: Princeton University Press, 1999.

Hill, Daniel Delis. *Advertising to the American Woman.* Columbus: Ohio State University Press, 2002.

hooks, bell. *Ain't I a Woman: Black Women and Feminism.* New York: Routledge, 2nd edition, 2014.

Kealing, Bob. *Tupperware Unsealed: Brownie Wise, Earl Tupper, and the Home Party Pioneers.* Gainesville: University Press of Florida, 2008.

Lears, Jackson. *Fables of Abundance: A Cultural History of Advertising in America.* New York: Basic Books, 1995.

Payne, Robert. *Report on America.* New York: John Day Company, 1949.

Rothstein, Richard. *The Color of Law: A Forgotten History of How Our Government Segregated America.* New York: Liveright, 2017.

Royce, Edward. *The Origins of Southern Sharecropping: Labor and Social Change.* Philadelphia, PA: Temple University Press, 1993.

Ruiz, Vicki. *From out of the Shadows: Mexican Women in Twentieth-Century America.* New York: Oxford University Press, 2008.

Schaefer, Richard T. *Encyclopedia of Race, Ethnicity, and Society.* Thousand Oaks, CA: Sage Publications, 2008.

Schrecker, Ellen. *Many Are the Crimes: McCarthyism in America.* New York: Little, Brown, 1998.

Sowards, Stacey.*¡Sí, Ella Puede!: The Rhetorical Legacy of Dolores Huerta and the United Farm Workers.* Austin: University of Texas Press, 2019.

CHAPTER THREE: INTELLECTUAL LIFE

Alvarez, Julia. *Once upon a Quinceañera: Coming of Age in the USA.* New York: Penguin, 2007.

Ashby, LeRoy. *With Amusement for All: A History of American Popular Culture since 1830.* Lexington: University Press of Kentucky, 2012.

Bisbort, Alan. *Beatniks: A Guide to an American Subculture.* Westport, CT: Greenwood, 2009.

Brandt, Jenn, and Callie Clare. *An Introduction to Popular Culture in the US: People, Politics, and Power.* New York: Bloomsbury Academic, 2018.

Burnham, John. *Health Care in America: A History.* Baltimore, MD: Johns Hopkins University Press, 2015.

Cameron, Ardis. *Unbuttoning America: A Biography of "Peyton Place."* Ithaca, NY: Cornell University Press, 2015.

Cary, Alice. "Unveiling the CIA Book Club." *BookPage*, September, 2019.

Charters, Ann, ed. *The Portable Beat Reader.* New York: Penguin Books, 1992.

Cirincione, Joseph. *Bomb Scare: The History and Future of Nuclear Weapons.* New York: Columbia University Press, 2008.

Douglas, Susan J. *Where the Girls Are: Growing Up Female with the Mass Media.* New York: Three Rivers Press, 1995.

Franklin, Ruth. *Shirley Jackson: A Rather Haunted Life*. New York: Liveright, 2016.

Hartman, Andrew. *Education and the Cold War: The Battle for the American School*. New York: Palgrave Macmillan, 2012.

Ignotofsky, Rachel. *Women in Science: 50 Fearless Pioneers Who Changed the World*. New York: Ten Speed Press, 2016.

Jacobs, Jane. *The Death and Life of Great American Cities*. New York: Random House, 1993.

Johnson, Claudia Durst, and Vernon Elso Johnson. *The Social Impact of the Novel: A Reference Guide*. Westport, CT: Greenwood, 2002.

Kröger, Lisa, and Melanie R. Anderson. *Monster, She Wrote: The Women Who Pioneered Horror and Speculative Fiction*. Philadelphia, PA: Quirk Books, 2019.

Messick, Dale. *Brenda Starr, Reporter: The Collected Dailies and Sundays, 1940–1946*. Neshannock, PA: Hermes Press, 2012.

Mettler, Suzanne. *Soldiers to Citizens: The G.I. Bill and the Making of the Greatest Generation*. New York: Oxford University Press, 2007.

Oswald, Diana. *Debutantes: When Glamour Was Born*. New York: Rizzoli, 2013.

Pasternak, Anna. *Lara: The Untold Love Story and the Inspiration for "Doctor Zhivago."* New York: HarperCollins, 2017.

Perry, Imani. *Looking for Lorraine: The Radiant and Radical Life of Lorraine Hansberry*. Boston, MA: Beacon, 2018.

Pursell, Carroll. *Technology in Postwar America: A History*. New York: Columbia University Press, 2007.

Shetterly, Margo Lee. *Hidden Figures: The Story of the African-American Women Who Helped Win the Space Race*. New York: William Morrow, 2016.

Solomon, Barbara Miller. *In the Company of Educated Women: A History of Women and Higher Education in America*. New Haven, CT: Yale University Press, reprint edition, 1986.

Strickler, Dave. *Syndicated Comic Strips and Artists, 1924–1995: The Complete Index*. San Simeon, CA: Comics Access, 1995.

Sumner, David. *The Magazine Century: American Magazines since 1900*. New York: Peter Lang, 2010.

Urban, Wayne, and Jennings Wagoner. *American Education: A History*. New York: Routledge, 2013.

Walker, Nancy A. *Women's Magazines, 1940–1960: Gender Roles and the Popular Press*. Boston, MA: Bedford/St. Martin's, 1998.

CHAPTER FOUR: MATERIAL LIFE

Albee, Sarah. *Why'd They Wear That? Fashion as the Mirror of History*. Washington, DC: National Geographic, 2015.

Brown, Robin. *Materialism*. New York: Routledge, 2019.

Chandler, Adam. *Drive-Thru Dreams: A Journey through the Heart of America's Fast-Food Kingdom*. New York: Flatiron Books, 2019.

Cunningham, Michael, and Craig Marberry. *Crowns: Portraits of Black Women in Church Hats*. New York: Doubleday, 2000.

Handley, Susannah. *Nylon: The Story of a Fashion Revolution*. Baltimore, MD: Johns Hopkins University Press, 1999.

Heimann, Jim. *Car Hops and Curb Service: A History of American Drive-in Restaurants 1920–1960*. San Francisco: Chronicle Books, 1996.

Heitmann, John. *The Automobile and American Life*. Jefferson, NC: McFarland, 2009.

Hulme, Alison. *Consumerism on TV: Popular Media from the 1950s to the Present*. New York: Routledge, 2016.

Ikuta, Yasutoshi. *Cruise O Matic: Automobile Advertising of the 1950s*. San Francisco: Chronicle Books, 2000.

Jakle, John, and Keith Sculle. *Fast Food: Roadside Restaurants in the Automobile Age*. Baltimore, MD: Johns Hopkins University Press, 1999.

Jones, Gerald. *Honey, I'm Home! Sitcoms: Selling the American Dream*. New York: St. Martin's Press, 1992.

Kasser, Tim. *The High Price of Materialism*. Cambridge, MA: MIT Press, 2003.

Lamm, Michael, and Dave Holls. *A Century of Automotive Style: 100 Years of American Car Design*. Stockton, CA: Lamm-Morada Publishing Company, 1996.

Lovegren, Sylvia. *Fashionable Food: Seven Decades of Food Fads*. Chicago: University of Chicago Press, 2005.

Miles, Steven. *Consumerism: As a Way of Life*. Thousand Oaks, CA: Sage Publications, 2006.

Moore, Jennifer Grayer. *Fashion Fads through American History: Fitting Clothes into Context*. Santa Barbara, CA: Greenwood, 2015.

Samuel, Lawrence R. *Brought to You by: Postwar Television Advertising and the American Dream*. Austin: University of Texas Press, 2002.

Schor, Juliet. *Overspent American: Why We Want What We Don't Need*. New York: Basic Books, 1998.

Shapiro, Laura. *Something from the Oven: Reinventing Dinner in 1950s America*. New York: Penguin Books, 2005.

Smith, Andrew F. *Eating History*. New York: Columbia University Press, 2009.

Taylor, Candacy. *Overground Railroad: The Green Book and the Roots of Black Travel in America*. New York: Harry N. Abrams, 2020.

Tiburzi, Bonnie. *Takeoff!: The Story of America's First Woman Pilot for a Major Airline*. New York: Crown Publishers, 1984.

Trounstine, Jessica. *Segregation by Design: Local Politics and Inequality in American Cities*. New York: Cambridge University Press, 2018.

Walford, Jonathan. *1950s American Fashion*. New York: Shire Library, 2012.

CHAPTER FIVE: POLITICAL LIFE

Belofsky, Nathan. *The Book of Strange and Curious Legal Oddities*. New York: Perigee, 2010.

Campbell, Amy Leigh. *Raising the Bar: Ruth Bader Ginsburg and the ACLU Women's Rights Project*. Bloomington, IN: Xlibris, 2004.

Cohen, Adam. *Supreme Inequality: The Supreme Court's Fifty-Year Battle for a More Unjust America*. New York, Penguin, 2020.

Cohen, Lizabeth. *A Consumers' Republic: The Politics of Mass Consumption in Postwar America*. New York: Vintage Books, 2003.

Collins, Robert M. *More: The Politics of Economic Growth in Postwar America*. New York: Oxford University Press, 2002.

Craig, Campbell, and Fredrik Logevall. *America's Cold War: The Politics of Insecurity*. Cambridge, MA: Belknap Press, 2012.

Critchlow, Donald. *American Political History: A Very Short Introduction*. New York: Oxford University Press, 2015.

De Hart, Jane Sherron. *Ruth Bader Ginsburg: A Life*. New York: Knopf, 2018.

Gaddis, John Lewis. *The Cold War: A New History*. New York: Penguin Books, 2006.

Han, Lori Cox, and Caroline Heldman. *Women, Power, and Politics: The Fight for Gender Equality in the United States*. New York: Oxford University Press, 2017.

Hendricks, Nancy. *Notable Arkansas Women: From Hattie to Hillary, 100 Names to Know*. Little Rock, AR: Butler Center Books, 2016.

Hendricks, Nancy. *Ruth Bader Ginsburg: A Life in American History*. Santa Barbara, CA: ABC-CLIO, 2020.

Hirshman, Linda. *Sisters in Law: How Sandra Day O'Connor and Ruth Bader Ginsburg Went to the Supreme Court and Changed the World*. New York: Harper Perennial, 2016.

Isaacs, Jeremy, and Taylor Downing. *Cold War: An Illustrated History, 1945–1991*. New York: Little Brown, 1998.

Michaels, Jonathan. *McCarthyism: The Realities, Delusions and Politics behind the 1950s Red Scare*. New York: Routledge, 2017.

Stathis, Stephen. *Landmark Legislation 1774–2012: Major U.S. Acts and Treaties*. Thousand Oaks, CA: CQ Press, 2014.

Strebeigh, Fred. *Equal: Women Shape American Law*. New York: Norton, 2009.

Swers, Michele L. *Women in the Club: Gender and Policy Making in the Senate*. Chicago: University of Chicago Press, 2013.

Voss, Kimberly Wilmot. *Women Politicking Politely: Advancing Feminism in the 1960s and 1970s*. Lanham, MD: Lexington Books, 2019.

CHAPTER SIX: RECREATIONAL LIFE

Anderson, Kent. *Television Fraud: The History and Implications of the Quiz Show Scandals*. Westport, CT: Praeger, 1979.

Ashby, LeRoy. *With Amusement for All: A History of American Popular Culture since 1830*. Lexington: University Press of Kentucky, 2012.

Bontemps, Arna Alexander. *Forever Free: Art by African-American Women*. Alexandria, VA: Stephenson, 1980.

Browne, Pat, and Ray B. Browne, eds. *The Guide to United States Popular Culture*. Madison: University of Wisconsin Press, 2001.

Bufwack, Mary, and Robert Oermann. *Finding Her Voice: Women in Country Music, 1800–2000*. Nashville, TN: Vanderbilt University Press, 2003.

Creedon, Pamela, ed. *Women, Media and Sport: Challenging Gender Values*. Thousand Oaks, CA: Sage Publications, 1994.

Davies, Richard O. *Sports in American Life: A History*. Malden, MA: Wiley-Blackwell, 2017.

Davis, Jeffery. *Children's Television, 1947–1990*. Jefferson, NC: McFarland, 2011.

Edwards, Elisabeth. *I Love Lucy: A Celebration of All Things Lucy—Inside the World of Television's First Great Sitcom*. New York: Running Press, 2011.

Farris, Phoebe. *Women Artists of Color: A Bio-critical Sourcebook to 20th Century Artists in the Americas*. Westport, CT: Greenwood, 1999.

Gabler, Neal. *Winchell: Gossip, Power, and the Culture of Celebrity*. New York: Vintage, 1995.

Gilbert, Thom. *Blue Suede Shoes: The Culture of Elvis*. New York: Glitterati Editions, 2016.

Grant, Barry Keith. *American Cinema of the 1960s: Themes and Variations*. New Brunswick, NJ: Rutgers University Press, 2008.

Hall, Mitchell. *The Emergence of Rock and Roll: Music and the Rise of American Youth Culture*. New York: Routledge, 2014.

Heller, Nancy G. *Women Artists: An Illustrated History*. New York: Abbeville Press, 2003.

Hendricks, Nancy. *Popular Fads and Crazes through American History*. Santa Barbara, CA: ABC-CLIO, 2018.

Ignotofsky, Rachel. *Women in Sports: 50 Fearless Athletes Who Played to Win*. New York: Ten Speed Press, 2017.

Javna, John. *Cult TV*. New York: St. Martin's Press, 1985.

Jentleson, Katherine. *Gatecrashers: The Rise of the Self-Taught Artist in America*. Oakland: University of California Press, 2020.

Kallir, Jane. *Grandma Moses in the 21st Century*. New Haven, CT: Yale University Press, 2001.

Kanfer, Stefan, *Ball of Fire: The Tumultuous Life and Comic Art of Lucille Ball*. New York: Knopf, 2003.

Leaming, Barbara. *Marilyn Monroe*. New York: Three Rivers Press, 2000.

Lisle, Laurie. *Portrait of an Artist: A Biography of Georgia O'Keeffe*. New York: Washington Square Press, 1997.

Mankiewicz, Frank, and Joel L. Swerdlow. *Remote Control: Television and the Manipulation of American Life*. New York: Times Books, 1978.

Moses, Grandma. *Grandma Moses: My Life's History*. Edited by Otto Kallir. New York: Harper, 1952.

Saffer, Max. "Dollars but No Sense: Golf's Long History of Shortchanging Women." *ESPN.com*. https://www.espn.com/espnw/sports/story/_/id/15160220/undefined.

Santoli, Lorraine. *The Official Mickey Mouse Club Book*. New York: Disney Editions, 1995.

Stone, Joseph, and Tim Yohn. *Prime Time and Misdemeanors: Investigating the 1950s TV Quiz Scandal*. New Brunswick, NJ: Rutgers University Press, 1992.

Watts, Steven. *The Magic Kingdom: Walt Disney and the American Way of Life*. Columbia: University of Missouri Press, 2001.

Welch, Rosanne, ed. *When Women Wrote Hollywood: Essays on Female Screenwriters in the Early Film Industry*. Jefferson, NC: McFarland, 2018.

Wiggins. David. *Separate Games: African American Sport behind the Walls of Segregation*. Fayetteville: University of Arkansas Press, 2016.

Winn, Marie. *The Plug-in Drug*. New York: Viking, 1977.

CHAPTER SEVEN: RELIGIOUS LIFE

Balmer, Randall. *Religion in Twentieth Century America*. New York: Oxford University Press, 2001.

Butler, Jon, and Grant Wacker. *Religion in American Life: A Short History*. New York: Oxford University Press, 2011.

Findlay, James F. *Church People in the Struggle: The National Council of Churches and the Black Freedom Movement, 1950–1970*. New York: Oxford University Press, 1993.

Hertzberg, Arthur. *The Jews in America*. New York: Columbia University Press, 1998.

Hyman, Paula, and Deborah Dash Moore. *Jewish Women in America: An Historical Encyclopedia*. New York: Routledge, 1997.

McClymond, Michael. *Encyclopedia of Religious Revivals in America*. Westport, CT: Greenwood, 2006.

McGuinness, Margaret M. *Called to Serve: A History of Nuns in America*. New York: New York University Press, 2013.

Myers, Robert J. *Celebrations: The Complete Book of American Holidays*. New York: Doubleday, 1972.

Putnam, Robert, and David E. Campbell. *American Grace: How Religion Divides and Unites Us*. New York: Simon & Schuster, 2012.

Schultz, Debra L. *Going South: Jewish Women in the Civil Rights Movement*. New York: New York University Press, 2002.

Sicherman, Barbara, and Carol Hurd Green, eds. *Notable American Women: The Modern Period: A Biographical Dictionary*. Cambridge, MA: Belknap Press of Harvard University Press, Volume 4, 1986.

Williams, Peter W. *America's Religions: from Their Origins to the Twenty-First Century*. Urbana: University of Illinois Press, 2015.

INDEX

Page numbers in *italics* indicate photos.

About the Author

NANCY HENDRICKS, PhD, is an award-winning author whose book *Senator Hattie Caraway: An Arkansas Legacy* was named by *Cosmopolitan* magazine as one of the "Twenty Political Books Every Woman Should Read."

Her other books include *Notable Women of Arkansas: From Hattie to Hillary*, *America's First Ladies: A Historical Encyclopedia and Primary Document Collection of the Remarkable Women of the White House*, *Daily Life in 1950s America*, *Haunted Histories in America: True Stories behind the Nation's Most Feared Places*, *Ruth Bader Ginsburg: A Life in American History*, and the two-volume *Popular Fads and Crazes through American History*. She is also the author of the Civil War novel *Terrible Swift Sword: Long Road to the Sultana*.

As a playwright, her works include *Miz Caraway and the Kingfish*, *Second to None*, and *Boy Hero: The Story of David O. Dodd*.

Her writing can also be seen on *Smithsonian.com* as well as in ABC-CLIO's *Historic Sites and Landmarks That Shaped America*; *Disasters and Tragic Events: An Encyclopedia of Catastrophes in American History*; *Political Groups, Parties, and Organizations That Shaped America*; *Technical Innovation in American History*; and *Women in American History*.

Hendricks is a founding member of the proposed National Women's History Museum in Washington, DC. She earned the Pryor Award for Arkansas Women's History, the Arkansas Governor's Arts Award, National Society Daughters of the American Revolution "Women in American History" Award, and the White House Millennium Award.